# Saudi Arabia
# and Ethiopia

# Saudi Arabia and Ethiopia

## Islam, Christianity, and Politics Entwined

### Haggai Erlich

LYNNE
RIENNER
PUBLISHERS

BOULDER
LONDON

Published in the United States of America in 2007 by
Lynne Rienner Publishers, Inc.
1800 30th Street, Boulder, Colorado 80301
www.rienner.com

and in the United Kingdom by
Lynne Rienner Publishers, Inc.
3 Henrietta Street, Covent Garden, London WC2E 8LU

**Library of Congress Cataloging-in-Publication Data**
Erlich, Haggai.
   Saudi Arabia and Ethiopia : Islam, Christianity, and politics entwined /
Haggai Erlich.
     p. cm.
   Includes bibliographical references and index.
   ISBN-13: 978-1-58826-493-0 (hardcover : alk. paper)
   ISBN-10: 1-58826-493-9 (hardcover : alk. paper)
   1. Religion and politics—Saudi Arabia. 2. Religion and
politics—Ethiopia. I. Title.
   BL65.P7E75   2006
   322'.109538—dc22

                                              2006023204

**British Cataloguing in Publication Data**
A Cataloguing in Publication record for this book
is available from the British Library.

Printed and bound in the United States of America

 The paper used in this publication meets the requirements
of the American National Standard for Permanence of
Paper for Printed Library Materials Z39.48-1992.

5   4   3   2   1

*To my grandchildren,*
*Yuval,*
*Yonathan,*
*Maya*

# Contents

# Preface

THE IDEA TO STUDY ETHIOPIAN-SAUDI RELATIONS WAS BORN AT A somewhat embarrassing moment. In September 2002, I was invited to a conference on Christianity and Islam in Ethiopia organized by the Addis Ababa branch of the German Goethe Institute. My paper was on Lij Iyasu, the young Ethiopian emperor from 1913 to 1916, who was said to have adopted Islam. I addressed the political complexities of that episode, underlining the relevant reservoirs of mutual Christian-Islamic concepts. There followed a long, lively discussion. The 1990s revival of Islam in a land that had been, for sixteen centuries, dominated by Christians created new perspectives, and the subject was pivotal enough to inspire a vibrant debate in the packed hall. Ethiopians love to argue and do so with a sophisticated combination of bluntness and humor. This atmosphere was suddenly interrupted when a gentleman stood up and presented himself as the Saudi Arabian ambassador to Ethiopia. He expressed surprise that he himself had not been invited to address the conference and admonished the organizers for inviting an Israeli "to spread Zionist propaganda and incite Christians against Muslims." Silence prevailed for some seconds, then was broken by a member of the audience. "Sir," he said, "I ask you as an Ethiopian Muslim. Before we invite you to speak on Islamic-Christian relations, please do tell me: Can a debate like the one we are having here be held in your country?" The Saudi, much to his credit, responded with a big smile, as the whole audience burst into laughter.

A few months earlier, I had won a grant from the Israel Science Foundation to study "Islam and Revolution in Today's Ethiopia." By the time of that visit, it was already apparent to me that the subject I had proposed was too broad. The redefinition of contemporary Ethiopia is indeed multifaceted, and its religious aspect is in itself multidimensional. It is too varied to be grasped fully with my tools as a historian.

That moment in the Goethe Institute helped me to identify my own perspective for observing the current dynamics and their historical roots. Saudi involvement in the revival of Islam in Ethiopia was discernible nearly everywhere. Even on the Ethiopian Airlines flight on which I returned home, along the Red Sea and over Jerusalem, passengers were frequently informed of the plane's speed, its altitude, and the direction and distance to Mecca.

Studying the relations between what used to be a Christian state in Africa and the fundamental Islamic Arab kingdom of the Saudis naturally turned into an inquiry about the interplay between religion and politics. I should like to believe that this analysis contributes new perspectives to the modern annals of both countries. Mainly following the periodization of Ethiopian developments, the history presented here is also an attempt to understand the intriguing interplay between religion and politics in today's Saudi Arabia. As in Ethiopia, this was never a one-dimensional story.

The research for this book was generously supported by the Israel Science Foundation of the Israeli Academy for Science and Humanities. Additional financial help was offered by both Tel Aviv University's Department of Middle Eastern and North African History, headed by Eyal Zisser, and the Open University of Israel. I am grateful to the staff members of these bodies, as well as to those of the Institute of Ethiopian Studies at Addis Ababa University, the Public Record Office in London, the Archivio Storico of the Italian Foreign Ministry, and the Israel National Archive. I am also most grateful to my two research assistants, Avi Mor and Avishai Ben Dror, for their unfailing resourcefulness and goodwill. Special thanks are due to friends and colleagues who helped by reading various chapters. Notable among them are Mustafa Kabha, Avraham Hakim, Sara Yizraeli, Uzi Rabi, Amit Bein, Mario Tedeschini-Lalli, and Muhammad al-Atawna. Valuable material was also provided by my students Amit Obeles, Roi Galili, and Shiri Ziv. Gila Haimovic of the Open University of Israel edited the manuscript. Her professionalism, patience, and sober sense guided me through the writing. Preparing the book for publication with the staff of Lynne Rienner Publishers, and notably with Lynne Rienner herself, was a great pleasure, as always.

I was especially fortunate to be corrected and advised by leading scholars who read the entire work in its final stages. The Ethiopian aspects benefited from the comments of David Shinn and Paul Henze. In addition, Paul's knowledge, perceptions, and generosity have inspired my studies on Ethiopia for the past twenty-five years. The Saudi and Arab dimensions were reviewed by Joshua Teitelbaum, Joseph Kostiner, James Jankowski, and Israel Gershoni, all of whom offered constructive criticism and helpful ideas. Beyond this book, Gershoni's penetrating scholarship and deep friendship have enriched me and my work in countless ways. Whatever faults there are in the book, needless to say, are entirely mine.

Finally, my deepest gratitude goes to Yochi, the love of my life.

*—Haggai Erlich*

# 1

# Politics and Religious Legacies: An Interplay

ETHIOPIA, ONCE A "CHRISTIAN ISLAND" IN AFRICA, IS UNDERGOING a fundamental revolution, perhaps the deepest in its history. Today's Ethiopia, recuperating from an old siege mentality that deepened during the dictatorship of Mangistu Haile Mariam (1974–1991), is no longer an isolated culture "encompassed on all sides by the enemies of [its] religion."[1] Instead, it is opening up to its own ethnic and religious diversity and intensively reconnecting to the neighboring Middle East. Islam and Muslims are rapidly entering the core of Ethiopian life across all conceivable dimensions—social, economic, and cultural. It is clear that Ethiopia is being redefined before our eyes, that Christianity is no longer comprehensively hegemonic as it was in the past sixteen centuries, that Islam is no longer the religion of the marginal and the deprived, and that the very cultural identity of the country is being modified in a most meaningful way.

But in what way, and in which direction? Does this Islamic momentum herald the pluralization of society, the diversification of culture, and the revival of an economy based on trade, commerce, technology, and international dynamism—namely, momentum that enriches the Ethiopian fabric? Or, does the rise of Islam herald a religious conflict, a struggle for political hegemony, a new round in the age-old cycle of Islamic-Christian collision?

The revolution inherent in Ethiopia's redefinition is too young to be assessed. One can derive comfort from the country's long tradition of relative religious tolerance. Over the centuries, the Ethiopian common denominator has often proved stronger than her religious differences. Ethnic, linguistic, and regional identities often turned out to be more

1

vibrant factors in internal politics than religious ones. Were the Ethiopians left on their own, one could expect a process of constructive transformation. However, as this process is taking place in close combination with Ethiopia's rapid integration into the economic, cultural, and strategic circles of the Middle East, much depends on external influences. Indeed, a major, determinant question is the nature of Middle Eastern involvement in the current Ethiopian process. What factors are involved, and how are Ethiopia and her future conceived by others in the region?

Islamic Middle Eastern states and Christian Ethiopia share a long and intensive history. The story of the Prophet Muhammad sending his first group of followers, still persecuted by Mecca's polytheistic leadership, to seek asylum with the neighboring Christian *najashi* (a negus, or king) of Ethiopia, molded Islam's concept of the Ethiopian "other." Islamic interpretations of Muhammad's relations with his contemporary *najashi* are still centrally relevant to the subject of this book.

The story—as narrated by Muslim historians of the period—has two main parts. The first begins in A.D. 615 with the Prophet telling his early followers—the *sahaba*—of a just king in Ethiopia "who oppresses no one" and instructing them to flee to Aksum. There, in the court of Najashi Ashama, they found shelter, and the *najashi* protected them from a Meccan mission seeking their extradition. The Christian *najashi* thus not only saved the whole Islamic community of the time, but went on to protect the *sahaba* in his kingdom and to help the Prophet Muhammad in Mecca.

The second part of the story begins later, in A.D. 628 In that year, Muhammad, already well established in al-Madina, initiated Islam's first international diplomatic effort. He sent letters to eight rulers, including the kings of Persia and Constantinople and the rulers of Egypt, Syria, and some Arab Peninsula entities, calling on them to adopt Islam. He also sent a similar letter to his friend the *najashi*. According to all Islamic sources (there is no trace of the story in Ethiopian sources), only the Ethiopian king responded positively. He replied that he appreciated Muhammad's mission and accepted Islam. Two years later, when Muhammad heard of the *najashi*'s death, he prayed for him as one would for a departed Muslim.

For the Islamic world, the Prophet-*najashi* story carried a double message. In the years to come, mainstream orthodoxy tended to emphasize the first part, that of Ethiopian generosity and the righteousness of the Christian *najashi*. The legacy of this part was that Ethiopia, in spite of its Christianity, deserved gratitude and was therefore legitimate. This interpretation was eternalized in the famous saying attributed to the Prophet: "Leave the Ethiopians alone as long as they leave you alone." For many Islamic jurists, Christian Ethiopia was a unique case, a "land of neutrality" (*dar al-hiyad*), exempt from jihad. Muslims in the Middle East should not interfere in Ethiopian affairs, on condition, naturally, that the Ethiopians did not mistreat Muslims. Moreover, Muslims in Ethiopia should live in peace under the Christian government. This early Ethiopian model, of Muslims accepting a non-Islamic regime as prescribed by the Prophet himself, still serves moderate Muslims the world over. The figure of the dark-skinned *najashi* later embracing Islam served the moderates mainly as an example of Islam's supraracial universality.

The second part of the story, however, carried a totally different message for more radical Muslims. As interpreted over the centuries by Middle Eastern advocates of anti-Ethiopian militancy, *Islam al-najashi* meant that Ethiopia was already an integral part of the "land of Islam" (*dar al-Islam*). The Muslim *najashi*, they contended, betrayed by his generals and priests, died in isolation. Ethiopia, therefore, represented Islam's first failure, and her Christian history was traitorous and illegitimate. Christian Ethiopia prevented Islam from spreading into Africa and continued to oppress its own Muslims. In the eyes of Islamic radicals, Ethiopia should be redeemed by again installing a Muslim ruler. Over the centuries, the slogan *Islam al-najash*—the contention that Ethiopia's king had been a Muslim and that the country should therefore be ruled by a Muslim—served those in the Middle East who sought to undermine Ethiopia's Christian system, and encouraged Muslims in the Horn of Africa to take over its political leadership.[2]

In my earlier studies on relations between Middle Eastern Muslims and Ethiopia, I made extensive use of the dichotomy between the concept of "leave the Ethiopians alone" and that of *Islam al-najashi*. This dichotomy was often the principal theme of internal Islamic discussions whenever Ethiopia was on the agenda. The Sudanese Mahdi (d. 1885), for example, initially pursued a flexible policy regarding Ethiopia and preached the "leave the Ethiopians alone" concept. He, and his successor, the *khalifa*, later changed their line and declared a holy war on Emperor Yohannes IV (1872–1889), calling on him to follow the *Islam al-najashi* precedent and to convert.[3] When Ethiopia was threatened by Benito Mussolini in 1935, this dichotomy polarized public opinion across the Arab world. Those who identified with Ethiopia's struggle recycled the Prophet's legacy about gratitude and acceptance. Those siding with the Fascists hoped that Mussolini would finally reinstall a Muslim *najashi*.[4]

In a previous book, *The Cross and the River*, I followed the internal Egyptian-Islamic discussion of Ethiopia from the time of the Mamluks (1250–1517) to the presidency of Husni Mubarak (1981–). Here too, the principal abstract argument underlying the strategic dilemmas revolved around these polarized interpretations of the initial Muhammad–*al-najashi* story. There is no doubt that Egypt has been the most relevant Islamic entity in Ethiopian history. It played a major role in shaping both Ethiopia's Christianity and its Islam, and it remained centrally influential in practically all related developments in Ethiopia. In general, however, most Egyptian leaders tended to follow a rather pragmatic, flexible Ethiopian policy. Dependent on the Nile, ever anxious that Ethiopia might interfere with its flow, Egyptians often pursued the "leave the Ethiopians alone" policy. The *Islam al-najashi* concept was always ready—kept alive and revitalized by their own radicals—to be addressed and used in time of confrontation and peril.[5] However, over the past decade or two, Egypt lost its centrality in Ethiopian affairs. For reasons beyond the scope of this book, officials in Cairo preferred to keep a low profile in Ethiopia. The leadership of external Islamic involvement in Ethiopian affairs passed in the 1990s to the Saudis, who indeed, by the turn of the century, managed to practically monopolize the issue.

Saudi money is behind much of the current Islamic revival in Ethiopia, the construction of hundreds of new mosques and quranic schools, the establishment of welfare associations and orphanages, the spread of the Arabic language and translated literature, the expansion of the hajj, the organization of conferences of preachers, the monthly sub-sidies for the newly converted, the spread of the contention that Muslims are already an overwhelming majority in the country, and more. A good part of the Saudi effort focuses on the Oromo people and southern areas, where Islam, revolving mainly around the walled city of Harar, historically enjoyed long periods of political independence, but there is also a clear endeavor to influence people in the Christian core. There is a marked effort to promote education and to spread the notion that the Saudi aim is actually to advance general openness and assure democratic progress.

Saudi books, the press, and various other publications also dissemi-nate pieces describing the ideology behind this effort. One central argu-ment is that Christianity, revitalized throughout Africa by the same imperialist West that had subjugated the continent in the past, is again threatening to marginalize Islam and that the struggle for Islam in Ethiopia is crucial to its defense throughout the continent. A recurrent theme is that Islam is by nature tolerant, so its revival would benefit Ethiopian democracy. The spread in Ethiopia of Wahhabism—the Islamic radical doctrine of the Saudi state—is inconsistent with such openness and indeed is not always overtly encouraged by the Saudis.

Various Saudi nongovernmental organizations (NGOs) help in this effort, most of them under the umbrella of the Muslim World League (*Rabitat al-'Alam al-Islami*). Founded in 1962 "to disseminate Islamic *da'wa* [the call to join Islam] and expound the teaching of Islam," it is administered by the religious establishment but supported, financed, and controlled by the Saudi government. Though still part of the system, since the early 1990s the Muslim World League has led Saudi Arabia's more fundamentalist wing. By challenging the royal Saudi regime to implement Islamic morality and law more rigidly, it is said to have facilitated, at least indirectly, the cause of global Islamic militancy and its networks.[6]

What do the Saudis think about Ethiopia's religious worlds? Do they seek the revival of Islam as one dimension of Ethiopian openness, or do they seek its victory? What is Wahhabism's main concept of historical Ethiopia? How was the old, neighboring Christian kingdom perceived by the spiritual founders of the Saudi state? Was it "a land of righteousness," legitimate and worthy of acceptance in spite of its religious difference? Or was Ethiopia a painful reminder for them of Islam's first defeat (the demise of the Muslim *najashi*), which can only be redeemed by Islamization? Or, did the Saudis vacillate, coping with a dynamic mixture of these dichotomous approaches, shifting their conceptual emphasis in accordance with historical change, as indeed was the case with most other Islamic communities vis-à-vis Ethiopia? What is behind Saudi "exported" Al-Qaida radicalism in the 1990s and its impact on the Horn of Africa and Ethiopia? Is Al Qaida's terrorism and assistance to local subversive organizations another dimension of Wahhabism? Is there still a voice of Saudi moderation and of acceptance of the Ethiopian "other?" Addressing these crucial questions of the Wahhabis' attitudes and policies, our analysis will follow Saudi strategic and religious complexities over the past seven decades.

It will also follow the Ethiopian role in these dialectical relations. Christian Ethiopia—meaning the core culture and the hegemonic elite groups—also developed its own perceptions of the Islamic, Middle Eastern "other." The Christians' concepts were equally dichotomous and similarly shifting. They, too, were shaped during formative processes and events. During the very early medieval emergence of Ethiopia's Christian culture, there arose a vital urge to retain a constant connection with the lands of the Middle East. However, there was also the ingrained fear, which in the early sixteenth century became a resilient trauma, that opening up to the Middle East would result in Islamic momentum in the Horn of Africa and the destruction of the Christian state. I shall elaborate below on these polarized attitudes and especially address how they influenced the complex relations with the Wahhabis. Both Ethiopian Christianity and Saudi Wahhabism, though connected to universal religions, did, and still do, manifest local identities and cultures and are integrally related to concrete political systems. The relations between Ethiopia and Saudi Arabia, therefore, can not be understood without following their religious premises and transformation. Equally, following interstate political relations is an essential background to understanding today's religious redefinition of Ethiopia on one hand, and to appreciating today's transformations, and indeed, the new global impact of multidimensional Wahhabism on the other hand.

A third pillar of the history analyzed in this volume is that of the Muslims of Ethiopia itself. Caught between their position within the "Christian empire" and the influences, messages, and involvement of their Middle Eastern co-religionists, they have also developed their own perceptions and concepts. We shall address several dimensions of their modern history as it flowed toward current dilemmas. Are the Muslims of today's Ethiopia ready to follow the initial Islamic message of accepting their state—provided it is "righteous"? Or will they follow the *Islam al-najashi* concept and strive for a political Islamic victory in Ethiopia?

Internal Islamic-Ethiopian dynamism is perhaps the most important single issue on the country's contemporary agenda and has an impact on the more comprehensive Islamic-Christian and Arab-African dialogues. Interestingly, it has acquired an even broader significance. One of the most interesting intellectual struggles splitting today's greater Islamic world is an argument over the very essence of Islam between Wahhabi activists and a group called "the Ethiopians" (*Al-Ahbash*), on the other. The latter, centered in Beirut, has branches all over the world and preaches peaceful Islamic-Christian coexistence in the Middle East, Europe, America, and elsewhere. Their Wahhabi rivals accuse them—in a comprehensive war of Internet exchanges, pamphlets, books, sermons, and *fatwas*—of distorting the true nature of Islam. Both camps are led by old shaikhs from the Ethiopian Islamic capital of Harar. One dimension of our story will follow the rivalry between Shaikh 'Abdallah ibn Yusuf al-Harari (now in Lebanon) and Hajj Yusuf 'Abd al-Rahman (now in Saudi Arabia) as it developed throughout seven decades of the Saudi-Ethiopian story. Indeed, the history of the relations between Ethiopia, the last Christian state, and the fundamentalist Islamic kingdom of Saudi Arabia reflects issues that trouble not only Ethiopia, but also the entire globe.

Ethiopia, we saw, was the first, early medieval meeting ground between Christianity and Islam. As Christian-Islamic relations have become a pivotal issue, often portrayed as a global "clash of civilizations,"[7] our Saudi-Ethiopian story may contribute a new perspective. It offers a glance at the heritage of the longest Christian-Islamic dialogue and the way it developed outside Western-Eastern relations. Ethiopia's Christianity emerged from fourth-century Eastern Christianity and remained the state religion from A.D. 334 to 1974. Saudi Arabia developed from the eighteenth-century adoption, by a ruling family, of a rigid quranic-centered doctrine. Both states, cultures, and societies have remained strongly history-oriented, and their modern relations continue to be influenced by their respective, formative, Christian and Islamic concepts.

Our analysis will revolve around the dialectical interplay between formative religious legacies and concrete issues of international politics. Muslims and Christians across the Red Sea, like members of all human groups, continue to resort to their own reservoir of common historical memory, concepts, symbols, and images when they form attitudes and policies. We shall follow Saudi-Ethiopian relations as they unfolded from 1930 to 2005 and will reconstruct the inner debates they energized. We shall discuss the relevant literature, newspaper articles, speeches, school textbooks, official declarations, and—more recently—Internet debates, as we attempt to understand the mutual conceptualizations of the "other" and their evolution, transmission, and reinterpretations.

The bottom line of our study is that in this interplay of politics and religious legacies everything is possible and all is changeable. Even the more past-oriented, conservative reservoir of concepts is diverse enough to be interpreted and reinterpreted. Our Islamic-Ethiopian case is a good example, because the early, formative events from the *najashi*-Muhammad episode offered distinctively dichotomous legacies. History shapers on both sides, we shall see, were therefore both captives and masters of history: they were driven by legacies of the past, yet were able to choose according to interests and legitimize whatever policy they adopted.

Among criticisms of the "clash of civilizations," there is the contention that the main confrontation today is not Christian-Islamic, but Islamic-Islamic. It is believed that the worldwide, internal debates and conflicts over the interpretation of Islam, not its conflict with Western,

Christian civilization, are the main cause of today's international insta-
bility.[8] Our study supports this argument. The chapters below describe
the gradual development of an inner-Islamic debate, beginning in the
1930s and developing into a polarized drama in the 1990s. We shall follow the dialogue between the Wahhabi doctrine and the Saudi state,
from the Wahhabi-influenced pragmatism of Ibn Sa'ud in the 1930s, to
the fundamentalization of the Saudi-Wahhabi combination in the 1970s
and 1980s, through the radicalization and globalization of Wahhabism
and its complex relations with today's Saudi state—all as reflected in
Saudi Arabia's Ethiopian policy. Even more closely, we shall follow the
development of Islam in Ethiopia during these years as influenced by
Wahhabi-Saudi inputs. What began in the 1940s as sporadic tensions
between imported Wahhabi concepts and Ethiopia's local, popular, Sufi,
mildly orthodox Islam, by the 1990s became a struggle over the very
nature of Islam in Ethiopia and the redefinition of the country. We shall
discuss the dilemmas and options of Ethiopia's Muslims as they rebuild
their identity amid an ongoing dialogue with the dichotomous legacies
of Islamic-Ethiopian history.

Our narrative will follow Ethiopian periodization. Chapter 2 discusses the early 1930s and the simultaneous solidification of both Saudi
Arabia and Ethiopia as religious states. Having expanded his rule to
dominate the Arabian Peninsula, in 1932 'Abd al-Aziz Ibn Sa'ud gave
the Wahhabi kingdom its present name. At the time, he was the strongest
Arab Islamic sovereign, believed by many admirers in the Middle East
to be a candidate for a caliph who would lead the entire Islamic nation.
Haile Selassie was proclaimed emperor of Ethiopia in late 1930 and
began to intensively deepen the ancient alliance in Ethiopia between the
cross and the crown. This chapter will also examine Christian-Ethiopian
concepts of Muslims in Ethiopia and in the Middle East as well as fundamental Wahhabi concepts of Ethiopia. In 1934, the Muslim king and
the Christian emperor began to develop a neighborly dialogue.

Chapter 3 begins with the outbreak, in early 1935, of the Abyssinian
Crisis—Mussolini's threat to conquer Ethiopia, and from our perspective, to do so for the sake of Islam and the Muslims. Facing total
destruction and fearing a fifth column at home, Haile Selassie hastened
to redefine the position of Muslims in Ethiopia. He sought Middle
Eastern backing for this policy and sent diplomatic missions to a number of Arab countries. That year, the Fascist-Ethiopian confrontation
turned into a major dilemma for Arab, Egyptian, and Islamic nationalists
in the Middle East, which had far-reaching consequences for all
involved. Aware of Ibn Sa'ud's position in the Islamic world, the

Ethiopians repeatedly asked for a symbolic treaty with Saudi Arabia, or at least some token of solidarity. They got only sweet words and declarations of complete neutrality. Behind those declarations, however, the Saudis, inspired by their fundamental, Wahhabi concepts of Ethiopia, followed the advice of the more militant anti-Ethiopian Islamic-Arab nationalists. In practice, they paternalistically dismissed the Ethiopians and sold vitally needed camels to Mussolini's invading army. The Saudis were thus among the few countries that helped the Fascists' campaign to destroy Ethiopia.

Chapter 4 discusses the Islamic dimension in Ethiopia's history between 1936 and 1948 and its connections with Arabia and Wahhabism. These were years when Ethiopian Islam seemed to be reasserting itself as a political entity. First, the Italian Fascist occupiers of the country (1936–1941), with their eyes on the Arabian Peninsula, worked to revive Islam throughout the region. Then, as of the end of World War II, the struggles over the former Italian colonies of Eritrea and Somalia further encouraged Islam as an anti-Ethiopian identity. Our discussion will mainly follow the story of Harar, the historic capital of Islam in the Horn of Africa. The Islamic community of Harar was split throughout the period. One wing, led by many who, with Italian help, had made pilgrimage to Mecca, tried to spread Wahhabism in Harar, and led to Harar's secession from Ethiopia. The other wing, more loyal to Harar's tradition of popular Islam, remained oriented toward Ethiopia and worked for Islamic-Christian collaboration. The Harari story of those years, replete with rivalries and plots, left enduring legacies that are still recycled today, involving competing "Ethiopian" and Wahhabi values.

Chapter 5 deals with the period from the end of World War II to the fall of the imperial regime in 1974. This period was, from our perspective, marked by the weakening of Islam as a political identity in both Ethiopia and the Middle East. In Ethiopia, the 1950s and 1960s witnessed the culmination of Haile Selassie's power as a Christian king. Aspects of growing Christian hegemony and the further marginalization of Muslims in Ethiopia will be addressed, with Harar again a case in point. Muslims in Ethiopia who opposed centralizing imperial politics and culture did so mainly in the name of modern Arab revolutionism rather than in the name of Islam. An Arab-Eritrean nationalist movement became a major issue for Ethiopia. It oriented itself toward the pan-Arab revolutionaries of the Middle East: the Nasserites, the Ba'thists, and others, forces that, at the time, also threatened the Islamic kingdom of Saudi Arabia. The chapter will discuss these international complexities and also the aspects of the traditional-royal solidarity that developed between the emperor of Ethiopia and the Saudi royal house. However, when this solidarity was put to the test, the Islamic-Christian dichotomy won out. The chapter will discuss how the Saudis viewed Haile Selassie's Ethiopia and conclude with their indirect contribution to his downfall.

Chapter 6 analyzes the period of Mangistu's dictatorship, 1974–1991, which was marked by mutual Saudi-Ethiopian enmity and demonization. Mangistu introduced Marxist terminology and declared religious equality, which in the beginning seemed favorable to Islam. In practice, however, he turned to oppressing both Christianity and Islam. His effort to uproot religiosity in Ethiopia proved disastrous and his communist methods only aggravated old problems, cultural isolationism, and internal conflicts. After the reopening of the Suez Canal in 1975, the Red Sea became, for a time, a focus of international tensions. These culminated with the Somali-Ethiopian Ogaden War (1977–1978) that led to a battle over Harar, which reactivated the old Christian and Islamic-Arab legacies. Various Arab regimes in the Middle East were portrayed as backward reactionaries in Ethiopia, the newly rich Saudis—who contributed significantly to the deterioration toward the Ogaden War—were depicted as the ultimate, feudal-capitalist, jihadi enemy. Ethiopia's image in the eyes of the Saudis fared no better. It was now the worst combination of Communists and black crusaders. In the 1980s, the strategic focus of the region shifted from the Red Sea to the Persian Gulf, and by the end of his reign, Mangistu was forced to tolerate both Christianity and Islam, even opening the doors of Ethiopia to Saudi influence.

Chapter 7 will analyze post-1991 Ethiopia and the nature of the current Saudi involvement. It will address the contemporary issues of Islam's resurgence in Ethiopia and discuss Saudi involvement in this multifaceted process. Against the background of the histories presented in this book, and the Saudis' own contemporary developments and splits, it will present various Saudi-Wahhabi inputs in promoting three Islamic options in Ethiopia: Ethiopian Islam, fundamentalist Islam, and militant anti-Ethiopian Islam. Following Saudi attitudes and policies toward the Ethiopian "other," it will provide a new perspective for understanding the current dilemmas of the Wahhabi kingdom. The chapter will also reexamine the old Ethiopian-Saudi and Christian-Islamic concepts of dialectical mutuality as they are reinterpreted today in Ethiopia. In recording some of the relevant Ethiopian voices, both Christian and Islamic, the chapter will present a new understanding of the nature and directions of Ethiopia's current redefinition.

The conclusion will briefly examine the global significance of our Saudi-Ethiopian, Christian-Islamic history. It will do so also by returning to the two Harari shaikhs, 'Abdallah and Yusuf, whose rivalry, followed throughout these chapters, continues to reflect Islam's main dilemmas. While the aging Shaikh Yusuf still persists in working from Saudi Arabia to promote the fundamentalization of Ethiopia's Islam, Shaikh 'Abdallah, the founder of *Al-Ahbash*, still works quite effectively from Beirut to spread Ethiopian-modeled flexible religiosity throughout the Islamic world. A third native of Harar has meanwhile appeared on the global scene to represent the third option, that of militant, terrorist Islam. In 1989, the young Muslim, Hamdi Isaac, left his native Harar for Europe, and in July 2005, was arrested in connection with a bombing attempt in the London Underground. The question of what Islam is in the eyes of its believers—the Ethiopian-Saudi aspects of which are discussed in this volume—will undoubtedly

## Notes

1. Edward Gibbon's famous sentence is the classical manifestation of Ethiopia's image as a Christian island: "Encompassed on all sides by the enemies of their religion, the Æthiopians slept near a thousand years, forgetful of the world, by which they were forgotten. They were awakened by the Portuguese, who, turning the southern promontory of Africa, appeared in India and the Red Sea, as if they had descended through the air from a distant planet." Gibbon, *Decline and Fall of the Roman Empire*, vol. 5 (1788), pp. 78–79. (For a discussion of the Portuguese help against Islam, see Chapter 2 of this book.)

2. The passage above is based on my book, *Ethiopia and the Middle East*, especially Chapter 1, "Muhammad's Message: 'Leave the Abyssinians Alone,'" pp. 3–20. It should also be mentioned here that in the internal Islamic context, the figure of the Muslim *najashi*, the prophet's Ethiopian friend, also served the call of those who stood for purifying Islam of racial tendencies and enhancing it as a supra-ethnic universal faith. For this aspect, see Lewis, *Race and Slavery in the Middle East*. See a discussion of Lewis's book in *Ethiopia and the Middle East*, pp. 12–14.

3. See Erlich, *Ethiopia and the Middle East*, pp. 65–72: "Yohannes and the Mahdiyya: The Legacy of Radical Islam."

4. See Erlich, *Ethiopia and the Middle East*, Chapter 8: "The Arabs, Mussolini, and the Abyssinian Dilemma," and Chapter 9: "Pan-Arabism, Arslan, and Conquered Ethiopia."

5. Erlich, *The Cross and the River*. See mainly Chapter 2: "Christianity and Islam: The Formative Concepts," pp. 15–33; also Chapter 9: "Egyptian Concepts of Ethiopia, 1959–1991," pp. 145–182.

6. See, for example, "The Muslim World League" in http://law.about.com/library/911/blmuslim.htm.

7. See Huntington, *The Clash of Civilizations*. Huntington's attempt to portray a global clash between Christian and Islamic civilizations has come under attack from various quarters. His short references to Ethiopia do indeed reflect overgeneralizations seemingly made to fit a sweeping theory. Recycling the concept of Ethiopia as a Christian island (which follows "Coptic Orthodoxy") and is besieged by external Islamic factors (p. 136), he identifies Christianity with Amharas and Ethiopia's Islamic minority with Oromos (p. 256). Moreover, he explains the Ethiopian-Eritrean struggle as one between Christians and Muslims ("On the Horn of Africa, largely Christian Ethiopia and overwhelmingly Muslim Eritrea separated from each other in 1993"), p. 137; see also p. 275.

8. See Sivan, "The Clash Within Islam," pp. 24–25, and even more strongly, Sivan, *The Crash Within Islam*, mainly the Preface.

# 2

## The Christian State
## and the Islamic State

ETHIOPIA WAS THE THIRD POLITICAL ENTITY TO EMBRACE Christianity (after Rome and the Armenians). It did so in A.D. 334 and preserved the unity of the cross and the crown until 1974. It was also the first Christian entity to meet Islam, which was born next door, across the Red Sea. Chapter 1 has already mentioned the beginning of this interreligious dialogue and the dichotomy regarding Christian Ethiopia on the Islamic side. Some elements of this dichotomy were inherited by the followers of Muhammad from the pre-Islamic history of the Arab Peninsula.[1] Aksumite Ethiopia occupied Yemen between A.D. 524 and 590. The Ethiopian ruler of Yemen, Abraha, was said to have raided Mecca in 570 in order to destroy the Kaaba, a polytheistic shrine at that time, and to divert all attention to his church in San'a. The Kaaba, as attested by the "Sura of the Elephant" in the Quran, was miraculously saved, and the concept of the Ethiopians as the ultimate enemies was preserved in a hadith, a saying attributed to the Prophet Muhammed: "the lean-legged Ethiopians will [eventually] destroy the Ka'ba."[2] The Prophet himself was born in the same year, but his later experience with Ethiopians of his acquaintance and his knowledge of the neighboring monotheistic kingdom led him to order his persecuted followers to seek asylum with Ethiopia's "righteous" king. Indeed, the Arabian Peninsula, the immediate neighbor of Ethiopia, was the cradle of Islam and its diverse reservoir of concepts. The Islamic dichotomy regarding Ethiopia—interpretation of the black, *habashi* Christian "other" as a legitimate neighbor vs. the conceptualization of the Ethiopian as the ultimate enemy—was born in those formative years in the Hijaz.

When the center of political Islam shifted away from the Arabian Peninsula, the dual conceptualization of Ethiopia survived. It continued through the ages to inspire Muslim rulers whenever Ethiopia appeared on their agendas. The initial double message, enriched with new experiences and legacies, was always there to resort to and derive from, according to need. In time, this dichotomy, with a new vocabulary, was transmitted to the modern nationalist identities of Arabians, Egyptians, Sudanese, and so forth. The history of Ethiopia's relations with its Middle Eastern neighbors developed alongside this Islamic duality.

In the late 1920s and early 1930s, the Arabian Peninsula regained its political prominence in the Middle East and the world of Islam. The Saudi state of Najd, renewed in Riyadh for the third time in 1902, expanded to unite most of the peninsula and did so in the name of a fundamentalist Islamic doctrine. Having occupied the holy places of Mecca and Medina (1924–1925), and having restrained a more militant coalition of religious purists and tribal leaders that he himself had created (the *Ikhwan* movement, 1929), the state's charismatic re-establisher, 'Abd al-Aziz ibn Sa'ud, in 1932 proclaimed the Kingdom of Saudi Arabia in its current boundaries. In June 1934, he defeated his neighbor the Imam Yahya of Yemen (who attempted to regain a region the Saudis had occupied). Ibn Sa'ud and the defeated imam were now the only independent Arab-Islamic sovereigns; the Saudi was by far the stronger. For many in the Arab world, Ibn Sa'ud was at that time not only "the custodian of the Holy Places" but also the ideal candidate to become the caliph, the leader, in Sunni eyes, of the entire Islamic nation. He did not, however, respond to this presumptuous call, which would have challenged the authority of the region's other states, nor did he dare to defy the British hegemony in the Middle East and the Red Sea. Ibn Sa'ud was a cautious politician. But he was also a Wahhabi, an adherent to a radical Islamic school to whose interpretations of the aforementioned Islamic concepts of Ethiopia we shall soon turn.

## Haile Selassie: The Christian King

The emergence of the Islamic state of Saudi Arabia corresponded to the revitalization of nearby Ethiopia as a Christian empire. In November 1930, Emperor Haile Selassie I was crowned by the *abuna* Qerilos V, the head of the Ethiopian Church. The ambitious monarch, already an experienced politician and the country's strongman for fourteen years, embarked upon a quick road to absolute power. His formula included various aspects of modernization in major fields, combined with strengthening Ethiopian Christianity as a source of legitimacy and control. A devout believer, he had long worked to turn the church into a pillar of Ethiopian uniqueness and modern self-awareness. Already as Crown Prince Ras Tafari (1916–1930), he had made an effort to increase the autonomy of the Ethiopian Church under the Egyptian Coptic mother church. His main goal, to see an Ethiopian appointed by the Egyptian patriarch as *abuna*, was not achieved at that time. In May 1929, the Egyptian Abuna Qerilos V was sent from Cairo to succeed the late Abuna Matewos (d. 1926) as head of the Ethiopian Church. Tafari was also unsuccessful in his effort to obtain from the Egyptians the keys to the gate of the old Ethiopian monastery of Deir al-Sultan in Jerusalem (which had been paternalistically held by the Copts since 1838). He would nevertheless strive for decades to attain these religious goals and, in due course, achieve them. He was more successful, however, in achieving an important related aim. Prior to the arrival of the new Egyptian *abuna*, three Ethiopian monks had been sent to Egypt and returned with him as bishops. In early 1930, the Coptic patriarch himself visited Addis Ababa and appointed a fourth Ethiopian bishop. It was the first time in sixteen centuries of Ethiopian Christianity that Ethiopians held such positions, so vital to the expansion of the priesthood and the sanctioning of churches. The new Ethiopian bishops took part in the coronation of Haile Selassie as a Christian king.[3]

In the four peaceful years ahead, Haile Selassie took major steps toward centralizing his regime. In July 1931, he enacted Ethiopia's first modern constitution which defined the limited powers of all other forces and depicted the emperor as a representative of divinity.[4] Reforms were introduced in administration, armed forces, education, the judiciary system, church management, and others.[5] These were all initiated and led by the all-powerful emperor who acted as both a modernizing monarch and as the actual head of the Ethiopian Church. This last position had been traditionally held by all of his predecessors, but with Haile Selassie I, heading the Church became a dynamic reality. He strove to identify the emerging modern nationalism with Ethiopia's orthodox Christianity. Perhaps the most significant step in this direction during those years was his initiative to translate the Bible from Geez into Amharic. Very few in Ethiopia of that time, including many of the priests, understood the messages of the holy scriptures conveyed in the ancient language of Geez. Rendering them in all-Ethiopian Amharic was a revolutionary step of the utmost significance. The Emperor arranged for the publication of the Gospels and liturgy with the texts in Geez and Amharic in parallel

columns. In 1934, a full translation of the Bible was completed in manuscript form, but spreading the printed books had to wait until after World
War II.[6] Thus by strengthening the identification of the cross with the
crown, Haile Selassie was able to combine the traditional with the modern. On the one hand, he supported the church establishment. In 1930,
sixty youngsters were sent to Egypt to be educated in Coptic institutions. A theological college was planned, to be opened in Saint George
Church in Addis Ababa. On the other hand, reforms in education and in
the judiciary eroded the power of the clergy. Moreover, unlike his predecessors, Haile Selassie was appreciative of the role of foreign missionaries (he himself had been educated by French missionaries in Harar). By
1935, some 200 European missionaries were active throughout the
country. Many of them, like those in Harar, were deliberately sent to
spread their word among non-Christian populations.[7]

The ancient concept of Ethiopia as a "Christian island" would survive
into the 1970s and beyond. In the years under discussion, Haile Selassie
continued to work to soften the old sense of isolation and to connect
Ethiopia with the wider world. But his concept of his country remained to
the end that of a Christian citadel. Nearly half of the population in the
early 1930s was Muslim: 2,250,000 compared to 2,625,000 Ethiopian
Christians, as estimated by the Italians in 1930.[8] But almost all positions
of significance in all public fields were held by Christians. Muslim communities were marginalized and administered by Christian governors.
They were geographically scattered, divided by deep linguistic and ethnic
differences, and defined themselves in terms of language and ethnicity.
Most Muslims lived according to popular Islamic customs and rituals and
had only scant knowledge of Arabic,[9] the language of education, law, and
intercommunal communication. Islamic centers of learning were spread
throughout the country, but those of historic significance were in Harar,
Wallo, and Jimma. Of these, only Jimma survived the nineteenth-century
political expansion of the Christian state as an autonomous entity, thanks
to the submission in 1883 of its ruler, Sultan Muhammad bin Daud Abba
Jifar II, and his full acceptance of Ethiopian hegemony. He committed
himself to helping Emperor Menelik II (1889–1913) to expand further in
the south and in return was promised that no churches would be built in
his autonomous territory. Under his rule, Jimma flourished economically
and as an Islamic center. In the 1880s, Jimma was believed to have had
around sixty Islamic schools, and it continued to develop its religious education and legal systems, as the pious ruler supported scholars and Sufi
leaders. However, on 19 September 1934, when Abba Jifar II died, Haile
Selassie abolished the Jimma autonomy altogether and appointed a

Christian governor over this last and only administrative manifestation of Islamic existence in Ethiopia.[10]

In the early 1930s, the emperor could thus treat Islam as if Christian dominance were natural. The Ethiopian empire seemed stronger than ever. Its elite was still feeding on the memories of its late-nineteenth-century victories over other local peoples and over Western imperialists. Islamic and Arab societies in the Middle East and in the Horn of Africa were long conquered (with the notable exception of Saudi Arabia and Yemen), occupied by either Europeans or Ethiopians. Contacts between Muslims in Ethiopia and their co-religionists in the Middle East were now quite remote. Long distance commerce, traditionally handled in Ethiopia by Muslims only, was slow. There was an acute economic crisis in Egypt and in the developed Arab countries, and slave trade between Ethiopia and Arabia, another long-standing Arab-Islamic enterprise, came to a practical halt. In the first half of the 1930s, only one suspected slave dhow was spotted in the Red Sea from a distance by a British ship.[11] The number of Muslim Ethiopian pilgrims to Mecca in the year 1932 was 49, and in 1933, only 11.[12]

## Christian Ethiopian Concepts of Islam

This was not always the picture. In the past—and indeed during the later twentieth century—whenever momentous political or religious movements united Muslims in the Middle East, and whenever this momentum reached the Red Sea, it injected fresh energy among the Muslims of the Horn of Africa. The ultimate manifestation of this Islamic Middle Eastern–African connection was the sixteenth-century case of Ahmad ibn Ibrahim, better known by his Ethiopian nickname, "Gragn." Prior to his emergence in 1520 as an amir in the town of Harar, the Muslims in what is today southern Ethiopia and Somalia had been divided into various independent emirates, torn among themselves by ethnic, linguistic, and tribal differences. The neighboring Ethiopian empire of the Solomonian dynasty (as of 1270) had enjoyed two and a half centuries of military superiority over these Islamic entities. The Christian armies raided and occasionally occupied the area of the Muslims. Ahmad Gragn's early career in Harar was marked by resumed contacts with the Islam of the Arab Peninsula. The contact itself was not new. In the tenth century, Harar had emerged as practically the only medieval urban center of Islam in the inland of the Horn. It was said to have been established by immigrants from Mecca and continued to occasionally attract roving Islamic scholars from Arabia. When Gragn seized power, his followers were already under the influence of a wave of migrating Islamic scholars from Hadarmawt and Mecca, which had begun in the 1490s. The amir of Mecca, Barakat II (1495–1522), sent Gragn his blessings together with green holy war flags, like those of the Prophet. The religious momentum in Arabia only heralded a new wave of political inspiration from beyond the Red Sea. In 1517, the Ottomans occupied Egypt and continued in their successful enterprise of creating the mightiest empire in the world at that time. They united the Islamic Middle East, occupied most of the Red Sea coasts, and became entrenched in Yemen. This powerful revival of Middle Eastern Islam directly and diversely influenced Ahmad Gragn's local Islamic revolution. Gragn united the various Islamic communities around an anti-Ethiopian holy war, to which Islamic scholars from various parts of Arabia brought the spiritual drive. They also helped to spread Arabic, the language in which the entire campaign was conducted and later recorded. The Ottomans in Yemen supplied Gragn with auxiliary military units and artillery. It was due to this Arabian–Middle Eastern connection that Gragn managed to unite Islam in the Horn and to launch a devastating campaign against the Christian kingdom. Between 1529 and 1543, Gragn's armies occupied the entire country in the name of Islam. From an Ethiopian point of view, this was the greatest defeat ever, the only time (prior to Mussolini's occupation of 1936–1941) that the Christian empire had been subjugated. According to Ethiopian tradition, nine of every ten Christians were forced to adopt Islam. Salvation came through the help of the Portuguese who enabled the Ethiopians to regroup and finally to kill Gragn.[13]

If the Prophet-*najashi* dialogue was the formative experience that shaped the initial Islamic concepts of Ethiopia, the history summarized above seems to have shaped the Christian Ethiopians' concepts of the Middle East. They were similarly dichotomous. On one hand was the awareness, fed by both history and myth, that Ethiopia as a Christian culture was part of the greater Middle East; that it had developed in Oriental Semitic languages and as an extension of Eastern Christianity; that keeping in touch with the Middle East, the source of material innovations and religious legitimacy, was vital for Christian Ethiopia's survival and progress. This urge to continue to belong to the Middle East was manifested in sixteen centuries of voluntarily accepting the position of a junior branch of the Egyptian Church. It was also manifested in the royal political ethos, couched in biblical Christian religiosity, of the "Glory of Kings" legend. Namely, the conviction that Ethiopian monarchs were direct descendents of King Solomon of Jerusalem.

The strong sense of affiliation with the East and the maintenance of its practical aspects—a bishop from Egypt, a pilgrimage to Jerusalem—necessitated a continuous dialogue with the rulers of Islam. Where these Ethiopians' needs met with the parallel Islamic concepts of tolerance towards Ethiopia, there was wide space for constructive mutuality. This was especially true of Egypt, whose relations with Ethiopia revolved around a dual dependency—Egypt as the source of the patriarch (and the road to Jerusalem), Ethiopia as the source of Egypt's Nile. Altogether, the Christian Ethiopian sense of belonging to the Middle East also worked to develop a sense of pragmatic proximity with Islam. In a previous book, *The Cross and the River*, I analyzed this Ethiopian concept under a section called "The Ethiopians and the Egyptian *Abun*."[14]

On the other hand, Christian Ethiopians developed an antithetical concept, that of deep suspicion of Islam and fear of the proximity of the Middle East. This can be labeled the "Ahmad Gragn trauma." The sixteenth-century experience of total collapse in the face of unified Islamic communities in the Horn of Africa is perhaps the single most vivid historical collective memory of Christian Ethiopians. The Gragn conquest was a unique episode, total and abrupt. The legacy it left was not fear of the Muslims in the Horn or Ethiopia. In themselves, the Muslims of the region returned to their fragmentation and were never again able to achieve similar power. Nor was it fear of the Middle East itself. The Islamic dynasties of the core Land of Islam continued to "leave Ethiopia alone." The Gragn trauma was the fear of a potential connection between a revitalized Islamic Middle East and local Islamic communities in the Horn, which could result in the politicization and unity of Islam at the expense of Christian hegemony.[15]

This Christian Ethiopian conceptual duality had a geographical aspect. With those areas of the Islamic Middle East with which Ethiopia had Christian connections, and especially with Egypt over which Ethiopia had its Nile leverage, relations were multidimensional. But with the Arabian Peninsula, it was somewhat different. There were no Christian connections in Arabia nor any leverage over it, and it was from there that religious and material support for Gragn came.


## Harar and Islam in Ethiopia

No less important was the role of Harar as the place that Christians identified with the Gragn trauma. Since Harar is a pivotal dimension of our modern story, it is worth expanding on its historical role.[16] Prior to

1887, the town was never under Ethiopian control. It was a busy Islamic juncture of ethnic and commercial relations, as well as an urban center with its own self-identity and political and cultural continuity.

From its inception, Harar remained connected to the greater Islamic world, mainly to Mecca and Yemen. Traditions are contradictory about when Shaikh Abadir 'Umar al-Rida actually founded the town. One tradition mentions the years 945–964; another tells of Abadir's arrival in 1216. But they all agree on his origin. He is said to be an Arab, a descendent of the first caliph, Abu Bakr, who came from Mecca with 143 Arab followers who set up the urban community.[17] The same Shaikh Abadir was also said to have been a disciple of Shaikh 'Abd al-Qadir al-Jaylani, the twelfth-century founder of the Sufi (mystical Islamic) *tariqa* (order, or fraternity) of *al-Qadiriyya*, who himself came to Harar for a short period. Under Abadir's leadership, the Qadiriyya was rooted in Harar. Later, mainly after the fall of Gragn, the town became the *tariqa*'s regional center and radiated Sufism in all directions. In the fourteenth and fifteenth centuries, Harar was directly mentioned in the histories of Somali, Afar, and Sidama speakers, their various political entities, and their conflicts with the Ethiopians. Harar's all-regional and Arab-connected role culminated in Gragn's campaigns. The conquest of Christian Ethiopia, however, proved also to be a costly gamble. After the demise of Gragn, his Harar capital was reduced from a dynamic regional center to a town struggling to survive and retain its identity. Amir Nur ibn Mujahid (1551–1569) built the famous walls to defend Harar from the rising power of the Oromo peoples. From his time until 1875, Harar conducted a most complicated dialogue with the Oromos which is beyond our scope.[18] More related to the background of our story were Harar's relations with Somali speakers. The town remained integrally connected to the Somali clans of the Ogaden desert. Many Somali speakers lived in Harar itself, and many of the Ogaden nomads followed the Qadiriyya. Though some Hararis made an effort to retain their pure Harari identity, there was always a very vivid Somali dimension in this Harari concept. The ultimate manifestation of Harari uniqueness was the language of the Adari, maintained and spoken within its walls.

Harar's own vitality gave it the stamina to survive the challenge of the Oromos and even to influence their own gradual Islamization. In 1578, the local dynasty was forced to move to Awsa in the Afar area, but in 1647 it was revived and remained in power until 1875. Closed behind its walls, never allowing any Western traveler to enter (in 1855 Richard F. Burton was the first to enter, in disguise), the town remained an agricultural and commercial center, trading in coffee, the narcotic *qat,* skins, ivory, cloth, and slaves with the coast and the Arab Peninsula. It was famous for its permissive life on one hand,[19] and for its lively Islamic religiosity on the other. Harar's Islam was vibrant. It included Sufi Islam with its reverence of saints, sensual ceremonies, and tomb visitations (*ziyara*—particularly those of Abadir and Amir Nur[20]) as well as orthodox Islam, of both the Shafi'i and Hanafi legal schools. Dozens of quranic schools, mosques, and other institutions of learning operated over the centuries. Generations of local scholars retained Arabic as the language of learning, law, and prayer.[21] Amir Muhammad bin 'Abd al-Shakur (1856–1875), for example, built a library which contained classical interpretations of the Quran, collections of the hadith, legal literature, and Arabic historical texts. Harar was known as an Islamic center in Arabia and Egypt and was occasionally visited by scholars.[22] Hararis kept in constant touch with Mecca through the hajj. Though we lack statistics on the precolonial periods, the annual pilgrimage was clearly well organized in Harar. In 1874, it is said, Harari pilgrims in Mecca invited the Egyptians to come and save the town from the Oromos.[23]

Between 1875 and 1885 Harar was occupied by the Egyptians, who, for their own purposes, worked to modernize its infrastructure and to encourage the spread of orthodox Islam. Islamic scholars were brought from Al-Azhar to work inside the walls and among the Oromos outside. The Egyptians did not open new schools in Harar, but they did upgrade the existing system by introducing Egyptian teachers and the study of mathematics and geography in Arabic. Some outstanding local students were sent to Al-Azhar in Cairo. When Ethiopia regained its regional hegemony under Emperor Menelik II, the entire south was conquered and annexed to the Christian empire. Harar was occupied in January 1887, and its new governor, Ras Makonen (Haile Selassie's father), was quite efficient at absorbing the town into the all-Ethiopian fabric. He built churches, introduced some modern administrative methods, and turned Harar, now the capital of an Ethiopian province named Hararge, into a major power base in imperial politics. Within this policy, he also worked to appease the conquered Muslims. He appointed 'Abdallah al-Sadiq as "Head of the Muslims" and saw to the welfare of the community and its religious institutions.[24] Under Makonen and his Christian establishment, Harar became one of the most important towns in the Ethiopian empire and has remained so to this day. When an envoy of the Ottoman Sultan visited the town in 1904, he was an enthusiastic witness to an Islamic community flourishing under the "righteous" *najashi*, Menelik II.[25]

During the reign of Menelik II, a process of co-opting and assimilating the elite of the various Islamic communities began. Jimma, as mentioned, was the only community to obtain autonomy. Another important Islamic community worth briefly noting here was Wallo. Wallo's community was established by Oromos who invaded this core region of highland Ethiopia in the sixteenth-century and adopted Islam in the eighteenth. Their Islamization process was a result of the transformation of the society of Wallo Oromos from a tribal, egalitarian system into hierarchical dynasties, combined with their growing religious contact with Arabia. Indeed, before we continue with the development of Ethiopia, we need to briefly cross the Red Sea again.

The second half of the eighteenth century in the Arabian Peninsula witnessed another wave of religious and political Islamic momentum, ignited by the rise of the first Saudi-Wahhabi state in Najd in 1745–1746. The new state combined the political skills of the Al Sa'ud family with the Islamic doctrine of Muhammad bin 'Abd al-Wahhab (1703–1792). It was a radically Quran-centered, Sunni fundamentalist doctrine that rejected all later theological and mystical innovations and was strongly anti-Sufi. The first Saudi-Wahhabi state stretched mostly through central Arabia and was still unable to dominate the Peninsula. In 1802, the Saudi-Wahhabis captured Mecca, but in 1811 Muhammad 'Ali Pasha of Egypt sent his army, liberated Mecca two years later, and gradually destroyed the Saudi polity.

One response to the eighteenth-century rise of the first Wahhabi state was a revitalization in Arabia of its Islamic rivals, moderate orthodoxy, and Sufism. One prominent scholar teaching in Mecca between 1800 and 1813 who stood up to the Wahhabis was Ahmad ibn Idris al-Fasi (1760–1837). A native of Morocco, he invested a great deal in his African students. Ibn Idris al-Fasi was one of many scholars who at that period granted Sufism a milder interpretation, closer to moderate orthodoxy. He discouraged the use of narcotics and the reverence of saints and emphasized the centrality of the Quran and Shari'a. His students, upon returning to their countries, were indeed ready to establish important Sufi movements of Islamic and political revival. Among his disciples were the founders of the *Sanusiyya* in Libya and the *Mirghaniyya* in the Sudan. The *Mirghaniyya* was behind the nineteenth-century Islamization of the western Eritrean clans of the Banu 'Amir, which would, in the late 1950s, become the backbone of the Eritrean Liberation Front. Ibn Idris al-Fasi also inspired the *tariqa* of the *Salihiyya*, which would be the spiritual source of the early-twentieth-century Somali anticolonial revolt led by Muhammad bin 'Abdallah Hasan.[26]

The rise of Islam in Wallo was related to this comprehensive revival of Sufism. Quite a number of young Oromo Islamic scholars also studied in Mecca and Medina of that time and were inspired by this Sufi-intellectual momentum. Back in Wallo they spread this kind of Islam under the patronage of the local Oromo dynasties. In the first half of the nineteenth century, Wallo's Islam, in terms of learning and legal institutions, reached dimensions equal to Harar's. However, unlike Harar, Wallo was already well-interwoven in Ethiopian life. Wallo's elite participated in, and occasionally even dominated, the all-imperial Ethiopian political game, and some of it members voluntarily adopted Christianity. Islam in Wallo, as analyzed by Hussein Ahmed, developed quite flexibly, and along popular Islamic lines. Its spiritual leaders who studied in Arabia and were acquainted with the *Wahhabiyya*, refused to import

> the *Wahhabis'* call for the rejection of established Islamic institutions and practices such as the mystical orders and the veneration of saints. . . . Of the main nineteenth-century forms of Islamic militant movements in the Muslim world—*Wahhabism, Mahdism* [of the Sudan], and *tariqa* revival—it was only to the last that the Ethiopian Muslim 'Ulama, especially those of Wallo, responded favorably.[27]

Generally speaking, the Islam that was thus developing helped to preserve the Wallo Oromos' autonomy and identity but also coexisted with Ethiopia's politics and constituted part of Ethiopia's diverse culture.

This state of coexistence was challenged when emperors Tewodros II (1855–1868) and Yohannes IV (1872–1889) destroyed the political base of the Wallo Oromo. In 1878, Imam Muhammad 'Ali, the Wallo Oromo leader, converted to Christianity. He adopted the name of Ras Mikael and became a major figure in the courts, first of Yohannes IV, then of Menelik II. Yet, though Islam occasionally inspired vivid protest movements in Wallo of the nineteenth and twentieth centuries, it remained, generally speaking, closely affiliated with Ethiopian culture and identity.[28]

Harar, in contrast, was never a part of Ethiopia prior to 1887 and was never really uprooted from its long, independent history. It soon returned to its role of embodying the Islamic political challenge to Ethiopia's Christian domination. Menelik's successor, his grandson Lij Iyasu, was the son of Ras Mikael of Wallo. After the death of Menelik, Iyasu began to build a new coalition based mainly on peripheral forces and newly annexed populations. A year into this process, in late 1914, with the outbreak of World War I, political Islam in the greater Middle

East was revitalized. The Ottomans declared a holy war against the Allies, the powers (Britain, France, and Italy) that, in the Ethiopian context, supported the elite that Iyasu was attempting to replace. In June 1915, Iyasu moved to the Ogaden and stayed there until April 1916. Without even notifying Tafari, Ras Makonen's son and the governor of Harar, Iyasu appointed 'Abdallah al-Sadiq vice-governor of Hararge. He then married 'Abdallah's daughter and made his father-in-law his tutor on Islam and his contact with Somali leader Muhammad bin 'Abdallah Hasan (the "Mad Mullah"). The latter had begun an anti-British holy war in 1899 and was trying to inspire the Somali clans of the Ogaden to follow the militant *Salihiyya* order rather than the mellower *Qadiriyya* order. In August 1916, Iyasu removed Tafari from Harar and made it his headquarters. A short time later, he was reported to have declared himself a Muslim. Though some of the story still remains a mystery, it is quite clear that Iyasu gambled on an Ottoman victory in the war, and on himself as the ruler of an Islamic Horn of Africa, with Harar as its capital.[29] It seems that Iyasu began his dialogue with Islam following his native Wallo model of religious Ethiopian coexistence, but he ended up in Harar siding with the Middle Eastern–inspired political victory of Muslims. However, an Ottoman defeat in the Arabian Peninsula (by the "Arab Revolt" of the pro-British Hashemites of the Hijaz) rendered this gamble disastrous. On 27 September 1916, a coalition of Ethiopian strongmen and the *abuna* exposed Iyasu as a Muslim and therefore no longer a legal ruler. In his autobiography (written between 1937 and 1940), Haile Selassie cited the indictment against Iyasu read on that occasion. It was most probably composed by the future emperor and surely reflected Haile Selassie's political-Christian concepts:

> The Christian faith, which our fathers had hitherto carefully retained by fighting for their faith with the Muslims and by shedding their blood, Ledj Iyasu exchanged for the Muslim religion and aroused commotion in our midst; in order to exterminate us by mutual fighting he has converted to Islam and, therefore, we shall henceforth not submit to him; we shall not place a Muslim on the throne of a Christian king.[30]

Zawditu, Menelik's daughter, was crowned as empress, and Ras Tafari (Haile Selassie), the leading figure of the coalition, was proclaimed heir to the throne. Iyasu himself was captured and arrested in 1921. His deposition was legitimized by his supposed pretension at being an "Islamic *najashi*" and evoking the Gragn trauma in its original Harar setting.

By the early 1930s, however, the Islamic political challenge to Christian dominance in Ethiopia seemed to have been long defeated. In May 1932, Lij Iyasu escaped from his prison and for a moment Haile Selassie's regime was threatened. But the plot was attributed to rivalries within the ruling elite, and little was said about Iyasu's Islamic history. In any event, he was caught within less than a week and transferred to a new prison in Hararge province. Three years later, the Italians would threaten to invade Ethiopia, and their propaganda would revitalize political Islam in the Horn of Africa. We shall turn to this dramatic change in the next chapter.

Before the appearance of the threat of Mussolini, Haile Selassie's Christian empire still enjoyed growing confidence. Throughout 1930–1935, Addis Ababa continued to expand, thriving on commerce led mostly by Muslims, who were hardly recognized as a community. Back in 1904, Emperor Menelik had promised the Ottomans he would build a mosque for the capital's Muslims, but neither he nor Haile Selassie authorized the enterprise. An initiative to issue a newspaper in Arabic, raised in the early 1930s by an Egyptian schoolmaster in Addis Ababa, was not approved.

However, Muslims were accepted, even encouraged, as traders. The leading merchants of Addis Ababa and of Harar enjoyed imperial favor and shared business with the royal family. A trading firm named Muhammadali, registered in India, had branches in the capital, in Harar, and in other places. With imperial support—a leading middleman was Shaikh Barasu, member of a prominent Harari family—the firm dominated much of the import-export business in Ethiopia at the time. The firm combined the interests of many local Islamic leading families and of Indian Muslim merchants who had been favored since the days of Emperor Menelik. The Addis Ababa community of Arab traders, mostly immigrants from Yemen and Aden, had a strong presence in the *mercato,* the capital's huge market. A similar and closely related community of leading locals, Indians and Arabs, also developed now in Harar, gradually depriving the local trading middle class of their old privileges. The Arab traders in the capital had their social club (*Nadi Sa'id*), and on some occasions they could gather and receive imperial attention. The firing of guns during Ramadan, however, was not allowed.[31]

Haile Selassie's policy toward the Muslims of his empire was a mixture of suspicion, exploitation, and patronizing tolerance. The latter dimension seemed to grow with the general stabilization of the early 1930s and the remoteness of the Middle East. Haile Selassie's governor of Harar in the early 1930s, Ras Imru, was his closest friend and one of the enlightened members of the greater royal family. Under his authority, a more relaxed atmosphere prevailed in the town. A related aspect was the resumption of Muslims' cultural and social initiatives. Some time before 1933, an Islamic Voluntary Association (*Jam'iyyat al-khayriyya al-islamiyya*) was founded by a group of some sixty local Harari and Yemeni traders (the latter were headed by Shaikh Ahmad Shamsan). The new association members, called *firmach,* the signatories, and led by Hajj Abu Bakr 'Ayun, tried to address various issues on the Muslims' agenda, including how the big, regime-connected merchants were depriving the local middle class of their assets. They blamed traditional costly Harari burial and wedding customs for impoverishing the masses and called for abiding by stricter orthodoxy. Their major contribution, however, was the initiative in 1933 to establish the first modern Islamic-Arabic school in Harar. The town, to reiterate, had been an ancient center of traditional Islamic education, and shortly before the Ethiopian occupation, some twenty elementary Quran schools functioned there. After the Ethiopian annexation of Harar, the number of those schools dwindled and, most significantly, Amharic replaced Arabic as the language of education.[32] As Harar gradually lost its Arab-inspired Islamic identity, the cream of its Islamic youth began to emigrate to Addis Ababa. The founders of the new school viewed their enterprise in terms of Islamic-Harari national revival. Under the management of Shaikh 'Ali 'Abd al-Rahman, better known as 'Ali al-Sufi, the new school, popularly called *Jam'iyya* (association), reintroduced Arabic and strove to construct a modern Islamic and general curriculum. Little is known about the history of the school in the two years prior to the Italian occupation. It was said to have been tolerated by the Ethiopian authorities, and the emperor was said to have donated 5,000 birr for the school. Books were brought from Egypt through Addis Ababa's Muslim-owned bookshops, and some conservative Islamic leaders in town opposed the new curriculum.[33] The story of this first modern Islamic school in Ethiopia would soon acquire greater significance.

## Wahhabi-Saudi and Arabian Concepts of Ethiopia

Haile Selassie was now fully ready to restore a dialogue with Arabia. In February 1934, when war broke out between Yemen and the Saudis, the Yemeni imam approached the emperor to buy 2,000 mules. Haile Selassie, with the help of his Muslim traders, managed to hurriedly ship

100 animals, but most did not survive. However, he lost no time in pursuing the commercial and diplomatic opportunity. In the first week of June, a three-member Ethiopian delegation was dispatched via Aden to San'a. It was composed of David Hall, a Polish-German Jew who served as a director of the agency in charge of government purchasing and as an adviser to the foreign ministry;[34] Kassa Maru of the foreign ministry; and Shaikh 'Umar al-Azhari, a Somali from Harar and Addis Ababa with connections in Egypt who was long involved in ensuring the loyalty of the Ogaden Somalis to the Ethiopian crown.[35] The declared aim of the mission was to demonstrate Ethiopia's goodwill toward its Arab neighbors and to mediate between the Yemenis and the Saudis. Beyond that was interest in building commercial, as well as diplomatic, relations. The mission was cordially received in San'a. It then proceeded to Jedda in the first week of July 1934 and remained in Saudi Arabia until 15 July.[36] It brought the following letter from Haile Selassie to Ibn Sa'ud:

> We and the Ethiopian nation still remember the relations and friendship which have existed between us and the Arab Nation since olden times until to-day, a relation which history has recorded within its pages and which we shall never forget. We wish from the depth of our heart success and greatness for the Arab Governments of Western Asia. We are therefore grieved to hear that war broke out between Your Majesty and His Majesty the king of Yemen the Imam Yahya ibn Muhammad Hamiduddin. We are also grieved that concord does not prevail between the two brotherly Governments. Such grief will doubtless not be confined to the Arabs only but it will be prevalent among all those related to you and will also affect all friends.
>
> In order to show our affection and friendship we send Your Majesty a delegation composed of our honest servants David Hall, Ato Kassa Maru and Sheikh 'Umar al-Azhari, to prove the affection we have in our hearts to Your Majesty and in order to see peace and amity established between Your Majesty and His Majesty King Yahya. . . . We hope that this special delegation we have deputed to Your Majesty will receive Your Majesty's attention and we beg Your Majesty to accept our wishes.
>
> Written on 19 Genbot 1926 [27 May 1934] in the fourth year of our reign in our capital Addis Ababa.
>
> (Sd.) Haile Selassie[37]

By the time the delegation reached Jedda, the Saudi-Yemeni war had ended and the Ethiopians' mediation services were not needed. The Saudis received their guests hospitably, and the Mecca weekly *Umm al-Qura* of 6 July 1934 mentioned that this was the second Ethiopian delegation to Arabia; the first one had been sent by the righteous *najashi* to

the Prophet.[38] Beyond that courtesy, there were no practical consequences of the Ethiopian initiative, except for the following letter from
Ibn Sa'ud:

> In the name of God the Most Merciful the Compassionate. To His
> Majesty Emperor Haile Selassie I, Emperor of Abyssinia.
>     We have had great pleasure in receiving your honorable delega-
> tion that brought us Your Majesty's letter, and thus renewed the
> remembrance of the old relations which existed between your people
> and the country of the Arabs. Our Arab nation shall never forget that
> strong friendship which aided and supported the rise of Arab and
> Islamic nation at the beginning of the development of Islam. We
> appreciate Your Majesty's high feelings and that generous spirit shown
> by you in respect to the small dispute which existed between us and
> His Majesty our brother the King and Imam Yahya. We are glad to
> convey to Your Majesty the good news of the end of that dispute. In
> this connection we cannot but offer our thanks for Your Majesty's
> mediation and your good wishes.
>     We greatly welcome the idea of inaugurating relations between us
> and Your Majesty and between our peoples and countries. We wish
> that such relations will bring forth the best of good results for the two
> countries. We wish Your Majesty and your people all success and hap-
> piness.
>     Written in our palace in Ta'if in the 26th Rabi' Awwal 1353 [10
> July 1934].
>     (Sd.) 'Abd al-'Aziz Al Sa'ud[39]

Ibn Sa'ud's written response to the "first Ethiopian delegation since
the days of the Prophet" was in the spirit of cordial acceptance. He was
glad to resume relations with a Christian *najashi* and to base these relations on the memory of ancient Ethiopia having saved Islam. In the summer of 1934, the issue was still a minor one on Ibn Sa'ud's agenda. His
interests and worries were elsewhere, and it seemed practical to respond
to Haile Selassie expressing noncommittal kindness. Ibn Sa'ud was a
shrewd politician who had masterfully created, retained, and expanded
his power through flexible pragmatism. He did so not only by facing
various rivals but also by facing the initial dichotomy between the new
Middle Eastern Arab state he had built and the Wahhabi doctrine and
movement of fundamentalist, *jihadi* Islam he himself had reignited and
re-enlivened. Combining the religious radicalism of the *Wahhabiyya*
with the institutions, concepts, boundaries, and considerations of the territorial state—a state built on tribal norms and family interests—represented, from its very inception, the pivotal complexity of Saudi Arabia.
Every dimension of its modern history is a product of this inner tension.

The Ethiopian dimension is no exception; rather, it is a classical example of the complex Saudi conceptualization of the "self" and the "other."

Before we turn to the *Wahhabiyya* and its conceptualization of Ethiopia, we need to remind ourselves that it was only in the 1920s that the Saudi state managed to force that doctrine over most of Arabia. Prior to that, the Hijaz and its holy places were centers of various Islamic trends. We have already mentioned the Islamic orthodox, the Sufi revivalist, as well as the political *jihadi* connections and influences that Mecca had over the centuries with Ethiopia and with the Horn's Muslims. Arabian and Hijazi contact with Ethiopia had another central dimension—slavery. From very ancient times the Horn of Africa was a source of slaves for Arabia and from there to the rest of the East. The relevant history of this pivotal issue cannot be discussed here.[40] By the 1930s, when we begin our concrete Ethiopian-Saudi story, the Red Sea, as mentioned, had ceased to be the major slave trade route it had been until World War I. In the 1930s, the Saudis, in their dialogue with the League of Nations, began trying to hide slaving and slavers, while Haile Selassie's Ethiopia began, as of July 1931, to combat the trade legally and actively. The emperor was now also ready to cover the costs of reabsorbing, in Ethiopia, slaves manumitted by the British in Arabia.[41]

But the recent abolition of trade activities could not erase slavery nor the impact that the institution had on cultural concepts. Actual enslaving of Ethiopians by Muslims centered in Arabia. Their import to Arabian ports and markets had just reached its historical peak. In practice, the 1857 Ottoman declaration abolishing slavery was not applied to Arabia. Various studies of the subject estimate that, throughout the nineteenth century, up to 5,000 Ethiopian slaves were bought and sold in Arabia annually. Ethiopian, *habashi* slaves, as distinguished from other blacker Africans (*sudan* or *zunuj*), were considered the best. Their life in Arabia (and in other parts of the Islamic world to which they were taken) were not necessarily miserable. They were all converted to Islam, served in households, and occasionally integrated into families as concubines, nurses, domestic servants, tutors, and so forth. Very many prominent Arabians throughout history were descendants of Ethiopian women. The population of Mecca, it was observed in the nineteenth century, was somewhat more "golden" and darker, attesting particularly to such Ethiopian connections.[42]

Both the institution of slavery and the term *habasha*—"Ethiopians" in Arabic—had only an indirect connection to the Christian culture and state of Ethiopia. Most of the *habashi* slaves brought over the centuries from the Horn of Africa to Arabia were not Ethiopian Christians. They

were mostly Oromo, Sidama, and members of other peoples and tribal
societies from southern Ethiopia and the Nile basin. Many of these were
also enslaved by Ethiopians, both Christian and Muslim. But long-distance slave trade was in the hands of Muslims only, an Arabian and local
co-enterprise. *Habashi* was a term that referred to color, not religion.[43]
In classical Arabic it designates "a certain race of blacks," and it was
popularly believed that the basic concept of this Arabic name is "mixture [of peoples]," suitable for the multi-ethnic Horn and Ethiopia.[44] The
browner skin color of the people or the peoples of *al-habasha* was conceived in Arabia as less inferior in comparison to other, darker African
slaves. As all *habashi* slaves brought to Arabia were converted to Islam,
their image was boosted also by the memory of the initial story of the
Prophet and the *najashi*. A sixteenth-century manuscript written in
Medina (in 1583–1584) contains the following example of Arabian attitudes to slavery and the *habasha*:

> Praise be to Allah Who created man from a clay of mud and preferred
> some of them to others. The disparity between them was like the dis-
> tance between the sky and the earth. Each group [however,] praises
> and pleases Allah. . . . He made them servants and masters, rulers and
> ruled. Allah distinguished some of the descendants of Noah . . . with
> prophethood and sovereignty, and He predestined servitude and slav-
> ery for some of them until the Day of Resurrection. . . . But he blessed
> some of the servants with distinction by which they became masters.
> He distinguished a group of Ethiopians with grace, leadership and
> faith—like Bilal,[45] like al-Najashi . . . and others who believed [in
> Him] and adhered [to Islam]. Many of them became Companions [of
> the Prophet], successors and holy and righteous men. Moreover, they
> became eminent men on earth and in Paradise, and religious guides
> and temporal leaders.[46]

The author, 'Abd al-Baqi al-Bukhari al-Makki, studied in Mecca
and was a judge and a preacher in Medina. He wrote this passage as an
introduction to a booklet entitled, "The Colored Brocade Concerning the
Good Qualities of the Ethiopians." It is a compilation of all the praises
for Ethiopians he could find in various Islamic texts, notably the famous
Egyptian Jalal al-Din al-Suyuti's "Raising the Status of the Ethiopians,"
published a century earlier. Al-Makki's book has four parts and all
revolve around the Prophet-*najashi* story, the merits of the Ethiopian
king, his hospitality and righteousness, and the exalted virtues that he
and the Ethiopians in general possess. There is a strong emphasis
throughout on Ethiopians as faithful Muslims, and on the *najashi*'s conversion to Islam, but there is no mention of the other Ethiopians'

Christianity as a negative culture. The *habasha*, in general, even though they were destined to slavery, had kind virtues due to which many of them, as Muslims, could lead Islamic communities as free men. There is also a strong recommendation to marry Ethiopian concubines.[47] In short, though racially different, the Ethiopians were considered superior to other Africans. Though born to serve, they had very positive virtues. Through Islam a *habashi* slave could become a most distinguished individual; he could even be a ruler.[48] Many Muslims of some darker complexion were nicknamed *al-Habashi*, and throughout history dozens of prominent personalities of various backgrounds adopted this name.

What were the initial Wahhabi concepts of Ethiopia? The roots of Saudi-Wahhabi principles do not stem from Hijazi traditions and experiences but rather from the doctrinal legacy of Taqi al-Din Ahmad ibn Taymiyya (d. 1328). This medieval Islamic scholar, who resided in Damascus, was the spiritual founder of Sunni fundamentalism. His main intention was to most strictly follow the Quran and the hadith, and he considered religion and the state to be indissolubly linked. Without the coercive power of the state, he wrote, religion was in danger, but between them was the ruler—the absolute servant of strict Islamic law. The writings of Ibn Taymiyya continue to inspire Islamic radicals the world over.[49] More to the point, Ibn Taymiyya molded the main political Islamic concepts that directly influenced the eighteenth-century scholar Shaikh 'Abd al-Wahhab (d. 1792), founder of the *Wahhabiyya* movement in Najd, and the spiritual founder of the Saudi state. 'Abd al-Wahhab recycled Ibn Taymiyya's formula of rulers–*'ulama* (scholars) harmonic partnership, designed to implement true Islam. Their Islam was based on the principles of God's oneness, on the quranic text and the early Sunna tradition, and on the strict following of the model and inheritance of the medieval founding fathers (*al-salafiyyun*). It totally rejected any later innovation and any method of reaching God through intercession. It called for a holy war against the infidels beyond the land of Islam, as well as against Muslims deviating from their fundamental interpretation of Muhhamad's legacy.

Turning to Ibn Taymiyya and 'Abd al-Wahhab is indeed the first step in understanding the Wahhabi concepts of the *habasha*, their interpretation of the formative Prophet-*najashi* dialogue, and their ideas about the legitimacy of Ethiopia's Christianity. A search in Ibn Taymiyya's books reveals the following traditional views:

- The *najashi* was a good Muslim even though his knowledge of Islam was only partial. (Ibn Taymiyya addressed the question of whether someone could be considered a good Muslim because of his pious intentions even though he was unable to perform all duties. He answered in the positive, giving the *najashi* as a model. The *najashi* was unable to follow the fundamentals of Islam, he wrote, and it was said he never even prayed all five daily prayers. He also never prayed in the direction of Mecca, but in the direction of Jerusalem. Yet the Prophet fully recognized him as a Muslim.)[50]

- The *najashi* could not apply Islamic law in Ethiopia, judge his people according to the Quran and spread the holy book, or even appear as a Muslim. Once exposed as a Muslim, Ibn Taymiyya wrote, his people would alienate him and fight against him, and he could not stand up to them.[51]

- The Christian Ethiopians, when they ruled Yemen (A.D. 524–590), aimed at destroying the Kaaba in Mecca. They wanted to do so in order to force all Arabs to make pilgrimages to a church they had built in San'a. Eventually, at the end of the days, "the lean-legged Ethiopians will destroy the Ka'ba."[52]

- The Christian Ethiopians are a model of heresy. Ibn Taymiyya quoted, "God's curse on the Jews and the Christians who turned the graves of their prophets into houses of prayer. It was transmitted by the name of 'Aisha that Umm Habiba and Umm Salma [who had been among the emigrants to Ethiopia] told the Prophet of a church they had seen in Ethiopia with paintings in it. He [the Prophet] said: those people, if one of their righteous men died, they built a house of prayer over his grave and painted those paintings in it. *These are the worst of human beings in the eyes of God on the day of insurrection*" [italics added].[53]

Each of these traditions quoted by Ibn Taymiyya was naturally recycled from earlier sources. They were reinterpreted as part of his general fundamental militancy (still canonized in early-twenty-first-century Saudi Arabia). Within that conceptual framework, Christian Ethiopia, when addressed, was the embodiment of evil and danger. Nowhere in Ibn Taymiyya's writings is there a mention of the other Islamic image of Ethiopia, that of a land and a people who saved the *sahaba,* nor is there mention of the Christian Ethiopians whom the Prophet ordered to "leave [peacefully] alone."[54] Ibn Taymiyya's categorical condemnation of worship of shrines and reverence for saints was not aimed only at Christians. It would also be a reflection of the *Wahhabiyya*'s principal fight against intercession, against all forms of popular Sufi Islam, against such permissive habits like the chewing of *qat*—identified derogatorily with Ethiopia[55]—and other manifestations of flexible religiosity followed by most Muslims in Ethiopia and the Horn.

However, even a radical doctrine like the *Wahhabiyya* was never fully monolithic. 'Abd al-Wahhab, the spiritual father of the Saudi state and originator of its doctrine, resorted to other traditions about Ethiopia as well. On one hand, he repeated the Prophet's saying that the Christian Ethiopians were "the worst of human beings in the eyes of God on the day of insurrection."[56] Yet, on the other hand, unlike Ibn Taymiyya, he reproduced a lengthy description of the "first *hijra*" to Ethiopia. In his "Short Biography of the Prophet," he dedicated seven pages to the story. The greater part of his description focused on the *najashi* as still a Christian and on his saving the first Muslims. The atmosphere of 'Abd al-Wahhab's version in those pages is one of Christian-Islamic affinity.[57] However, he never developed this discussion further or quoted the Prophet's saying on Ethiopia's legitimacy.

Wahhabi scholars, like Muslims of all schools, continued to mention the formative case of Ethiopia in their deliberations on the principles of Islam. For example, 'Abd al-Wahhab's grandson, the important scholar Sulayman bin 'Abdallah bin Muhammad bin 'Abd al-Wahhab (executed by the invading Egyptians in 1818), mentioned the first *hijra* to Ethiopia in his discussion of the "satanic verses." Of the various early sources that dealt with the issue of the Devil's temporary interpolation with the Divine Revelation, he chose the one that asserted that the Devil made a special effort to ensure that his verses would "spread until they reached the land of Ethiopia." At that time—before the *hijra* to Medina—Muslims lived only in Mecca, where they were still persecuted, or in Ethiopia. The Devil's plan was to trick them into returning to Mecca from the asylum they found with the *najashi*. Ethiopia was thus portrayed as a safe refuge for Muslims, a land that saved them even from the Devil's plot. In another place in the same book, however, Sulayman 'Abd al-Wahhab repeated at length the story about the church in Ethiopia with its paintings and the Prophet's saying that the Christians, and indeed all worshipers of saints, "are the worst of human beings in the eyes of God on the day of insurrection."[58]

The establishment and crystallization of the Saudi state in the early 1930s made Wahhabi Islam the dominant doctrine in Arabia. The peninsula was no longer a source of diverse influences on Ethiopia's Muslims, including—as we have seen—ideas and values quite compatible with popular Islamic Ethiopian systems. With regard to Christian Ethiopia, the *Wahhabiyya* did preserve some memories of grace, but these were marginal compared to the negative concepts. The *Wahhabiyya* was also an antithesis to the kind of Islam prevalent in Ethiopia, mostly Sufi, and mostly adapted to coexist with Christians. In the past the *habasha*, both Christians and Muslims, had hardly been relevant to Najd, nor were they favored by the fundamentalist Islam the Saudis imposed on Arabia. The Wahhabi doctrine itself, however, was often balanced by Ibn Sa'ud's more earthly considerations. In the summer of 1934, with little active interest in Ethiopia, he could derive from his religious reservoir the concept of good neighborliness. However, within a few months, the whole situation in the Red Sea theater would change. Amid the global storm of the "Ethiopian Crisis," relations between the Ethiopian and the Wahhabi-Saudi states would reach a moment of truth.

## Notes

1. For a succinct summary of relations between Aksumite Ethiopia and the Arab Peninsula, see Munro-Hay, "Arabia: Relations in Ancient Times," in *Encylopaedia Aethiopica*, vol. I, pp. 294–300. All articles in this encyclopedia have extensive bibliographies for further reference.

2. The tradition about the "lean legged (*dhu al-suwayqatayn*) Ethiopians [that] will destroy the Ka'ba in the end of time" is widely quoted and can be found in the earliest and the most revered canonical hadith compilations, those of al-Bukhari and Muslim. See al-Bukhari, *Sahih*, vol. 2, ed. al-Bagha, pp. 577–599 (Beirut: 1997); Muslim, *Sahih*, vol. 4, ed. 'Abd al-Baqi, p. 2232 (Beirut: 1983).

3. See details and analysis in Erlich, *The Cross and the River*, pp. 94–100; Erlich, "Ethiopia and Egypt," pp. 64–84; and Erlich, "Identity and Church," pp. 23–46.

4. See text in Perham, *The Government of Ethiopia,* pp. 423–432.

5. See Marcus, *Haile Selassie I*.

6. See Ullendorff, "Bible Translations," in his *Ethiopia and the Bible*; Perham, *The Government of Ethiopia*, pp. 120–122; see more in Stoffregen-Pedersen, "Bible Translation into Amharic," pp. 574–575.

7. See Kaplan, "Christianity."

8. See Perham, *The Government of Ethiopia*, p. 103.

9. See Gori, "Arabic Literature," pp. 301–304.

10. See Foreign Office (hereafter FO) 317/19189, "Ethiopia, Annual Report, 1934," Public Record Office (London). See also Hassan, "Abba Gifaar II," pp. 15–16.

11. See Perham, *The Government of Ethiopia,* pp. 223–224. For general analysis, see FO 371/16101, "Slave Traffic in the Red Sea," in "Ethiopia, Annual Report, 1931," Barton to Simon 20 January 1932; FO 371/16996, "First

Annual Report on Slavery in Abyssinia, 1932," in S. Barton to Simon, 20 February 1933.

12. Tuson and Burdett, eds., *Records of Saudi Arabia, Primary Documents 1902–1960* (hereafter *Records of Saudi Arabia*), vol. 5 (1932–1935), Public Record Office (London), p. 441, "The Pilgrimage, 1933." There was no mention of pilgrims from Ethiopia in the years 1930, 1931, 1932 (see p. 38, "Annual Report, 1932").

13. See the chapter "Ahmad Gragn, Ethiopia, and the Middle East," in Erlich, *Ethiopia and the Middle East*, pp. 29–33.

14. See Erlich, *The Cross and the River*, pp. 15–22.

15. See "The Ahmad Gragn Trauma," in *The Cross and the River*, pp. 48–50.

16. The summary below is also based on Cerulli, *L'Islam di Ieri e di Oggi*, mainly chapter 14, "Harar, Centro Musulmano in Etiopia," pp. 281–327; chapter 16, "Gli Emiri di Harar dal secolo XVI alla conquista egiziana (1875)," pp. 365–362; and chapter 17, "La fine dell'emirato di Harar in nuovi documenti storici," pp. 383–395.

17. See Wagner, "Abadir 'Umar ar-Rida," pp. 4–5.

18. See Hassen, *The Oromo of Ethiopia*.

19. See Burton, *First Footsteps in East Africa,* vol. 2, mainly pp. 14–18; see also Hecht, "Cat in Harar," p. 698.

20. Emile Foucher, "The Cult of Muslim Saints in Harar," pp. 71–83, and Zekaria, "Harar: The Land of Ziyara, Pilgrimage," pp. 1–9.

21. For a short discussion of Arabic literature in Harar and of the various studies on it, especially by Ewald Wagner and Enrico Cerulli, see Gori, "Arabic Literature," pp. 305–307.

22. See examples in Cerulli, "Documenti Arabi per la Storia dell'Etiopia," in his *L'Islam di Ieri e di Oggi*, pp. 135–206.

23. See Hill, *Colonel Gordon in Central Africa*, pp. 312–313; also Hassen, "The Relations Between Harar and the Surrounding Oromo," p. 20.

24. See Erlich, *Ethiopia and the Middle East*, p. 79; also, Tafla, "Abdullahi 'Ali Sadiq," p. 38.

25. Al-'Azm, *Rihlat al-Habasha*, pp. 138–143, 234. (A new, widely distributed Arabic edition of this important book, republished in 2001 by the Arab Institute for Studies and Publication, Beirut, is titled: "The Voyage to Ethiopia, from Istanbul to Addis Ababa 1896." The editor confused the Ethiopian calendar with the European one and wrongly added the date 1896 throughout the book. See also a long article on the new edition in *Al-Hayat*, 24 October 2001. The journey of Sadiq al-'Azm to Menelik's Ethiopia took place in 1904. See Erlich, *Ethiopia and the Middle East*, pp. 77–82.)

26. See O'Fahey, *Enigmatic Saint*. See also Levtzion, "Tnu'ot hitangdut vereforma baislam bame'a ha-18," pp. 48–70.

27. See Ahmed, *Islam in Nineteenth-Century Wallo,* pp. 73–74.

28. See Ahmed, *Islam in Nineteenth-Century Wallo*. See also his article "Traditional Muslim Education in Wallo," pp. 94–106. See also Ficquet, "Interlaces of Mixity."

29. See Erlich, "Iyasu, the Somali Mawla, and the Demise of the Ottoman Empire," in *Ethiopia and the Middle East*, pp. 83–91.

30. Haile Selassie I, *My Life and Ethiopia's Progress,* p. 48.

31. Borruso, *L'Ultimo Impero Cristiano*, pp. 178–179.

32. For more on Harar's traditional education and also on its connections to Arabia, see Edris, "Traditional Islamic Centers of Learning in Harar."

33. See also Edris, "Traditional Islamic Centers of Learning in Harar," and Rahji Abdella, "The Kulub-Hannolato Movement by the Harari."

34. See Holtz and Holtz, "The Adventuresome Life of Mortiz Hall," pp. 49–66.

35. See a report on 'Umar al-Azhari in Ministero degli Affari Esteri, Archivio Storico (Rome), EFG, Etiopia Fondo la Guerra, Affari Politici (hereafter ASMAE, EFG), Busta 60, 30 September 1935.

36. On the Ethiopian mission of June–July 1934 to Yemen and Saudi Arabia, see FO 371/17828, Barton to FO, 13 June 1934; 4 July 1934; Calvert to FO, 15 July 1934; 24 July 1934.

37. The text of the letter as in FO 371/17828, Calvert to FO, 24 July 1934.

38. See text of *Umm al-Qura,* 6 July 1934, translated in FO 371/17828 in Calvert to FO, 15 July 1934: "This is the second time the Abyssinian Government sent an official mission to the Hejaz to establish relations between the two countries, and that the first one was sent by the *Nagashi* at the appearance (rise) of Islam to the Prophet."

39. The text of the letter as in FO 371/17828, Calvert to FO, 24 July 1934.

40. For slavery and its Ethiopian-Arabian contexts, see Pankhurst, *Economic History of Ethiopia*, chap. 3, mainly pp. 124–128; Abir, *Ethiopia: The Era of the Princes*, chap. 3; Toledano, *The Ottoman Slave Trade and Its Suppression*, chap. 1, 2, 6; Willis, *Slaves and Slavery in Muslim Africa*, vol. 1 and 2 (see mainly the articles by the editor, Ephraim Isaac, William Sersen, Nehemia Levtzion, Mordechai Abir, and Akbar Muhammad). See also Lafin, *The Arabs as Master Slavers*, chap. 6: "Saudi Arabia: Slavery as Part of Lifestyle"; Miers, "Britain and the Suppression of Slavery in Ethiopia," pp. 257–288; Fernyhough, "Slavery and the Slave Trade in Southern Ethiopia," pp. 680–708.

41. See "Slavery and Slave Trade," in "Annual Report, 1932," *Records of Saudi Arabia*, vol. 5, pp. 43–44; FO 371/16996, "First Annual Report on Slavery in Abyssinia, 1932," in S. Barton to Simon, 20 February 1933.

42. See Lewis, *Race and Slavery in the Middle East*, pp. 90–91.

43. See a detailed analysis of the term *habasha* and discussions (throughout the book) of various cases in point in Lewis, *Race and Slavery*. See also the section "Habasha," in Farias, "The Enslaved Barbarian," pp. 36–41.

44. See Voigt, "Abyssinia," pp. 59–65. See "Hbsh," in Ibn Manzur (al-Ifriqi), *Lisan al-'Arab* v. 6 (Beirut: n.d.), pp. 278–279.

45. On Bilal bin Rabbah, "Bilal al-habashi," see Erlich, *Ethiopia and the Middle East*, pp. 6, 10, 37, 81.

46. See Muhammad, "The Image of Africans in Arabic Literature," pp. 47–74.

47. Muhammad, "The Image of Africans in Arabic Literature."
48. See Patricia Crone, "'Even an Ethiopian Slave': The Transformation of a Sunni Tradition," pp. 59–67. The emphasis in Crone's analysis is on the concept that a Muslim of any ethnic origin can be a legitimate ruler and should be obeyed even in the nearly absurd case of his being from such a low background.
49. For Ibn Taymiyya's history and political theory, see a summary in Sivan, *Radical Islam*, pp. 94–104.
50. Ibn Taymiyya, *Sharh al-'umda*, vol. 4, p. 548; Ibn Taymiyya, *Kutub warasa'il*, vol. 19, p. 217.
51. Ibn Taymiyya, *Kutub waras'il*, vol. 19, p. 218.
52. Ibn Taymiyya, *Sharh al-'umda*, vol. 4, p. 494, and *Kutub warasa'il*, vol. 27, pp. 355–356.
53. Ibn Taymiyya, *Sharh al-'umda*, vol. 4, p. 427.
54. This harsh criticism of the Christians and the Jews made through the Ethiopian model of worshipping graves was recycled and discussed by Muhammad bin 'Abd al-Wahhab in several places. See 'Abd al-Wahhab, *Taysir al-'aziz al-hamid fi sharh kitab al-tawhid*, pp. 277–280. However, it is worth noting here that 'Abd al-Wahhab did narrate the whole Prophet-*najashi* story, including a long description of the Ethiopian saving of the *sahaba*. See 'Abd al-Wahhab, *Mukhtasar sirat al-rasul*, pp. 61–67.
55. The Wahhabis categorically forbid chewing the qat, and because it is widely believed that the narcotic plant was brought to Arabia by Abraha—the Ethiopian sixth-century ruler who aimed at the destruction of the Kaaba—the sin and the crime do sometimes add to Ethiopia's negative image. It is also worth noting that most Wahhabis of Najd were members of the 'Anaza tribe, which belongs traditionally to the Qays family of tribes. The Qays were pushed out of Yemen in ancient times by the tribes of Yaman. The Yaman were said to later collaborate with the Christian Ethiopians of Abraha, one of them even guided his army toward Mecca. Thus the concept of Ethiopia in Wahhabi eyes became indirectly connected with elements of the historical enmity they recycled against the Yaman tribes and families. (Based on oral information, mainly from Mustafa Kabha.)
56. See al-Rumi, Baltaji, and Hijab, *Mu'alafat al-Shaykh al-Imam Muhammad bin 'Abd al-Wahhab*, vol. 1, pp. 45–46.
57. 'Abd al-Wahhab, *Mukhtasar sirat al-rasul*, pp. 61–67, 132–138.
58. 'Abd al-Wahhab, *Taysir al-'Aziz al-hamid fi sharh kitab al-tawhid*, vol. 1, pp. 244, 277–280.

# 3

# Camels for Mussolini

H AILE SELASSIE'S INITIATIVE OF JUNE 1934 TO ESTABLISH RELATIONS
with Ibn Sa'ud and Imam Yahya was an effort to rebuild an old, but
barely operational, bridge. The Red Sea occasionally had connected the
Arabian Peninsula with the Islamic communities in the Horn of Africa,
but it was much less of a bridge to the Christian state. The history of
diplomatic relations between Ethiopia's emperors and the various
Islamic rulers of Arabia was more like a collection of rare episodes. A
famous case in point, the mid-seventeenth-century attempt of Emperor
Fasiladas to begin a dialogue with Yemen's Imam al-Mutawwakil 'ala
al-Allah, only emphasized the inherent difficulties. The Yemeni imam
rejected the idea of commercial and political relations prior to the
Ethiopian monarch's "following in the footsteps of the *Najashi*" and
converting to Islam.[1] In the early 1930s, the chances of these relation-
ships' occurring seemed equally slim. By this time, Ethiopia had grown
stronger as a "Christian empire." The Arabian Peninsula, hitherto the
home of various Islamic trends, was now under the hegemony of Saudi
Arabia. Centered on Najd, the Saudi house had almost no record of a
Red Sea orientation. Based on the *Wahhabiyya*, the Saudi kingdom was
hardly receptive to the idea of accepting Christian Ethiopians as regional partners.

The concept of the Red Sea as a bridge between the Horn and
Arabia, however, was much more relevant to the strategy of Italian
imperialists. Since 1890, when they established their local colony of
Eritrea, named after the Red Sea (*Mare Erithraeum*), the Italians had
dreamt of spreading their influence on both shores. Under Mussolini,
this abstract vision became an active policy. In 1926, having solidified

his dictatorial grip on Italian society, Mussolini declared "a Napoleonic year" during which the fascist empire would assert itself in the Mediterranean and the Red Sea. Jacopo Gasparini, the energetic governor of Eritrea, began a dual action. On one hand, he deepened Italian subversion of Ethiopia and, on the other, worked to build alliances in Arabia. In September 1926, Gasparini signed a treaty of friendship with Imam Yahya, which paved the way to Italy's arming of Yemen. Though the new Asmara-San'a alliance was a threat to Ibn Sa'ud (he was already in conflict with the imam), in 1927, Gasparini initiated diplomatic overtures with the Saudis as well.

Gasparini led Mussolini to believe that Italy could force the British into a deal by which London would accept Italian hegemony in greater Yemen, while Britain would retain its influence over the Saudis. But the Italian dream of becoming the major power in the Red Sea was to face the mighty Britain of the 1920s. In February 1927, British Foreign Secretary Austin Chamberlain spelled it out clearly to Mussolini: "His Majesty's Government regards it as a vital interest that no European Power should establish itself on the Arabian shore of the Red Sea." Facing such British resolution (the British hinted they were ready to take military action in Yemen), Mussolini had to shelve his Red Sea dreams. Gasparini was removed from Eritrea, no direct Italian aid was rendered to Yemen in its effort to stem the Saudis, and diplomatic overtures toward the Saudis came to a complete halt. Subversion in Ethiopia also slowed, and in August 1928, Italy signed a twenty-year treaty of friendship with the Christian empire.[2]

In 1932, with the global "Grand Crisis" and the apparent weakening of Britain, Mussolini regained his taste for Red Sea domination. Action was resumed on both shores. In Eritrea, Governor Corrado Zoli rerecruited Gasparini to help resume the undermining of Haile Selassie's regime. The renewed policy of encouraging centrifugal forces in Ethiopia focused on the Tigrean ethnic group and on their old resentment of Shoan-Amhara hegemony (*"politica tigrigna"*). This was now gradually reinforced by the idea that Islam in Ethiopia could be cultivated as a centrifugal factor. In Arabia, the Italians signed a "Treaty of Friendship and Commerce" with the Saudis on 29 March 1932,[3] but the real emphasis was again on Yemen. In practice, the Italians intensified their activities in San'a and encouraged Imam Yahya to resist Saudi control over the disputed region of 'Asir. However, the Italians' Yemeni card in Arabia was a disappointment. On 20 May 1934, as mentioned, Yahya, defeated in the field, had to acknowledge Saudi rule in 'Asir and Wahhabi hegemony over the peninsula. Italian policy in Arabia was now reoriented toward placating the Saudis and preparing them gradually for accepting fascist regional supremacy, once achieved.[4]

Seven days after the loss of the Arabian-Yemeni card, the Ethiopian option gained momentum. On 27 May 1934, the ruler of Eastern Tigre, Haile Selassie Gugsa, secretly promised the Italians that he would open the road into the heart of Ethiopia to their armies. Four days later, Mussolini ordered his ministers to prepare for the conquest of Ethiopia, and in July, he began to supervise the plan personally.[5] On 5 December 1934, an incident was staged on the Ethiopian-Somali border (at Wal-Wal) to ignite the "Abyssinian Crisis." Throughout 1935, Mussolini's threat and his preparations for the conquest of Ethiopia gradually shattered the League of Nations' "collective security" concept. Facing Mussolini's aggressive determination and his threat to join Hitler's Germany, the British did not dare to stare him down this time. Though they tried to exert diplomatic pressure, by the summer of 1935, they had decided to sacrifice Ethiopia. As they tried to cope with the mounting global threat, British policymakers conducted a very cautious policy in the Red Sea. When the Fascists finally invaded Ethiopia on 3 October 1935, Mussolini was convinced, correctly, that he was not actually risking a conflict with Britain.[6]

But Mussolini's war on Ethiopia was merely a stepping stone in his eyes. The Italian dictator made no secret of his dream to revive the Roman empire throughout the East. His conquest of Ethiopia was labeled an African war, but the East African empire he sought was also to be a springboard to the Middle East. Ethiopia was the rear door to the Nile, to the Red Sea, and to a Mediterranean empire. In the long run, therefore, there was no escape from an Italian showdown with Britain and France. Moreover, Mussolini clearly realized that his vision of Roman hegemony in the great East would not materialize without the help of local forces. He thus considered tapping the energies of Islam and of Arabism and preparing them to join his future struggle with Britain and France.[7] He had begun flirting with Islam in the 1920s but then became stuck in Libya. Facing the Sanusi revolt, Mussolini could not avoid brutally crushing it. In September 1931, the public hanging of Sanusi leader 'Umar al-Mukhtar brought Mussolini's image in the Islamic-Arab world to its lowest level. The war he planned on Ethiopia was therefore crucial in his effort, after 1932, to regain his reputation as a savior of Islam. Apart from the account that Italy had to settle with the 1896 victors, and the strategic springboard to be gained, the conquest of Ethiopia was to be portrayed as a fight for the cause of Islam. By 1934, an Italian pro-Islamic, pro-Arab propaganda effort, led by many of

Italy's leading orientalists, was revived with fervor. Its main message, that Ethiopia was a semibarbarous Christian state that throughout history had oppressed Muslims, was radiated to the Islamic Middle East and amplified by local supporters, creating a controversy throughout the Arab world. We shall soon discuss its impact on the Saudis.

## Haile Selassie and Islam: Seeking Saudi Help

The message that Mussolini was the protector of Islam, together with the hint that Lij Iyasu was the legitimate monarch of Ethiopia, was also conveyed to Ethiopia's Muslims. According to Italian reports, the hope that Mussolini would remove Haile Selassie and restore Islam as a political factor spread most effectively in Harar, the Ogaden, among the Oromos of southern Ethiopia, and in the Arab-Islamic trading circles of Addis Ababa. For all intents and purposes, the Fascists and their agents worked to mobilize the various Muslim communities to undermine Ethiopia's defenses.[8] When preparing their invasion, the Italians recruited some seventy thousand Muslim fighters, *askaris*, in Eritrea and Somalia. They also sought recruits in Arabia and volunteers in other Arab countries. During the war itself, many Oromo Muslim fighters would indeed join the Italian invaders.[9]

For Haile Selassie and his regime, 1935 was a year of mounting anxiety. His attention was focused on European diplomacy and on military preparations, but the issue of Islam could not be ignored. The deep-rooted Gragn trauma—the fear that outside inspiration would move the Muslims of the Horn to unite against the Christian hegemony—was now fully re-evoked. The regime's response was threefold. First, the old methods of intimidation and repression were employed again. These would culminate, a few weeks after the Italian invasion, in the mysterious death of Lij Iyasu in his prison cell. Second was a sudden resort to a totally new approach. As of very early 1935, Haile Selassie began presenting himself as the leader of a diversified society. He made speeches about religious equality and about greater Ethiopia as the state of all its citizens. On 22 May 1935, he spoke to community leaders in Harar:

> I am the emperor of all black people and all black people are my subjects. I want to say that not only the black people of Ethiopia owe me allegiance, but also the black people who are now enslaved under the white men, in Somaliland, in Kenya, in French Somali, in Eritrea, and in Italian Somalia. They are foreign citizens legally only, not factually.[10]

Haile Selassie's new message was to unite all religious and ethnic groups behind a newly remolded Ethiopian identity, not Christian, but diverse. He now promised constitutional equality to all religions. His new effort to placate the Muslims included the authorization of an Arabic-language journal published in Addis Ababa and edited by an Egyptian Copt, a schoolmaster in the Menelik II school. He also—finally—authorized the construction of a grand mosque in Addis Ababa (one promised by Menelik in 1904). Under the influence of the Muhammadali company, the Arab-Islamic commercial circles of the Addis Ababa *mercato* issued statements in support of Ethiopia.[11] On 30 May 1935, the Amharic *Berhanena Selam* published a statement by Muhammad al-Sadiq, "the leader of the country's Muslim community" (and a relative of Harari 'Abdallah al-Sadiq, Lij Iyasu's old ally):

> Mussolini's men want to separate the Muslims and Ethiopia. My people, let us not fall into this trap. Let us prove that we are the same nation. Let us forget the old [Christian Ethiopian, mocking] saying 'Skies have no pillars, Muslims have no land.' It is no longer the case that in Ethiopia people are selected for governmental posts by their religion. This is my message to anyone who wants to see a free Ethiopia.[12]

On 18 July 1935, Haile Selassie delivered a speech to his parliament. He called on all Ethiopians to prepare for the coming war: "Soldier, trader, peasant, young and old, man and woman, be united! Defend your country by helping each other! . . . Although Italy is doing everything possible to disunite us, whether Christian or Muslim we will unitedly resist."[13]

The third measure taken by Haile Selassie was to seek support in Arab countries. Throughout 1935 he sent missions to Egypt, Libya, and Arabia. Their aim was not to gain military or other material aid. He needed tokens of identification with his new model of Ethiopia—a state of all *habashi* peoples—and his struggle against Mussolini in order to win the hearts of his Muslim citizens. He had mixed success. The mission to Libya was unsuccessful because the Sanusi anti-Italian movement had practically been shattered. The more important goal was Egypt's public. Indeed, the Egyptians needed no reminder from Ethiopia to be alert to the new situation created by Mussolini's preparations for war. In 1935, Ethiopia and its fate became a main issue that divided Egyptians as well as public opinion in Syria, Lebanon, Iraq, and Palestine. In the entire Arab Middle East, this was a formative year for rising pan-Arab nationalism as well as for the reemergence of Islam as a political platform. The "Ethiopian question" and its principal dilemmas went to the very heart of those identities, redefined now amid political uncertainties. Substantial parts of the Egyptian public sided with anything that could weaken Britain. Many were ready to support Mussolini and to wish Christian Ethiopia the worst. Books and articles described Ethiopia's crimes against Islam and made a mockery of Haile Selassie's last-minute pretension that he was enlightened. However, no less powerful were the sectors that rose up in support of besieged Ethiopia.[14] Here it is worth mentioning that Ethiopia's supporters in Egypt did in fact render the country important help. A "Committee for the Defense of Ethiopia" united liberals and Islamic moderates in Cairo. It raised donations and enlisted volunteers. In February 1935, two shaikhs were sent from Al-Azhar to open branches of the prestigious *madrasa* (Islamic school of higher education). A branch was opened in Harar by the Egyptian Shaikh Yusuf 'Ali Yusuf under the auspices and financial help of the emperor and the Egyptian consul in town. It was inaugurated by Ras Nasibu, the governor of Hararge province.[15] After the beginning of hostilities, three Egyptian Red Crescent medical units would be dispatched to treat Ethiopian wounded on the Harar front. One of the prominent activists for Ethiopia in Egypt was the distinguished leader of the *Salafiyya* movement for Islamic revival, Shaikh Muhammad Rashid Rida. Rida's political platform was strongly anticolonial and flexible enough to conceive Ethiopia not in narrow Islamic terms. Back in 1896–1897, he expressed admiration for Menelik II for having defeated the Italians and for building a strong independent, oriental empire.[16] When the 1935 crisis began, Rida established his own contacts with Ethiopian Muslims. He sent messages and books to fellow Muslims in Ethiopia who were ready to follow his fundamentalist yet politically flexible Islam and to remain loyal to Haile Selassie. Rida also corresponded with Ibn Sa'ud about Ethiopia. In many ways he had been close to the Saudi court and admired Ibn Sa'ud as an independent Muslim king. His emphasis on reforming Islam by following the model of the founding fathers, his insistence on purifying Islam from later innovations, mysticism, tomb cults, and other elements of Sufism, were quite similar to the major Wahhabi fundamentals.[17] In January 1935, he wrote to the Saudi king about the new atmosphere in "the land of the *Najashi*" and about the new opportunity to spread Islamic education there. He corresponded intensively about Ethiopia with his lifetime ally, Amir Shakib Arslan, a Syrian Druze. The latter, an even stronger admirer of Ibn Sa'ud, was now Mussolini's most ardent supporter in the Arab-Islamic world, and we shall soon discuss his influence over the Saudis.

In his book on Rida, Arslan later quoted parts of this correspondence. Ibn Sa'ud, Rida wrote to Arslan on 24 January 1935 (trying to persuade Arslan to stop supporting the Fascists), was curious and positive about the idea to spread Islamic education in Haile Selassie's Ethiopia. Ibn Sa'ud also gave his consent, Rida wrote, to open a center for Ethiopian Muslim scholars in Mecca.[18] Rida was to be proven wrong. It was not his version of fundamentalist yet politically flexible Islam that Ibn Sa'ud would follow in dealing with "the Ethiopian question."

On 7 April 1935, an Ethiopian delegation, including prominent Muslims, arrived in Jedda, after having spent a few weeks in Yemen where Imam Yahya, bitter now at the Italian openness toward Ibn Sa'ud, was ready to sign a treaty of friendship with Ethiopia. The main task of the mission, however, was to sign a similar treaty with Ibn Sa'ud, the guardian of Mecca, and the more significant independent Islamic ruler in the Arab East. Though in their preliminary contacts the Ethiopians had not hinted at such a proposal, in March, the Italians had already raised the issue with the Saudis and were reassured that no token of official friendship with Ethiopia would be declared. "Neither I nor [any of my men?] would wish to commit any act hostile to Italy which is our friend and with which we desire to increase our friendly relations," Ibn Sa'ud assured the Italian chargé d'affaires in Jedda, Giovani Perisco, on 31 March.[19] Five days later, the king's chief adviser and undersecretary for foreign affairs, Fuad Hamza, added, "His majesty will not authorize any act which might be interpreted in Italy or elsewhere as a modification of his friendly attitude towards the Italian Government."[20] On 10 April, Ibn Sa'ud himself hosted the Ethiopian delegation for a dinner on the road from Mecca to Jedda. He was given Haile Selassie's letter, which referred to Ibn Sa'ud's words of July 1934 that welcomed the inauguration of relations in the spirit of the Prophet-*najashi* friendship. The atmosphere at the meeting was correct and polite, it was reported, but there would be no letter of response. The Ethiopian emissaries were told that the time was not ripe for any official step, not even an anodyne treaty. Ibn Sa'ud stated that he was a friend of both Ethiopia and Italy and would not identify with either side before they ended their dispute.[21] During the meeting, Ibn Sa'ud told Ahmad Saliq, the Ethiopian Muslim member of the delegation, that "he knew all that Ethiopia had done to her Muslims: Abba Jifar was removed and his sons were exiled. An Islamic kingdom which existed for centuries [Jimma] was destroyed. No Muslim holds any position of significance in Ethiopia. I can do nothing for Ethiopia."[22] On 15 April, the mission left for Egypt empty-handed. Its only achievement was a promise that low-key secret contacts would continue. Pleased, Mussolini instructed his men in Jedda to thank the king and assure him of Italy's gratitude for his friendship to Italy.[23]

## Ibn Sa'ud, Arslan, and Ethiopia

When Ibn Sa'ud told his guests he could not help to unite Muslim and Christian Ethiopians in facing Mussolini because he had to remain neutral, he did not reveal the whole truth. By that time he had already authorized quite an active dialogue with Italy. In November 1934, his secretary for foreign affairs, Hamza, paid a visit to Rome, and in January 1935, ten young Saudi men were sent to Italy for training as combat pilots. They were designated to become the beginning of an Italian-equipped Air Force, a vital element in the kingdom's modernization and security.[24] Ibn Sa'ud himself was not entirely enthusiastic about this step. He still regarded Great Britain as the major power in the world and persistently sought British advice throughout that fateful year. Ibn Sa'ud was said to have little respect for Mussolini, and he remained suspicious of Italian designs in the Red Sea.

Although Ibn Sa'ud was the only decisionmaker in the kingdom, actual daily conduct of foreign affairs was in the hands of his advisers. At that time, none of his older sons was mature enough to deal with the global picture, and they were mainly entrusted with home administration. Prince Sa'ud was the heir to the throne and Prince Faysal was governor of Hijaz and minister of foreign affairs. Since the 1920s, Ibn Sa'ud's advisers on foreign affairs had been Egyptian Hafiz Wahba, Syrian Yusuf Yasin, and Lebanese Druze Hamza. In 1934–1935, Wahba was ambassador to Britain and somewhat outside the Saudi-Ethiopian story. Yasin and Hamza roved between Jedda, Riyadh, and Arab and European capitals, and it is from their telegraph communications with Ibn Sa'ud—intercepted by the British—that we can reconstruct Saudi policy toward Mussolini and Haile Selassie.

Both Hamza and Yasin were ideologically connected with a group of inter-Arab politicians called the "Syrian-Palestinian Congress." This body had been established in the immediate aftermath of World War I, and among its major leaders were Arslan and Rida. The group supported the more militant Palestinian wing of the mufti Amin al-Husayni and opposed the Hashemite kings of Iraq and Transjordan with their pro-British inclinations. In the 1920s, they flirted with the idea that Mussolini could help the Arab cause, but, like many others, they were disillusioned with the Fascists when they crushed the Sanusis. While

Rida, to his death, remained in strong opposition to Mussolini, Arslan and other members, and more covertly Hamza and Yasin, regained their faith in Italy in 1933–1934. To a large extent, Hamza was behind the Saudi-Italian rapprochement in the aftermath of the Saudi-Yemeni war, and the new Saudi-Italian aviation connection.

Hamza was not a Wahhabi himself; like his associate Arslan, he was a well-educated Druze who had become an orthodox Muslim. He nevertheless grew to be an admirer of the Saudi house whose service he entered in 1924 and considered the Arab Peninsula to be the center of Arab-Islamic history. He presented these concepts in his writings, mainly in his 1933 book, published in Riyadh, called *The Heart of the Arab Peninsula.*[25] Hamza's image of the Ethiopian role in Arab-Islamic history, as reflected in his book, was clearly negative. In telling the story of the Prophet, Hamza did mention the first *hijra* to Ethiopia, but he did so without mentioning that the Ethiopians saved the *sahaba* (pp. 262–271). In contrast, he devoted quite a long description to the Ethiopians' earlier conquest of Yemen and their threat to destroy the Kaaba (p. 252). The message he conveyed in that passage was that the Arabs had to unite in order to save their holy places from the invading Ethiopian Christians. In describing the Arabian Peninsula of his time, Hamza made a point of distinguishing between "pure Arabs" and some 435,000 non-Arabs he estimated lived in Arabia, among them 200,000 "blacks and Ethiopians." Though the latter were Muslims, they were, according to Hamza, descendants either of slaves or of invaders (pp. 85, 96–97).

Hamza was in constant touch with both the British and the Italian legations in Jedda. Time and again in March 1935 he assured the Italian chargé d'affaires, Perisco, that Ibn Sa'ud would sign no treaty with Haile Selassie. On 3 April, just before the arrival of the Ethiopian delegation, he told the Italian that "Italy was a great Power which could win the hearts of all Arabs and Muslims if it came out openly in support of the Palestinians. I say this because I know well the mufti of Jerusalem, the leader of the Islamic political movement in Palestine."[26] Indeed in the early spring of 1935, the Arab-Islamic group led by Arslan began to identify, for all intents and purposes, with Mussolini's challenge to Britain.

Arslan undoubtedly had more influence on Ibn Sa'ud in Ethiopian matters. Relations between the two stretched back to the early 1920s. Arslan was arguably the more prominent proponent of Islamic-Arab nationalism during the interwar period. He resided in Geneva, where he issued his journal *La Nation Arabe* and from where he traveled all over the Islamic-Arab world calling for militant solidarity. In his eyes, Islam and Arabism were inseparable. No Christian Arab could be a real patriot, he wrote, as Islam was the driving force behind the Islamic-Arab identity. He therefore identified with all Muslims who had some Arab affiliation, including the Berbers of Morocco and the Muslims of the Horn. But in seeking leadership for the entire Islamic-Arab nation, Arslan looked to the core land of Islamic history. After the abolishment of the caliphate by Turkey's Kemal Ataturk in 1924, Arslan had no doubt who should be the caliph of a reenergized Islamic-Arab nation. Ibn Sa'ud was his man, the pious desert warrior who had the strength to unite most of the Arab Peninsula and assure Islamic sovereignty over the holy places. Ibn Sa'ud, he wrote, was the strong Arab ruler who retained political independence. Arslan, like Hamza, was not a Wahhabi, but theological considerations did not bother him. Though Ibn Sa'ud did not respond directly to Arslan's idea of the caliphate—proclaiming himself a caliph would have alienated other Arab leaders, the British, and even many of his Wahhabi purists—Ibn Sa'ud nevertheless developed a close alliance with Arslan. The latter worked tirelessly to promote Ibn Sa'ud's image as the greatest of Arab kings, and the Saudi monarch rewarded Arslan with a most precious tool for his international activities: Saudi citizenship and a passport. In 1929, when Arslan made his pilgrimage to Mecca, for weeks he was a personal guest of Ibn Sa'ud. On 16 April 1934, Arslan returned to Mecca as a member of a reconciliation committee organized by Palestinian Amin al-Husayni that helped to end the Saudi-Yemeni war. Arslan remained in Saudi Arabia for nearly two months, spending weeks in the company of Ibn Sa'ud.[27]

By that time, Arslan had also become Mussolini's agent in the Arab world. In February 1934, he was twice summoned by the Italian leader and emerged from the meetings convinced that the Arabs would have no better deal than Mussolini's victory in the East. If such a victory were at the expense of Ethiopian existence, Arslan would not mourn. In fact he had already developed quite a negative attitude to the Christian empire. Back in 1928, Arslan had written to Ras Tafari demanding the restoration of basic rights for Muslims in Ethiopia. He received no reply and it was perhaps because of that insult that he continued to refer to Haile Selassie as Tafari throughout the 1930s. When Mussolini quelled the *Sanusiyya,* for a while Arslan lost his anti-Christian Ethiopian sting. In 1933, he published a long article, "The Muslims of Ethiopia," which included extensive passages from an Arabic manuscript recording the Ahmad Gragn conquest. The air of the article was that Islam in the Horn of Africa had had its share of victories and dignity. But, as mentioned, he soon returned to admiring Mussolini and spreading the Italian's word about saving Islam from Ethiopian oppression. In October 1934, Arslan returned from a tour in Eritrea and published an article in *La Nation Arabe* full of praise for Mussolini's treatment of Islam. In January 1935, he published another article in *La Nation Arabe* warning Ethiopia that it should restore autonomy to Jimma as well as to Harar or face destruction. In February 1935, he was again summoned to Mussolini and immediately afterward began an active campaign in support of the Italian cause in Africa and the Middle East. Of the dozens of articles he published in Arab media from that time until after the final collapse of Ethiopia, one example is worth quoting briefly, an article in the Palestinian newspaper *Al-Jami'a al-'Arabiyya*, on 4 March 1935: "All those who would like to defend Ethiopia have first to read about its history and particularly regarding the Muslims living there and what they received from the Ethiopians. They will see that apart from the Muslims of Spain no other Muslim people have suffered over the centuries such atrocities as the Muslims of Ethiopia." He then claimed that six million Muslims were living in Ethiopia, deprived of their rights, barred from governmental posts, and living in conditions worse than under European imperialism. Italy, he wrote, was a true friend of the Arabs and of Islam. He then asked, "Are we so strong and secure as to forget our own needs and give our attention and aid to the land of the *Najashi*? We should not alienate such a power as Italy just for the beautiful eyes of a certain people who for years did nothing but oppress Muslims who live on the same land."[28] Arslan, as mentioned, was in close touch with Hamza, Yasin, and Ibn Sa'ud himself. When in April 1935 the Saudi king told his Ethiopian guests that "he knew all that Ethiopia had done to her Muslims" and that he could do nothing for Ethiopia, he spoke not only as a student of Ibn Taymiyya and Muhammad 'Abd al-Wahhab, but also as an old patron of Arslan.

## Ibn Sa'ud's Dealings with Mussolini

On 15 May 1935, exactly a month after the Ethiopian delegation left empty-handed, a Saudi delegation embarked on an Italian ship, sent especially by Mussolini to Jedda, on its way to Rome.[29] It was headed by Prince Sa'ud and Hamza. They arrived in Rome on 20 May, amid pompous ceremony. The Italian leader was doing his best to shower honor on his guests. Prince Sa'ud met with the king of Italy and with Mussolini. He heard from the latter that he was most pleased with Saudi treatment of the Ethiopian delegation. Mussolini told Sa'ud: "I was and still am an admirer of His Majesty Ibn Sa'ud, and I am extremely pleased with the strengthening of our friendship." He told the prince to ask for whatever he wanted, for he, Mussolini, would do anything to prove his goodwill.[30] On 22 May, Hamza met with the Italian leader to discuss practicalities. According to British reports, a secret agreement of understanding was then reached with Prince Sa'ud. It stated that Mussolini was a friend of Islam and the true protector of the Muslims in Ethiopia, those suffering under the Christian yoke. The Saudis would block anti-Italian propaganda and facilitate the recruitment of workers and volunteers to help the Italian buildup in Eritrea and Somalia. They would also sell foodstuffs to the Italian army. In return, Italy would continue to build the nascent Saudi Air Force and pay the Saudis in arms, especially after the conflict in Ethiopia was resolved. Finally, Saudi Arabia would treat the conflict between Italy and Ethiopia as a war between two Christian states, and would therefore remain officially neutral. On this pretext, Saudi Arabia would cut off any diplomatic contacts with the Ethiopians.[31]

Prince Sa'ud remained as a guest of the Italian government for quite a while. He returned home in July via Egypt. In Cairo, he chose to spend time with the family's old friend Shaikh Rida. Rida, on his part, spared no effort in hosting Sa'ud. The old and weary Rida even disobeyed his doctors and took the trouble to see Prince Sa'ud off at the Suez port of Dahabiyya, most probably in an effort to talk Sa'ud out of the Italian connection. Rida, as mentioned, was one of the most prominent Islamic leaders to believe that Haile Selassie should be helped in his new Christian-Islamic policy. He felt that all the peoples of the East should identify with Ethiopia's struggle against Mussolini, whom he regarded as the worst manifestation of Western aggression and not as a champion of Islam. Rida, we have seen, had corresponded with Ibn Sa'ud on that issue. Unfortunately, we have no record of the conversations he now had with Prince Sa'ud, for on the train back to Cairo, Rida died.[32]

The Saudis indeed minimized their contact with the Ethiopians. Some time during the summer, Haile Selassie sent another envoy to Ibn Sa'ud that returned empty-handed.[33] A letter from the Ethiopian emperor to the Saudi monarch followed, but it was said to have been lost. In late August, Prince Sa'ud was again in Cairo for a three-day visit during which he met with the Syrian exile 'Abd al-Rahman Shahabandar, another proponent of aid to Ethiopia,[34] but no record of their talk exists. A letter sent on 2 September 1935 from the Ethiopian foreign minister, Heruy Walda-Selassie, to his counterpart, Prince Faysal, led to the resumption of some contact and to the arrival of yet another Ethiopian mission in Jedda on the last day of October, nearly a month after the beginning of the Italian invasion.[35]

Contact with the Italians, however, intensified in the spirit of the May understandings. In that same month, an Italian agent named Celso Odello, a lieutenant-colonel in the Italian Military Intelligence, arrived in Jedda. Accompanied by his wife and their daughter, he presented himself as a representative of various Italian commercial firms. The Odellos quickly became the center of Jedda's social life and established contacts with the local elite as well as with Yasin. In July, Odello and Yasin discussed the purchase of twelve thousand camels for the Italian army then building up in Eritrea. He offered to pay three times the regular price. By that time, the Saudis had made it clear that they would not authorize Italian recruitment of manpower in their land.[36] As international tension continued to grow, so did Ibn Sa'ud's anxiety. He was walking on a tightrope. On one hand, he was afraid of the Italian might and their long-range goal of penetrating Arabia. Mussolini was preparing to conquer not only Ethiopia; he might, soon after, also invade Yemen.[37] Ibn Sa'ud needed Mussolini's friendship, but at the same time, he could not afford to alienate the British. What would be the British response to Mussolini's war? Would a British-Italian conflict develop in the Red Sea? Could he succeed in placating Mussolini without risking relations with Britain? Throughout the early summer of 1935, the Saudis tried to understand the British position, but as the British were themselves wavering, they received no clear message. It was, however, clear that allowing the Italians to recruit Saudi manpower would be overidentifying with their cause. Vegetables were sold to the Italians through Odello, but by the time they reached Massawa they were of no use.[38] Camels were what the Italian war machine now needed.[39] As preparations for war continued, it became clearer to the Italian high command that mechanized transportation in Ethiopia would be quite limited. The Italian army would have to rely on camels for moving supplies and weapons in the mountainous Ethiopian theater. In fact, after the war began, the need for camels was proven even greater than anticipated.[40]

In July, Ibn Sa'ud authorized the gradual purchase of camels by Odello; only 300 a month. But Shaikh Yasin was pushing for more. He and Hamza supported deepening the Italian connection,[41] and Yasin was to gain personally from the deal. He finally managed to convince Ibn Sa'ud to meet with Odello in Riyadh on 20 August.[42] According to the Italian's report, Odello admitted that he was an Italian officer and said he was authorized to pay for the camels in Italian arms. He reported that

Ibn Sa'ud was very enthusiastic about the Italian connection. Odello quoted Ibn Sa'ud as saying that he mistrusted Britain and preferred to rely on Italy. In principle, he wanted Italian arms and airplanes. Meanwhile, however, they agreed on money for the camels. Odello, still as a private individual, would buy 12,000 camels through local merchants who dealt with tribesmen in Najd. The price agreed on was 15 pounds per head: 7 to the Saudi treasury, 7 to the vendors, and 1 pound to Yasin as the "broker."[43]

Odello's report on Ibn Sa'ud's willingness to rely on and be armed by Italy was exaggerated. The Italian agent was trying to push matters forward in Arabia quickly and without consulting the Italian chargé d'affaires in Jedda, Perisco. Ibn Sa'ud, in fact, was much more cautious. After allowing Odello to begin buying Najdi camels, the Saudi king kept a close eye on the deal. He was informed of every move and virtually dictated the pace of the transaction.[44] Ibn Sa'ud did this so as to leave time to get a British response, and on 25 August he ordered Yasin to inform the British of the deal and ask for their consent. He said he would cancel the enterprise should the British decide that it was anti-British, but if the conflict was only between Italy and Ethiopia, the Saudi government would follow its neutral policy and continue trading with the Italians.[45]

The British response was reassuring. As mentioned, in July 1935, the British government had decided in practice to sacrifice Ethiopia in order to appease Mussolini. In mid-August, the British (and the French) made yet another vain effort to offer Mussolini wide opportunities for indirect control of Ethiopia. To Ibn Sa'ud, the British now reiterated their commitment to their 1927 policy statement regarding the Arab peninsula. As to Ethiopia, they told the Saudis that their "opposition is not so much to Italian aims as to Italian methods."[46] Their advice to Ibn Sa'ud was to continue being polite to Mussolini and not to worry about the camel transaction. In fact, they disclosed, they themselves ignored the Italian purchase of camels in the Sudan.[47] In September, Mussolini and Ibn Sa'ud exchanged messages of friendship and mutual trust,[48] and on the 20th, the High Command of Africa Orientale drafted a thirty-two-page agreement for the purchase of camels.[49] In Jedda, Perisco admitted to Yasin that Italy had made mistakes in the past when it sided with Yemen, but that was all due to Gasparini's poor advice.[50] It was now clear to Mussolini that Ibn Sa'ud was his partner in Arabia, and he therefore wanted to pay for the camels in arms. Ibn Sa'ud's instructions to Yasin were to delicately put aside the arms offer and arrange for a sale of 1,000 camels, taking his time.[51]

## Humbling the Ethiopians, Helping the Fascists

On 3 October 1935, the Italians invaded Ethiopia. They captured Adwa within a few days, but their hopes to swiftly revenge their 1896 defeat to Ethiopia near that town were as yet not to materialize. Ethiopian defenses (partly due to the betrayal of Haile Selassie Gugsa) crumbled too quickly to enable a head-on collision in which, this time, Italian technological superiority could have crushed the Ethiopians. The Italians found themselves confronting guerrilla fighters in the mountains of northern Ethiopia and had to prepare for a prolonged war.[52] It was only on 8 November that they captured Makkale, the capital of Eastern Tigre, and it would be February 1936 before a chain of decisive battles made the war one-sided. Meanwhile, from our viewpoint, the Italians were in need of more camels for this kind of warfare, and the Ethiopians had gained time to seek diplomatic salvation. Emperor Haile Selassie could still hope to unite the Muslims of Ethiopia in support of his defensive effort. To promote this cause, a few days after the beginning of hostilities, yet another mission was dispatched to Arabia. It was composed of Blata Ayele Gabru and young Sayyid Muhammad Mahdi, both French-educated and fluent in Arabic (Gabru having been educated at the French Mission in Harar). They first went to Yemen, where they exchanged letters ratifying the treaty of friendship signed in April. They then crossed the Saudi border and arrived in Ta'if on 31 October, on their way to Riyadh. But instead of the Saudi capital, they were asked by Yasin's men to go to Jedda.[53] No official ceremonies were held and the *Umm al-Qura* newspaper mentioned their arrival only in two laconic lines.[54] Yasin arranged lodgings for them in a royal residence some five kilometers outside of Jedda. Yasin joined them at a dinner during which the Ethiopians repeated their proposal of a treaty of friendship and asked for the prompt opening of an Ethiopian consulate in Jedda. Yasin had been instructed by Ibn Sa'ud to merely repeat the statements that had been made to the previous Ethiopian delegation in April.[55] He told the emissaries to wait for Hamza, who arrived from Riyadh and met with the Ethiopians on 4 November. The dialogue can be reconstructed from Hamza's telegraphed communications to Ibn Sa'ud, which were monitored by the British. The Ethiopians first reiterated their proposal about a treaty and a consulate. Hamza politely replied that, as they had been told in April, Saudi Arabia was a friend to both Italy and Ethiopia and had to remain neutral. Signing a treaty with Ethiopia before the end of its war with Italy, he explained, would be viewed as an anti-Italian act. He then left the Ethiopian emissaries for a full week and returned on 11

November. He found Ayele Gabru much humbled. The Ethiopian diplomat said he had thought about it and understood that as friends they could not embarrass their Saudi hosts. Ethiopia would not want to create difficulties for Saudi Arabia, he said. He therefore suggested that they now merely draft the text of a treaty and sign it officially only after the war. Hamza asked if that meant that they would initial a treaty now and that the actual signing and ratification would take place in peacetime. Gabru agreed that this was more than acceptable. Hamza then told the Ethiopian that he was not authorized to promise anything. However—as he wrote in his telegraph to Ibn Sa'ud—he responded in a way that left Gabru very pleased. Hamza then asked the Ethiopians to be patient while he returned to Riyadh to put the issue to the king. "We approve it all," Ibn Sa'ud telegraphed Hamza. "Try to please them and entertain them lavishly."[56]

It is apparent that what the Ethiopians needed was not so much an official treaty but any written statement of friendship by Ibn Sa'ud. A friendly word from the ruler of the holy places could help Haile Selassie in his crucial dialogue with Ethiopia's Muslims. But Ibn Sa'ud had his own worries. In his eyes, the war in Ethiopia was a collision between Italy and Britain, and the Italians were pressuring him to side with them. Two days after they invaded Ethiopia, an Italian ship anchored in Jedda and unloaded a consignment of light arms and nine weapons experts. The surprised Ibn Sa'ud ordered it all to be left in the customs house, but he could not fail to understand the message.[57] Mussolini was exerting pressure to expedite the camels deal and was ready to pay in both cash and arms. As there were expectations for a very poor pilgrimage season (indeed, the number of pilgrims for 1935–1936 would be only 11,003[58]), Ibn Sa'ud's treasury men joined Hamza, Yasin, and Prince Sa'ud in persuading the king to cooperate with Italy.[59] Underlying the Italian promises was a barely hidden threat. Earlier, in April, the Ethiopian delegation, which left Saudi Arabia empty-handed, continued to Egypt. When they arrived in Cairo, the Italians issued a blunt warning to the Egyptian government that any official act of identification with Ethiopia would be considered by Mussolini as an act against Italy.[60] The text of that warning was sent to the Italian legation in Jedda, and there Perisco brought it to Hamza's attention. According to Hamza, Ibn Sa'ud was greatly alarmed by the Italian message. He had no intention of risking Italian wrath—he especially feared the Italian penetration of Yemen following their conquest of Ethiopia—and was not particularly concerned about Ethiopia itself.[61]

Ibn Sa'ud's main consideration was how Britain would face

Mussolini. He followed the issue very closely and sent his advisers time and again to get the British response and advice. The picture he got was that Britain would definitely not fight Italy and that he should remain on friendly terms with Mussolini.[62] Though the League of Nations, dominated by Britain and France, declared Italy the aggressor on 7 October, the British themselves told him that the Suez Canal would remain open for their use.[63] Sanctions were applied on Italy by the League on 18 November, but these were on arms and finances, which the Italians, at least in Saudi eyes, did not lack. The British, it was apparent, were still trying to appease Mussolini. If they would not protect Ethiopia, a member of the League, would they stand by Saudi Arabia, which was not? The persistent dialogue between Ibn Sa'ud's advisers and the British legation in Jedda finally yielded, on 22 December 1935, a more emphatic reiteration of the 1927 assurances that Britain would not allow any European power to penetrate the Arab Peninsula.[64] For his part, Ibn Sa'ud continued emphasizing his neutrality.[65] To make it clearer, on 22 October 1935, he arranged for the Egyptian *Al-Ahram* newspaper to report on this position as confided by a high-ranking Saudi source.[66] But his neutrality related to relations between Italy and Britain. On 20 November 1935, two days after the League's declaration on sanctions, 1,000 camels, already loaded on Italian ships, sailed from Yanbu' to Masswa.[67] The authorization must have come directly from Ibn Sa'ud who had followed all the details of their purchase and transfer to the port.[68] Because Saudi Arabia was not a member of the League, it was not legally obligated to refrain from selling war materials, and the British had indirectly approved the deal. The importance of the camels to the Italian war effort in Ethiopia now grew to such a level that both Perisco and Odello exerted growing pressure to promptly complete the deal for about 12,000 camels.[69] In December and in January 1936, the Italians, as reported by Hamza to the British, were ready to pay up to 100 pounds per head.[70] As the British were afraid that vetoing the transaction would result in Saudi financial and political demands from London, they continued to view it as merely a commercial issue. How many more Saudi camels were actually sold to serve the Italian war effort in Ethiopia is not clear.[71] After February 1936, the Italians gained enough military superiority in Ethiopia to switch back to a fully mechanized war. Ibn Sa'ud, always more fearful of British neglect than of Italian might, remained reluctant. Though Hamza, Yasin, and Prince Sa'ud supported further cementing the Italian connection, Ibn Sa'ud also listened to Prince Faysal[72] and to his own intuition. When in early January 1936 Odello tried to push matters, Ibn Sa'ud took a step back.

The Italian agent wrote to Ibn Sa'ud on 3 January 1936 suggesting an anti-British military alliance between Italy and Saudi Arabia, and that he, Odello, would be appointed over a Saudi army that would invade Transjordan and eventually free Palestine. Odello, an agent of Emilio De Bono's intelligence service in Eritrea, might have been overacting in the spirit of Mussolini's designs, for the Italian leader in the same month approved the transfer of arms and money to Palestinian leader Amin al-Husayni, and he ordered that this be done through Ibn Sa'ud and his men. In the coming years, Ibn Sa'ud would allow only the transfer of Italian money to the Palestinians, not arms. He would not openly defy Britain and would not see Odello anymore. On Ibn Sa'ud's instructions, Hamza showed Odello's letter to Perisco, hinting that the king was most unhappy with such ideas. Odello was duly summoned back to Rome and never returned.[73] Ibn Sa'ud's policy on the Ethiopian war finally took shape: friendship and business relations with Italy, no risk of a split with Britain.

Throughout November and December 1935, the two Ethiopian emissaries waited outside Jedda. Only on 24 December, two days after the repeated assurances from the British regarding the Arab Peninsula, did Hamza pay them another visit. He telegraphed Ibn Sa'ud in Riyadh and reported on another pleasant conversation. He told Ayele Gabru that no treaty of friendship was possible as long as there was war with Italy, but that they, the Saudis, were also friends of Ethiopia and had no intention of concealing this. Together, Hamza and Gabru drafted a letter to be sent from Ibn Sa'ud to the emperor that mentioned their earlier negotiations and their good intentions. The proposed draft included a statement that a treaty could not be signed at that time, but that the Saudi government was ready to open an Ethiopian consulate in Jedda and treat Ethiopian citizens staying in Saudi Arabia as if a treaty of friendship had been signed. In his cable to Ibn Sa'ud, Hamza asked for approval and also whether he should give the Ethiopians farewell presents.[74] We do not have Ibn Sa'ud's reply about any such presents. However, from the Italian correspondence, it is clear that on the more substantial aspects, the Saudis consulted the Italians. A few days later, Perisco was able to report to Rome that he had managed to defeat the Ethiopian mission completely.[75] When Ayele Gabru and Muhammad Mahdi embarked from Jedda on 29 December, they carried no draft treaty. Ibn Sa'ud refused to sign any treaty with Ethiopia. It is quite clear from the available documents that he even evaded signing the personal letter for Haile Selassie that Hamza and Gabru had drafted. Hamza told the Italians that the Ethiopian envoys carried two letters to the Ethiopian foreign ministry, one authorizing a consulate in Jedda, the other explaining why a treaty was not possible at that time.[76] According to Hamza's conversation with the British, the Ethiopians carried nothing in writing. The two weary Ethiopian envoys sailed to Port Sudan hoping to find a ship heading for Aden. No such ship was available to them. They took a boat back to Jedda on 8 January 1936, but this time they did not set foot on Saudi soil. They stayed on board in the harbor for a few more days, waiting for any vessel that would return them to their country.[77]

The Saudis' interpretation of neutrality meant that they could not officially express friendship for Ethiopia, but that Saudi Arabia would not join the League's sanctions on Italy. Camels were sold to the Fascists, the Saudis examined Italian arms samples, and young Saudi men were trained in Italy as combat pilots. In early February 1936, the "young eagles" were licensed as bomber pilots and began their advanced navigation training. They would return to Saudi Arabia in April, and in May, Italy would send Jedda a gift of six military airplanes.[78] Meanwhile, Hamza and Yasin were in constant touch with the British regarding the League's call for sanctions. The Saudi position was that as they were not members of the League they could not afford to take sides against Italy. Since the British were reluctant to push the Saudis in any way that would oblige them later to compensate the Saudis (for example, to work for Saudi admittance to the League in spite of difficulties regarding slavery), Ibn Sa'ud was able to continue to trade war materials with Mussolini.[79] On 28 January 1936, Prince Faysal, the foreign minister, sent an official letter to the League's Co-ordination Committee:

> As the Government responsible for the affairs of the Sacred Land of Islam, His Majesty's Government is above all anxious to maintain the most friendly and stable relations with neighboring countries or those inhabited by Muslims, so that pilgrims coming from all parts of the Muslim World may be able to perform their religious rites. . . . As a non-Member of the League of Nations it considers that its participation in economic sanctions would involve heavy responsibilities without the enjoyment of the privileges and advantages conferred on members of the League . . . it [is therefore] absolutely essential for it to observe complete neutrality in the present Italo-Ethiopian conflict.[80]

Mussolini was pleased with the Saudis and grateful. On 22 February, he personally cabled Ibn Sa'ud: "His Majesty will be delighted to learn about the deep satisfaction of the Italian people and of myself with the loyal attitude of his noble government and country in facing the call of the League to apply sanctions."[81] Ibn Sa'ud replied, expressing gratitude for the sympathy that the Italian people and their prime minister showed his country.[82] In the spring, as the Italians were quickly advancing in Ethiopia, they began to intensify their pro-Islamic propaganda in Arabia. Throughout Arabia, Italian agents distributed leaflets in Arabic heralding their imminent victory and promising that

> Italy will follow, in respect to the Muslim inhabitants of the new territories which she has conquered, the same line of policy since long adopted in her old colonies. . . . The Italian conquests in Ethiopia open a new era of freedom and progress for the Muslim population there, who were, until now, kept in a state of inferiority by the predominant Copt element, and were often hindered by the latter in the exercise of their cult.[83]

The Italian legation in Jedda saw to the spreading of Italian-Libyan Arabic newspapers in Hijaz, glorifying Mussolini's promotion of Islam in Libya.[84] Perisco and his staff informed the Saudis about the privileges given to Muslims in Ethiopian areas already under Italian control. Special emphasis was placed on Italian aid to pilgrims.[85] The hajj as a bridge between the Horn and Arabia, a bridge that also served Italy, would be an essential part of the Fascists' strategy after the fall of Ethiopia.

### "Leave the Ethiopians Alone": The Saudi Interpretation

What was the attitude of the Saudi public to besieged Ethiopia? The material available can offer only hints. The "Ethiopian question" that took the Arab world by storm in 1935 was also at the top of the Saudi agenda. But unlike in Egypt, Syria, Lebanon, Palestine, and Iraq, there was almost no educated, urban public to argue in writing about the inherent dilemmas. There were only two newspapers in Saudi Arabia at that time, *Umm al-Qura* and *Sawt al-Hijaz*, and reading them reveals very little. Until the very outbreak of hostilities in October 1935, items in both papers were merely chronological and laconic. After the outbreak of war, dozens of lengthy pieces about the international scene were published, some translated from the European or other Arab press. There were analyses of the military aspects and of global deterioration. The Italians, for their part, were not entirely happy with this kind of neutrality, and Rome instructed Perisco to see to a more pro-Italian line.[86] Perhaps more significant was the fact that no article was published throughout this period on the Ethiopians' predicament nor, naturally, on Haile Selassie's new effort to come to terms with Islam. Ethiopia itself, as mirrored in the Saudi press, was ignored. The British legation did try to randomly gauge some voices from below. It was observed that in Hijaz, in contrast with the more Wahhabi Najd, there were signs of some public sympathy with Ethiopia, which stemmed from its being the "land of the *najashi*." On 1 October, just before the Italian invasion, British Minister A. S. Calvert reported that in Jedda he had heard voices criticizing the government for not showing more solidarity with Ethiopia.[87] There were also voices raised in the Hijaz that opposed the sale of camels to Mussolini and condemned Ibn Sa'ud's Syrian advisers as being bribed by the Italians.[88] After the invasion, there were cheers of joy and some other pro-Ethiopia manifestations when a crowd in Jedda heard about some Ethiopian success over the radio. Shouts of "down with the Italians" were expressed, to the extent that Perisco officially complained about the breach of neutrality and the authorities warned the headmen of the quarters to make sure that it would not happen again. Still, in October 1935, when boys in Jedda were seen playing "Ethiopians and Italians," a game in which the rule was that Ethiopians should always win, the Italian chargé d'affaires lost his sense of humor and complained again. The boys were warned not to play the game anymore.[89] On the other hand, in December 1935, Perisco reported to Rome that he had met with local people in Jedda to gauge their attitudes. He was told that "if Italy managed to fulfill even half of its plans in Ethiopia, British prestige would be finished and we all would side with Italy."[90] A few days later (14 December 1935), Perisco told Prince Faysal in Mecca that Radio Asmara would begin to broadcast news in Arabic every Saturday and Tuesday night (Radio Bari, the Arabic station to the Middle East, could not yet be received in Arabia). He asked the Saudi newspapers to announce the broadcast schedule. When Faysal asked Ibn Sa'ud's permission, the response was negative. The King said that it was not up to his government to tell newspapers what to write. Apparently Ibn Sa'ud wanted to seem as neutral as possible.[91]

On 10 April 1936, Ibn Sa'ud gave an interview to *Al-Ahram* correspondents in Mecca. He spoke about developments in the Arab world in the shadow of the Italian-Ethiopian war. He said he hoped that "patience and restraint would prevail over haste and illusions, and that the present crisis would be solved for the benefit of all." As for the Arabs, his advice was that they "resort to patience and be calm. That they should think only about their own common interest, and not be dragged into futile affairs and pointless arguments over issues that would give them no benefit."[92]

Perhaps these words best reflected his fundamental attitude toward Ethiopia. In her hour of plight, Ibn Sa'ud chose to "leave the Ethiopians alone," but not in the orthodox interpretation of gratitude and grace. He rather "left them alone" in the more negative sense of indifferently ignoring Ethiopia. All three missions sent to Saudi Arabia in 1934–1935 included Ethiopian Muslims and thus conveyed the idea of Ethiopia's effort to build a new dialogue between Christians and Muslims. But Ibn Sa'ud had his own strategic anxieties and his own Wahhabi concepts. Under the cover of neutrality, he in fact helped Mussolini. In the end, the Saudis did not follow Rida's Islam, which at that time guided many Arabs and Muslims in other countries to actively identify with their besieged Ethiopian neighbors. It seems rather that the Saudis, hiding behind pleasing words, showed no consideration for Ethiopia.[93] Moreover, it would be fair to conclude that Wahhabi concepts combined with the Islamic-Arab militancy of Arslan to support Mussolini and his promise to bring victory to Islam, rather than encouraging renewed Christian-Islamic dialogue in the "land of the *najashi*."

## Notes

1. See Van Donzel, *Foreign Relations of Ethiopia*; Van Donzel, *A Yemenite Embassy to Ethiopia*; and Van Donzel, "Correspondence Between Fasiladas and the Imam of Yemen," pp. 91–100. For a summary see Erlich, *Ethiopia and the Middle East*, pp. 37–39.

2. See Erlich, "Mussolini in the 1920s, the Reluctant Imperialist," pp. 213–222.

3. For a discussion of Saudi-Italian relations in 1932–1934, see Pizzigallo, *La Diplomazia dell'Amicizia, Italia e Arabia Saudita*. For the 1932 treaty, see chap. 1, pp. 12–36. The chapters on 1935–1942 are rather slim and contain little new information. See also Salis, *Italia, Europa, Arabia*, chap. 8, "Dagli accordi di Gedda (1932) al conflitto Italo-Etiopico."

4. See also an analysis in FO 371/19020, Calvert to FO, 3 September 1935.

5. See Erlich, *Ethiopia and the Challenge of Independence*, chap. 7, "Tigrean Politics and the Approaching Italo-Ethiopian War," pp. 135–165.

6. For a succinct analysis of the pre-war diplomatic developments, see Sbacchi, *Ethiopia Under Mussolini*, chap. 2.

7. For a succinct analysis, see Segre, "Liberal and Fascist Italy in the Middle East," pp. 199–212; also Erlich, "Periphery and Youth: Fascist Italy and the Middle East," pp. 393–423.

8. Borruso, *L'Ultimo Impero Cristiano,* pp. 178–179.

9. Ibid., pp. 194–195.

10. Ibid., p. 178, quoting the Italian consul in Harar's letter to Mussolini.

11. Ibid, pp. 178–179.

12. *Berhanena Selam* (Addis Ababa), 30 May 1935.

13. Haile Selassie I, *My Life and Ethiopia's Progress,* p. 220.

14. See Erlich, *Ethiopia and the Middle East,* chap. 8, 9; *The Cross and the River,* chap. 6.

15. Zabiyan, *Al-Habasha al-muslima,* pp. 52–53, 60.

16. See Erlich, *The Cross and the River,* p. 90.

17. See Al-Salman, *Rashid Rida wa-da'wat al-Shaykh Muhammad bin 'Abd al-Wahhab.*

18. Arslan, *Al-Sayyid Rashid Rida,* pp. 763, 766, 783. For the Rida-Arslan dialogue on Ethiopia, see Erlich, *Ethiopia and the Middle East,* pp. 99–100, 114–118.

19. Perisco to Rome, 31 March 1935, in *Saudi Arabia Secret Intelligence Records 1926–1939* [British monitoring of Saudi telegraph system], Archives editions, London, 2003, (henceforward *SASIR*), vol. 5, pp. 55–56.

20. Perisco to Rome, 4 April 1935; *SASIR*, vol. 5, p. 56.

21. See "Jedda Report for April 1935," in Ryan to Simon, 1 May 1935, *Jedda Diaries 1919–1940* (Archive edition, compiled by R. Jarman, London, 1990, henceforward *JD*), vol. 4, p. 26. Also Perisco to Rome, 12 April 1935, and 14 April 1935, in Ministero degli Affari Esteri, Archivio Storico (Rome, henceforward ASMAE), Etiopia Fondo la Guerra, Affari Politici (henceforward EFG), Busta 101.

22. Foreign Ministry, Rome, to Perisco in Jedda, 26 July 1935, in ASMAE, EFG, Busta 60.

23. Pizzigallo, *La Diplomazia dell'Amicizia, Italia e Arabia Saudita,* p. 86. Also FO 371/19020, Calvert to FO, 3 September 1935.

24. "Annual Report for 1935," in *Records of Saudi Arabia,* vol. 6, p. 23.

25. Hamza, *Qalb jazirat al-'arab.*

26. Perisco to Rome, 3 April 1935, in ASMAE, EFG, Busta 60.

27. For Arslan's career, see Cleveland, *Islam Against the West.* For his bond with Ibn Sa'ud, see mainly pp. 65, 71–74, 81–83, 106, 115, 126–129.

28. For Arslan's concepts of Ethiopia and for references to the quotations in the above passage, see Erlich, *Ethiopia and the Middle East,* chap. 8, "The Arabs, Mussolini, and the Abyssinian Dilemma," and chap. 9, "Pan-Arabism, Arslan, and Conquered Abyssinia." For Arslan and Mussolini, see also Cleveland, *Islam Against the West,* mainly pp. 144–146.

29. "Jedda Report for May 1935," in *JD,* vol. 4, p. 32.

30. Prince Sa'ud in Rome to Ibn Sa'ud in Mecca, 22 May 1935, in *SASIR,* vol. 5, p. 60.

31. "Annual report, 1935," in *Records of Saudi Arabia,* vol. 6, pp. 23–24; also FO 371/19117, "Italian-Ethiopian Dispute, Extract from International Press Correspondence," 1 June 1935.

32. See a eulogy to Rashid Rida by 'Abdallah Amin, in *Al-Manar* (Cairo), 30 July 1935.

33. See Hamza to the King, 24 December 1935, in *SASIR*, vol. 6, pp. 145–147.

34. Cairo legation to Rome, 23 August 1935, ASMAE, EFG, Busta 102.

35. See Hamza to the King, 24 December 1935, in *SASIR,* vol. 6, pp. 145–147.

36. "Jedda Report for July 1935," in *JD*, vol. 4, p. 44; "Report for August," p. 50.

37. See, for example, FO 371/19130, Calvert, report of 20 August 1935 from Jedda, "Italo-Ethiopian Dispute: Reactions in Saudi Arabia": "The king appeared much engrossed in the situation and recurred to it often in conversation. Though he did not in so many words say so, he evidently felt that 'if not prevented by Great Britain,' Italy would find the conquest of Abyssinia an easy matter, and then, with victorious army on the spot would turn her attention to the Yemen. With a footing on Arabia soil, Ibn Saud would then find himself face to face with the Italians. . . . Ibn Saud should view so fundamental a disturbance of political equilibrium, at no great distance from his shores, with great mistrust and suspicion."

38. "Jedda Report for September 1935," *JD*, vol. 4, p. 56. "Annual Report, 1935," in *Records of Saudi Arabia*, vol. 6, p. 24.

39. De Bono to War Ministry, 2 August 1935, *Ufficio Storico Stato Maggiore del`Esercito*, SIM, Rac.5(B), fasc.1: "Fornitura governo saudino."

40. See FO 371/20056, Ryan to FO, "Saudi Relations with Italy," 3 January 1936. For the use of camels in military operations in Ethiopia (and bibliography), see the article "Camels," by R. Pankhurst, in Siegbert Uhlig, ed., *Encyclopaedia Aethiopica* (Hamburg: 2003), p. 677.

41. See the report "Fuad Hamza and the Italians," in FO 371/19020, 30 December 1935.

42. On Yasin's version as told to the British, see "Jedda Report for August 1935," *JD*, vol. 4, p. 50. Also FO 371/19020, Calvert to FO, 25 August 1935.

43. King to Faysal, 26 August 1935, *SASIR*, pp. 114–115; Suvich to Asmara, 18 September 1935, ASMAE, EFG, Busta 102; Calvert to FO, 22 October 1935, in Public Record Office (London), FO 371/19020.

44. See King to Ibn Sulaiman, 1 October 1935, *SASIR,* p. 131.

45. FO 371/19020, Calvert to FO, 25 August 1935.

46. See Ibid. (including the minutes).

47. Ibid.

48. See Yasin to King, 6 September, Perisco to Rome, 7 September 1935, in *SASIR*, pp. 116–118.

49. Draft of the agreement is in ASMAE, Gabinetto 1923–1943, Busta 519, fasc. 2.

50. Yasin to King, 8 September 1935, *SASIR*, pp. 119–120.

51. See telegraph communications between King and Yasin, 8, 18, 19, 26, 29, 30 September 1935 in *SASIR*, pp. 119–130.

52. See Erlich, *Ethiopia and the Challenge of Independence*, pp. 152–156.

53. Ministero Affari Esteri a Ministero delle Colonie, 10 December 1935, ASMAE, EFG, Busta 115.

54. See *Records of Saudi Arabia*, vol. 6, p. 321.

55. Yasin to King, 2 November 1935, *SASIR*, vol. 6, p. 133–134; Perisco to Rome, 2 November 1935, ASMAE, EFG, Busta 101; FO 371/19020, Calvert to FO, 5 November 1935.

56. Hamza to King, 11 November 1935, King to Hamza, 13 November 1935, *SASIR*, vol. 6, pp. 135–136; Hamza to King, 24 December 1935, *SASIR*, vol. 6, pp. 145–147.

57. See "Italy" in "Annual Report, 1935," *Records of Saudi Arabia*, vol. 6, pp. 23–26; Calvert to FO, 15 October 1935, and 29 October 1935, in *Records of Saudi Arabia*, vol. 6, pp. 317–320.

58. "Jedda Report for January 1936," *JD*, vol. 4, p. 84.

59. "Jedda Report for October 1935," *JD*, vol. 4, p. 63; De Bono to War Ministry, 14 October 1935, ASMAE, Gabinetto 1923–1943, Busta 519, fasc. 2; Pizzigallo, *La Diplomazia dell'Amicizia, Italia e Arabia Saudita*, p. 91.

60. Mussolini's letter of 26 April 1935 as forwarded to Perisco, in ASMAE, EFG, Busta 101.

61. Calvert to FO, 11 November 1935, Public Record Office (London), FO 371/19020.

62. See, for example, Calvert to FO, 6 September 1935, in Public Record Office (London), FO 371/19020; Calvert to FO, 14 September 1935, *Records of Saudi Arabia*, vol. 6, pp. 311–313.

63. See "Jedda Report for October 1935" (by A. S. Calvert), in *JD*, vol. 4, pp. 59–65.

64. "Jedda Report for December 1935," *JD*, vol. 4, p. 73; "Annual report, 1935," in *Records of Saudi Arabia*, vol. 6, p. 21.

65. See Perisco to Rome, 22 December 1935, *SASIR*, vol. 6, p. 139; "Italy" in "Annual Report, 1936," *Records of Saudi Arabia*, vol. 6, p. 385.

66. *Al-Ahram* (Cairo), 22 October 1935. See also translation in FO 371/19020.

67. FO 371/19020, Calvert to FO, 19 November 1935, Ryan to FO, 8 December 1935; FO 371/20056, Ryan to FO, "Saudi-Italian relations," 2 January 1936; see also "Annual Report, 1935," in *Records of Saudi Arabia*, vol. 6, p. 20.

68. Calvert to FO, 5 November 1935, 19 November 1935, in Public Record Office (London), FO 371/19020 and telegraph communications between the King and Yasin, 8, 18, 19, 26, 29, 30 September 1935, in *SASIR*, pp. 119–130.

69. See also "Jedda Report for January 1936," *JD*, vol. 4, p. 81.

70. Ryan to FO, 8 December 1935, Public Record Office (London), FO 371/19020.

71. "Italy" in "Annual Report, 1936," *Records of Saudi Arabia*, vol. 6, p. 385.

72. For Faysal opposing the pro-Italian line of Sa'ud and the Syrian advisers, see "Jedda Report for January 1936," *JD*, vol. 4, p. 79.

73. Perisco to Rome, 13 January 1936, ASMAE, EFG, Busta 102; Hamza to King, 4 January 1936, *SASIR*, vol. 6, pp. 152–154. On Italian money and arms to the Palestinians through Ibn Sa'ud, see Goglia, "Il Mufti e Mussolini." On 31 January 1936, Mussolini met with the Italian consul in Jerusalem, who presented him with a request by Amin al-Husayni for 100,000 British pounds, 10,000 rifles, and 6 antiaircraft guns. Mussolini agreed that arms should be sent from Eritrea to Ibn Sa'ud. But the Italians wanted to be asked for the arms by Ibn Sa'ud—which he never did. Money was transferred through this channel, at least 135,000 pounds by the end of June 1938.

74. Fuad Hamza to the King, 24 December 1935, *SASIR*, vol. 6, p. 145–147.

75. Italian Legation, Jedda to Rome, 25 December 1935, *SASIR*, vol. 6, p. 148; Perisco to Rome, 2 January 1936, ASMAE, EFG, Busta 102.

76. Fuad Hamza to King, 24 December 1935, and 4 January 1936, in *SASIR*, vol. 6, pp. 145–147, 152–154.

77. "Jedda Report for January 1936," *JD*, vol. 4, p. 83.

78. "Italy" in "Annual Report, 1936," *Records of Saudi Arabia*, vol. 6, p. 386.

79. See Ryan's report "Saudi Relations with Italy," 3 January 1936, and FO 371/20056, Sir R. Oliphant "Proposed Sale of Saudi Camels to Italians," 10 January 1936.

80. See *Records of Saudi Arabia*, vol. 6, p. 324. See also "Italy" in "Annual Report, 1936," *Records of Saudi Arabia*, vol. 6, p. 385.

81. Jacomoni to Legation in Jedda, 22 January 1936, in ASMAE, EFG, Busta 115.

82. Jedda to Rome, 29 February 1936, in ASMAE, EFG, Busta 115.

83. The quote is from a leaflet distributed in Yemen in early May 1936, available in ASMAE, EFG, Busta 113.

84. "Jedda Report for December 1935," *JD*, vol. 4, p. 74; "Jedda Report for May 1936," *JD*, vol. 4, p. 107.

85. "Italy" in "Annual Report, 1936," *Records of Saudi Arabia*, vol. 6, p. 386.

86. See reports in ASMAE, EFG, Busta 50, 115, and 124. The files contain translations from the Saudi press on the Italo-Ethiopian conflict.

87. Calvert to FO, 1 October 1935, *Records of Saudi Arabia*, vol 6, p. 315 and FO 371/19020.

88. FO 371/19020, Calvert to FO, 22 October 1935.

89. "Jedda Report for October 1935," *JD*, vol. 4, p. 64.

90. Ministero Affari Esteri a Ministero delle Colonie, 10 December 1935, ASMAE, EFG, Busta 115.

91. Faysal to King, 14 December 1935, King to Faysal, 15 December 1935, *SASIR*, vol. 6, pp. 137–138.

92. *Al-Ahram* (Cairo), 11 April 1936. The same interview was also published in *Umm al-Qura* (Mecca), 17 April 1936. See also analysis in "Jedda Report for April 1936," *JD*, vol. 4, p. 97.

93. In the words of Sir Andrew Ryan, British Minister in Jedda: "The King

watches, as best he can, events in Europe, but has little true comprehension of them. . . . He has little real interest in Abyssinia, and has seen in the recent conflict, not so much a war between Italy and an African power, as a struggle between Italy and Great Britain." See "Italy," in "Annual Report, 1936," *Records of Saudi Arabia,* vol. 6, p. 387.

# 4

## The *Wahhabiyya* and Ethiopia, 1936–1948

HAILE SELASSIE'S LAST-MINUTE STRATEGY IN 1935 TO APPEASE Ethiopia's Muslims and mobilize them to help to defend the country proved a failure. The question of whether more outside Islamic help—like a token of friendship from the Saudi ruler of the holy places[1]—could have made a difference is irrelevant. Mussolini's invading armies included over 70,000 Muslim soldiers from Somalia, Eritrea, and Libya. When hostilities began, many of the Emperor's Muslim subjects helped the Italians. Once the Italians occupied the country, local Muslim forces were entrusted with securing the new regime in sensitive places.[2]

### The Fascists and the Politicization of Islam in Ethiopia

Mussolini's aim in launching his war, to reiterate, was twofold. First was the ambition to create an East African empire on the ruins of Ethiopia. Immediately after the fall of Haile Selassie, the very concept of the ancient Christian state was practically erased. The name "Ethiopia" survived officially only in the name of the local Orthodox Church and in the new title of the Italian king, now addressed also as the "Emperor of Ethiopia." What used to be the empire of Ethiopia, together with Eritrea and Italian Somalia, were declared Africa Orientale Italiana ("Italian East Africa"). Second, was the long-term ambition to build the East African empire as a springboard to the Middle East. By controlling the Blue Nile and strengthening his hold on the Red Sea, Mussolini gained some of the leverage he needed to revive the Roman empire in the eastern Mediterranean. This long-term strategy also included a strong element of propaganda. Both Islam and Arab nationalism were to be manipulated by Italy in order, eventually, to incite anti-British and anti-French revolts in Egypt and the "fertile crescent" and to enhance Italian influence in Arabia. Though the word "Africa" was widely used, the Fascists' comprehensive design was to prepare the grounds for their victory in the Middle East. In fact, the modern Italian conceptualization of Ethiopia was barely connected to the rest of the black continent. The leading Italian Ethiopianists of the time were orientalists, and some, like Carlo Conti-Rossini, Enrico Cerulli, and Martino Moreno, served in the administration of the new African empire. The leading Italian journal of Middle Eastern studies, *Oriente Moderno*, edited by Carlo Alfonso Nallino, covered Ethiopian affairs. Italian politicians, strategists, and scholars were all well aware of Ethiopia's uniqueness, its ethnic diversity, and its tradition of regional identities. They were equally aware of the history of Islam in Ethiopia and its dissimilarity from Islam in the Arab East. But Mussolini's twofold Ethiopian–Middle Eastern strategy necessitated a strong emphasis on Islam. Consequently, the five years of Italian rule in East Africa were marked by an effort to enhance Islam and, as far as possible, to represent it as identical to Arabism. This was done in the tradition of divide-and-rule in Ethiopia proper and through propaganda in the context of the Arab East.

Italian East Africa was divided into six provinces according to ethnic and religious criteria. These were Somalia, including most of the Ogaden area; Harar; Galla [Oromo]–Sidama; Eritrea, including most of Tigre; Shoa; and Amhara. Shoa and Amhara were the smallest in size and were recognized as having both Christian and Amharic cultures. In Eritrea, the previous system of separating Christians from Muslims continued. In the other three provinces, Islam was declared the principal religion and culture. There, as well as in the capital, Addis Ababa, the Italians began to subsidize Islamic institutions, allowing Muslims to implement Islamic law and to rebuild their educational systems. In Galla-Sidama and other areas, they encouraged Christian Oromos to convert to Islam. Hundreds of new mosques were built throughout the country, including the great Al-Anwar Mosque in Addis Ababa (Mussolini personally saw to its completion). A new mosque in Harar was inaugurated on 13 December 1937.[3] Most significantly, the use and teaching of Arabic were institutionalized. Arabic was declared an official language in the four provinces outside of Amhara and Shoa. Arabic newspapers and school textbooks were published. Radio programs in Arabic were introduced. All newspapers had to include columns in

Arabic.[4] The Italians thus provided the historically divided and linguisti-
cally diverse Islamic communities of the Horn of Africa with an effective unifying factor.

The official Italian policy was of religious equality.[5] In practice, the
Italians discriminated against Christians in all respects. After many of
the clergy resisted the occupiers, priests were massacred and church
leaders were executed. The Italians intervened to the extent of cutting
the historical ties of the Ethiopian Church to the Egyptian Coptic
Church. In November 1937, the Egyptian Abuna Qerilos V was
replaced by Ethiopian Abuna Abraham, and the church, declared autocephalous, was placed under strict Italian control.[6] At the same time,
Minister of Colonies Alessandro Lessona instructed Governor Rodolfo
Graziani to support Islam in a way that would be echoed throughout the
Muslim world. The hajj, the annual pilgrimage to Mecca, was now reorganized by the Italians in unprecedented scope. Hundreds of Muslims
from all over the country were encouraged—and subsidized—by the
Italians to perform this ultimate religious obligation. The preparations
for and sending of the hajj missions during the years of the Italian occupation became a major new framework for all-Ethiopian Islamic activities, connecting communities and providing participants with an inspiring religious experience. The Islamic community of Addis Ababa,
mainly its some 1,400 Arabs from Yemen and the rest of the Arabian
Peninsula, as well as other Muslims from India, were treated to special
gatherings and were showered with compliments and promises.[7] In
December 1936, Graziani held an official *'Id al-Fitr* reception and, for
the first time in Ethiopia, Ramadan cannons were fired.[8] The recently
destroyed Islamic Jimma was restored. Abba Jobir, grandson of Abba
Jifar, accompanied the Italian column to Jimma in November 1936 and
was put in charge of the region.[9] He was later sent on a tour to spread
the news in Arab countries. An Islamic high school, fully subsidized by
the Italians, was reopened in Jimma.[10] Similar gestures of support—
symbolic, verbal, and practical—were made in various other Islamic
areas. The dozens of pro-Islamic declarations by various Italian officials in Ethiopia were recycled by the Italians and their supporters in
Arabia and the rest of the Arab world.[11] Mussolini's Islamic propaganda
campaign climaxed in March 1937 when the Duce visited Libya, wav-
ing "the sword of Islam" and riding a white stallion, and declared that
having proven his intentions in both Libya and Ethiopia, he was now
the champion of Islam and its chief defender after the caliphate had
been abolished.[12]

Harar was a major factor in this strategic Italian enterprise. During the invasion, the Italians symbolically arranged for the ancient capital of Islam to be captured by the Muslim soldiers in their service. They also made sure that the backbone of the local garrison throughout the occupation would consist of Libyans and Somalis.[13] The Italians had special plans for the town. Designed in Rome and repeated time and again by Graziani and others, Harar was now to finally fulfill its historical goal. "The sacred Muslim city of Ethiopia," Graziani promised, "is destined by the Italian government to a brilliant future and should become a great center radiating quranic study and Muslim civilization."[14] Inspired and influenced by the Arabs of the Peninsula to become the center of Islam in East Africa for centuries, it was now Harar's turn to radiate interregional influence. Harar, the Italians promised, would become a revitalized center of Islamic scholarship, eventually competing with Egypt's Al-Azhar in inspiring learning in the Red Sea basin and Arabia.[15] Beyond such declarations, the Italians did in fact invest in Harar's Islam. Arabic was declared the official language of the town and Islamic religious courts were fully empowered.[16] Christians in Harar were openly told by Graziani (during his visit of 7–10 February 1937) that "they would have to give up all thought of retaining the social privileges they had enjoyed under the old regime."[17] The local Italian-language newspaper, *Corriere Hararino*, included columns in Arabic. In May 1939, the leading Italian scholar of Ethiopian Islam, Enrico Cerulli (vice-governor of Africa Orientale Italiana as of December 1937) was appointed governor of Harar.[18]

Italian rule in Ethiopia was too short to demonstrate their true intentions and abilities. The idea of a scholarship center in Harar never developed. The *madrasa* that Haile Selassie opened hastily in 1935 with the help of Egyptian Al-Azhar remained small. Its head, Egyptian Shaikh Yusuf bin Yusuf, was most displeased with what he considered the Hararis' religious shallowness and preferred to remain in the nearby town of Dire Dawa.[19] More substantial was the change in Harar's elementary education. The Italians subsidized the local Islamic schools and opened a general, modern "fascist" school. Of central importance to our story was their policy regarding the modern Islamic school that had been opened in 1933 by the local Islamic Voluntary Association. The Italians now supplied the school with new furniture, sports facilities, and teaching equipment. They facilitated the import of elementary Arabic-language textbooks from Egypt and also supplied the school with Arabic translations of Italian teaching materials. The school's headmaster, Shaikh 'Ali 'Abd al-Rahman ('Ali al-Sufi), retained his position and so did most of the teachers. However, they were now under direct

Italian control and salaried by the Italian administration. The Fascists allowed the Islamic Voluntary Association to continue its social activities and fundraising, but it was no longer permitted to interfere with the running of the school.[20]

Many Muslims throughout Ethiopia welcomed the Italians and expressed their enthusiasm and gratitude for the changes they brought. The breaking of the Christian hegemony with all its discrimination against and humiliation of Muslims was accepted as a blessing that also had a taste of historical revenge. "So let the history of the world," declared Shaikh Ibrahim 'Abd al-Rahman of Harar in one speech, "record the great praise due to Italy for releasing us from the unbearable yoke which was around the necks of Muslims in the time of the brutal Negus. . . . Long live the Duce Benito Mussolini."[21] Gradually, however, some resentment appeared among the Muslims. The Italians were happy to divide and rule in Ethiopia and spread their propaganda in the Arab Middle East, but they were not really ready to reconstruct Islamic independence, and surely not in the spirit that their propaganda implied. Their occupation was interventionist and often insensitive. By the end of 1936, the British consul in Harar already discerned growing dissatisfaction in the town. The Italians covered the beautiful walled city with barbed wire, opened bars next to holy places, and dictated everything without bothering to listen or consult.[22] When Minister of Colonies Lessona visited the main mosque, he insisted on not taking off his shoes.[23] The Islamic Voluntary Association was practically ignored and stripped of its control of the modern school. The new administration centralized and controlled Harar's economic life, harming some local interests that had enjoyed commercial autonomy under the corrupt Ethiopian imperial regime.[24] The Muhammadali company, a Muslim-Indian-owned firm that, under Haile Selassie and with the indirect protection of British passports, had monopolized much of Ethiopia's long-distance trade, began to collide with the authorities. Combining the Islamic upper commercial circles of Harar and Addis Ababa, and with branches in places like Jimma, it was targeted by the Fascists. In March 1937—much to the relief of Harar's small merchants—it had to cease its activities and its property was confiscated by the Italians.[25] In some cases of regional resistance, Muslims cooperated with Christians on equal footing. Following an attempt on Graziani's life in February 1937, Muslims, including the chief Muslim judge, were among those arrested.[26] Altogether, the Muslims' response to Italian policy was mixed. The British intelligence expert on Ethiopia, Colonel R. Cheesman, summarized the issue this way in his 1943 report:

In the early period of their occupation the Italians enjoyed a certain success in their policy of favoring the former subject peoples in the non-Amharic areas of the Ethiopian empire. That the subject peoples were to a large extent Mahometans was, however, an irrelevant consideration, however much the Italians may have played upon it. The Galla and Somalis welcomed the Italian occupation as offering a prospect of relief from Amhara oppression and as a novelty. The reasons of their dislike of the Amhara were, however, racial, administrative, social and economic, rather than religious.[27]

In the same year, the British Foreign Office Research Department concurred with this underplaying of the religious dimension.

The customary role of Italy as the self-styled protector of Islam was expected to have especial advantages in a country where the dominant class was Christian and many of the subject peoples Moslem. . . . But the religious antagonism which these measures were intended to exploit did not in fact exist, for the Amhara had never put difficulties in the way of the practice of Islam.[28]

In contrast, Alberto Sbacchi, a prominent historian of the Fascists' occupation of Ethiopia, concluded the following from a later perspective:

The support given by the Muslims to the Italians from 1935 to 1941 was indeed impressive as the Muslims for the first time enjoyed freedom of worship and liberal financial support for their schools and mosques. While the Italian rule lasted, the Muslims dreamed of making Ethiopia Muslim and the Italians hoped to become a Muslim power.[29]

## The Hajj and Saudi Policy, 1936–1941

After the Fascist occupation of Ethiopia, the importance of Saudi Arabia grew in Italian eyes.[30] Saudi Arabia's significance as the guardian of Islam's holy places, its being an independent state free of British or French control, and its proximity to their African Empire and the contacts they had already built there made it a potential pillar of the Italians' Middle Eastern dream. The Italians did their best to spread their influence in Saudi Arabia and conceived of the country as a prospective corridor to the core of the Middle East. In May 1936, just after their capture of the Ethiopian capital, they notified the Saudis that the Italian chargé d'affaires in Jedda had been promoted to minister plenipotentiary.[31] On 29 May, six Italian airplanes landed in Jedda complete with training crews, as a present to the Saudis. With the pioneer Saudi airmen already back from Italy, these planes were to represent the basis for an Italian-equipped Saudi Air Force. Their effort to thus create Saudi military dependency was combined with the intensification of their propaganda campaign. In Saudi Arabia, as in the rest of the Arab world, the Italians' focus was on their pro-Islamic policy in occupied Ethiopia and on their Arabization of Ethiopian Islam. Italian diplomats in Jedda made an effort to convey this message to Ibn Sa'ud in person. During 1936, the Bari radio station was upgraded so that its broadcasts could be received in Hijaz.[32] The Italian legation made extensive use of Arabic newspapers flown in from Libya, like *Al-'Adl, Raqib al-'Atid,* and *Barid Barqa*. These contained articles praising pro-Islamic Italian enterprises in both Libya and Ethiopia and were distributed regularly in Mecca and Jedda.[33] Some of the articles were occasionally summarized and recycled in *Sawt al-Hijaz* (Jedda) and *Umm al-Qura* (Mecca), though not with the regularity the Italians desired.[34]

The hajj was undoubtedly the heart of the Italian effort to bridge both shores of the Red Sea in the service of their propaganda. Already on 10 May 1936, Perisco insisted on seeing Ibn Sa'ud to tell him that in the upcoming hajj season, some 1,900 Ethiopians would make the pilgrimage.[35] This was supposed to be good news for the Saudis whose financial situation was worsening for various reasons, among them the decline in the number of pilgrims throughout the 1930s due to the world economic depression.[36] In 1933, their number had reached the lowest point since the Saudi conquest of Mecca—19,500, only 11 of whom were from Haile Selassie's Ethiopia. In 1934–1935, only 29 recorded pilgrims came from Ethiopia, and in 1935–1936, only 7.[37] Now, the Italians declared they were ready to encourage Muslim Ethiopians to make the hajj and were furthermore ready to cover the transportation and travel expenses. In preparing for the 1936 hajj season, the Italians asked for Saudi authorization to open an Italian hospital in Mecca. In the end, they settled for a new dispensary with one doctor and five rented houses to see to the welfare of the Ethiopian pilgrims.[38] Estimates of their 1936 numbers ranged from 1,696 to 1,900, all subsidized, with the Italians having to exchange their Italian paper lire or Maria Theresa silver dollars for gold.[39] The new hajj enterprise in Ethiopia took the shape of a pioneering event, with missions organized in various provinces. In 1937, the momentum was only slightly lost, with the number of pilgrims reported from Africa Orientale Italiana as between 1,271 and 1,700.[40] Similar numbers were given for the remaining two years prior to Italy's entry into World War II.

The Ethiopian pilgrims were expected to serve the Italian cause during the hajj and many of them performed accordingly. During the 1936–1937 hajj, for example, author Muhammad Salim Batuq of Massawa made a speech in Mecca praising both the Fascists and Ibn Sa'ud; his words were quoted in *Umm al-Qura* (of 22 February 1937). A group of twenty-five pilgrims from Harar was paid by the Italians to spread the word in Mecca about Haile Selassie's anti-Islamic policy and the salvation brought by Mussolini.[41] They were occasionally countered by anti-Fascist pilgrims from other countries and by exiled fellow Ethiopians. In the 1937 season, for example, Shaikh 'Umar al-Azhari, the Harari who was one of the 1934 Ethiopian envoys to Saudi Arabia, worked to stem the pro-Italian propaganda. At the time, he was staying in Jibuti together with quite a number of other Ethiopian exiles, headed by Makonnen Habta-Wald, the chief Ethiopian Christian adviser on Muslim affairs of the now ex-emperor. In Mecca, 'Umar al-Azhari praised Haile Selassie's religious moderation and exposed Mussolini as a brutal imperialist.[42]

For the thousands of Muslim Ethiopians who made the hajj under Italian auspices, it must have been a most inspiring experience. The episode, however, was short-lived. In 1941, Ethiopia would return to Haile Selassie's hands and Christian domination would be intensively resumed. When World War II ended, the first hajj season of late 1945 witnessed a great revival of this all-Islamic institution, with the number of pilgrims that year exceeding 200,000 people (to compare, in 1937, there were 67,224; in 1938, 48,318; in 1939, 34,382).[43] Of these, only 57 adults and 5 children came from Ethiopia.[44] Yet, as we will see, in the long run the hajj connection during the Fascist occupation proved significant, especially in the Ethiopian-Wahhabi story in Harar.

One of the few pilgrims of the 1935 hajj season was Ibrahim Hasan, a leading member of the Islamic Welfare Association of Harar and a teacher in its school. In Medina, he made the acquaintance of Shaikh Yusuf 'Abd al-Rahman Ibrahim, a fellow native of Harar. The latter, born in 1916, had made the hajj with his parents in 1928 and had remained in Medina. After completing his Wahhabi education, in 1935 he was appointed a teacher in the local Madrasat Dar al-Aytam. The bond between the two Hararis forged in Medina would have a significant impact on the history of Islam in their native town. Ibrahim Hasan was already fully ready to contribute to the demise of Haile Selassie's Ethiopia. In Medina, he wrote an article exposing Ethiopia's crimes against Islam and saw to its publication in one of the Arab journals. It included firsthand evidence by an Ethiopian citizen confirming the accusations made by Shakib Arslan and many other Arab writers throughout the Middle East. Ibrahim Hasan remained in Medina for a while and returned to Harar after the Italians had occupied Ethiopia. Shaikh Yusuf 'Abd al-Rahman left Saudi Arabia in 1938, spent a year in Asmara, and then settled in Addis Ababa, teaching Islam and importing Arabic books, mainly textbooks from Egypt.[45]

Also making the hajj of 1935 was Syrian journalist Taysir Zabiyan al-Kaylani. A lifelong friend of Arslan, he was already informed about and interested in the cause of Islam in Ethiopia. Like Arslan, Zabiyan was an admirer of Ibn Sa'ud and thought the king should lead the entire Islamic-Arab nation. In 1931, Zabiyan had established a newspaper in Damascus and called it *Al-Jazira* (The Peninsula), to emphasize the centrality of Arabia in Islam. Later in his career, he would move to Jordan where he would write on Saudi history and remain (until his death in 1978) a supporter of fundamentalist Islam and Wahhabism.

In late 1937, Zabiyan's book *Muslim Ethiopia: My Experiences in Islamic Lands*, was published in Damascus.[46] It was an account of his visit to Ethiopia in June 1936. It all began in Mecca during the hajj of 1935, he wrote (pp. 10–11). There he met with pilgrims from Ethiopia who told him at length about the plight of Muslims in their country. He mentioned no names but, given there were only seven Ethiopian pilgrims that year and from the spirit of the conversations he described, it seems that Ibrahim Hasan and Yusuf 'Abd al-Rahman were among those he met. Following these discussions, and on the strong recommendation of one of the pilgrims, Zabiyan decided to go to Ethiopia to see things for himself. He crossed the Red Sea in early 1936, but with the war in full swing, the Italians would not let him in. He returned to Damascus and on 12 May 1936 celebrated the fall of Haile Selassie with an article in *Al-Jazira* stating that it was fitting punishment for what the emperor had done to Lij Iyasu. It was only on 4 June that he arrived in Addis Ababa. (On 5 June 1936, *Al-Jazira* accused the British of saving the emperor's skin.)

Zabiyan's book is an interesting record of the state of Islam in newly occupied Ethiopia. His visit began with a long interview with the governor, Graziani (pp. 39–45), which repeats the Italian promises and plans mentioned above. Though somewhat reserved, the author nevertheless barely concealed his admiration for the strong-willed Fascist and his gratitude for his help to Islam. Zabiyan then proceeded to Harar and nearby Dire Dawa (pp. 50–69). His impressions of the Muslims he met and interviewed can be characterized in two ways. First, he was much impressed with those Muslim outsiders who came to help to rebuild

Islam in Ethiopia. He visited the camp of the 15,000 Libyan soldiers stationed near Harar and met with their leader, a captain in the Italian army.
The man was the epitome of Islamic devotion and bravery. Zabiyan also
spent time with Shaikh Yusuf 'Ali Yusuf, the Egyptian scholar who
served under the Italians as the head of the *madrasa* in Harar—the same
man who had been sent from Al-Azhar to help Haile Selassie open the
school. Nevertheless, he was a proud anti-imperialist, extremely critical
of Haile Selassie's Ethiopia, and he shared with Zabiyan what he knew
about Christian hegemony and the maltreatment of Muslims in Ethiopia's
history. The Egyptian sent detailed reports to the head of Al-Azhar,
Shaikh al-Maraghi (who, meanwhile, had become a supporter of the pro-
Islamic Italian policy in occupied Ethiopia).[47] Zabiyan's book is full of
similar reports that the author collected in Harar and Addis Ababa.

The second impression Zabiyan had was one of disillusionment
with Ethiopia's Muslims. He said their Islam was shallow, full of super-
stition and ignorance. It contained too many Sufi influences of the worst
kind. Zabiyan concurred with his Azharite host that the Muslims of
Harar were lazy, self-serving, and shameless in their subordination to
the Fascists. Their children wanted handouts, and their traders were
eager for new opportunities. In Harar, Zabiyan also met with the president of the Islamic Voluntary Association, Abu Bakr 'Abdallah Ayyub,
but the man left too small an impression to deserve more than a mere
mention. Much more space was devoted to Zabiyan's meeting in Addis
Ababa with Hajj Barasu, Haile Selassie's chief Muslim adviser and a
member of the Muhammadali company (p. 79). Hajj Barasu, an old
womanizer, a heavy smoker, and a happy man of leisure, was the only
local Muslim who told Zabiyan that the emperor had been fair to
Muslims and to Islam.

Before publishing his book, Zabiyan wanted to interview Mussolini
himself. When the Duce came to Libya in March 1937 to wave "the
sword of Islam" and to proclaim himself its defender, Zabiyan hurried
there from Damascus. He was granted the interview (pp. 13–16), during
which Mussolini repeated his promise to liberate the Muslims of
Ethiopia and enhance Islam there. Mussolini also assured Zabiyan that
he had no plans to invade Yemen or to penetrate the Arab Peninsula.
Zabiyan included this interview at the very beginning of the book.
Though he stated that by relaying the words of Mussolini he was not
necessarily endorsing them, the spirit of the entire book is fully supportive of the change in Ethiopia. This attitude was strongly boosted by an
introduction to the book written by Arslan (pp. 4–7). Here again, the
main example is Harar. What had been a proud Islamic sultanate was

reduced to slavery under Christian Ethiopia and now, with proper help, would face a new dawn.

Although there is no direct evidence of dialogues between Zabiyan or Arslan with Ibn Sa'ud regarding the Italian occupation of Ethiopia, his book certainly reached the king and his men.[48] No doubt Arslan and Zabiyan remained in constant touch with Hamza and Yasin, who were close to Prince Sa'ud. After the final collapse of Ethiopia in early May 1935, the British assessed that Hamza's influence had skyrocketed. Rumor had it that Ibn Sa'ud was considering a treaty with Mussolini. In July 1936, the king was reported to be disillusioned with the British. According to one source, Ibn Sa'ud told his entourage that "due to the strength of Greater Italy, Britain and her empire will soon be swept away—like many other similar empires, the Roman and the Ottoman—leaving it only a matter of history. . . ." He exhorted his small audience to avoid British connection as best they could lest they fall victims to their game of chess. He asked them to be very cautious during these days and to make it a point to kill the very seed of British influence on any aspect in the country, but at the same time to show no outward opposition or hostility toward them. He told his audience that the Italian government had promised to give advice and help through their newly appointed minister at Jedda whenever needed and that "it would behoove his officials to look to the Italian representative at Jedda for guidance."[49]

As already mentioned, for Ibn Sa'ud, the entire international issue was a British-Italian collision, not an Ethiopian war. Documents indicate that after the occupation of Ethiopia, the Saudi elite persisted in its inherent indifference to the fate of, and developments in, the land of the *najashi*. I found very little Saudi interest in the Italian propaganda that aimed to impress them with Italy's pro-Islamic policy in Ethiopia. The only direct evidence of any interest was the retrospective words of Hafiz Wahba, the Saudi ambassador to Britain. On 22 January 1941, as the British were about to destroy Africa Orientale Italiana, he said that Italy had failed to impress the Arab world "with one important exception. The Italians have been treating the Muslims in Ethiopia comparatively well. Parties of pilgrims, to whom special facilities were given, had been organized by the Italians."[50]

By the hajj season of late 1936, Ibn Sa'ud had apparently recovered from his initial surprise at the British sacrifice of Ethiopia. The British were now making it clear that they were not about to allow the Italians to actually challenge them in the Middle East.[51] In Egypt, the British came to terms with the nationalist movements, and in Palestine, they demonstrated their resolve to quell the local Arab revolt. In October 1936, the British and the Saudis signed an agreement on slavery, which strengthened their bilateral relations and was seen in Riyadh as a step toward the admittance of Saudi Arabia to the League of Nations (both the British and Italian legations in Jedda continued to help a trickle of manumitted Ethiopian slaves return to their country).[52] Moreover, Ibn Sa'ud's inter-Arab policy now needed the British on its side. In April 1936, he signed an agreement with Iraq, and in May, with Egypt, both still under British rule.

Of greater significance from our Red Sea perspective was the new Saudi dialogue with Egypt. Though Ibn Sa'ud needed Egypt's friendship to counter his old rivalry with the Hashemites of Transjordan and Iraq, his relations with the country of the Nile had been marred since 1926. In that year, his Wahhabi warriors attacked the *mahmal*, the annual procession that carried the gold-embroidered cloth covering the Kaaba from Egypt. The "*mahmal* incident"[53] created deep enmity between Ibn Sa'ud and King Fuad of Egypt, himself a rival candidate for leadership of the Islamic world and an admirer of Mussolini. The death of Fuad in April 1936 and the coming to power of a Wafdist government in May paved the way for Egyptian-Saudi reconciliation. Not only was the new government ready to sign an agreement with the British, but its new consul to Saudi Arabia, appointed in November 1936, 'Abd al-Rahman 'Azzam, was one of the most prominent antifascists in the Arab Middle East. 'Azzam, a long-standing admirer of Ibn Sa'ud and already developing into a major figure in inter-Arab relations (he would be the first secretary-general of the Arab League established in 1945), had never forgiven the Italians for their atrocities in Libya. In Islamic circles, he lost no opportunity to denounce Mussolini and his interference in Middle Eastern affairs.[54] Though now disillusioned with the British for their weakness during the Abyssinian Crisis, 'Azzam still considered London capable of preventing Rome from applying much harsher imperialism in the region.[55] Again, I have no direct evidence of 'Azzam's dialogue with Ibn Sa'ud during his stay in Arabia but can safely assume that he joined with Prince Faysal in talking the king out of any pro-Italian inclination.

Ibn Sa'ud, to reiterate, had always been suspicious of Mussolini. In practice, he refused to recognize the Italian annexation of Ethiopia, at least not without British consent. The Saudi press reported that he was very pleased with the Italian initiative to send so many Muslims from Africa to the hajj, but beyond this, he showed no gratitude.[56] The Italian request, in March 1937, to build, staff, and finance a hospital in Mecca for the pilgrims from their colonies was never authorized. The Saudi press was instructed to report that these were pilgrims from Somalia and Eritrea and thus avoid mentioning the Italian conquest of Ethiopia. Apparently to minimize the Italian propaganda effect, in 1936, for the first time, the king did not address the pilgrims who made the hajj at one huge banquet. Instead, four separate banquets were arranged: for Muslims from the Middle East, for Egyptians, for Indians, and "for all others" (including from China and Africa).[57] This arrangement remained in place in the coming years.[58]

Mussolini's gestures helped only a little. By declaring in March 1937 that he was the defender of Islam, the Duce must have personally offended the ruler of the holy places. Ibn Sa'ud, the British reported in April and again in June, now humbled Hamza and told him to keep a low profile for a while. Rumors were spread accusing Hamza of taking bribes from the Italians. The king told the British that Mussolini was trying to squeeze tokens of support from him, but that he, Ibn Sa'ud, despised the Italian, who resembled the mad Roman emperor Caligula.[59] On 27 April 1937, three more Italian airplanes arrived and the Italians resumed their offer of more weaponry.[60] But Ibn Sa'ud began searching for a way to divest himself of the Italians' military involvement without overtly offending them.[61] In November 1937, he began negotiating secretly with Egypt about training his young pilots on their soil. In their correspondence with the Italians, the Saudis made it a point to refer to the king of Italy without mentioning that Vittorio Emanuele III was now officially also the emperor of Ethiopia. An Italian demand in January 1938 to correct the reference was politely rejected.[62] In early 1938, the Italians made yet another effort to warm up relations. The famous orientalist Carlo Alfonso Nallino, editor of *Oriente Moderno* and a member of the Royal Italian Academy and of the Academy of Arabic Language in Cairo, landed in Jedda on 9 February. Nallino came with his daughter Maria, an orientalist in her own right, and their declared aim was to enhance cultural relations between Italy and Saudi Arabia. In a book on Saudi Arabia that he published a year later, in Maria's articles, and in their private papers, their disappointment was evident. The visitors spent six weeks in the country but were not permitted to go to Riyadh. After weeks of pleading, Nallino was finally granted only a thirty-minute meeting with Ibn Sa'ud in Jedda on 28 February 1938. The Italian scholar had to listen passively while Ibn Sa'ud lectured to him on Islamic history. The meeting ended with the arrival of the British minister, without Nallino having said a word.[63] Whatever message he carried from Rome, the response was a cold shoulder.

On 16 April 1938, the Italians and the British finally signed their bilateral agreement. Of interest here is that it contained British recognition of Africa Orientale Italiana and a mutual commitment to retain the status quo in Arabia. In response, Ibn Sa'ud instructed Faysal in Jedda to shower compliments on the Italian minister and "praise him more than usual."[64] He further telegraphed:

> Write to him and thank him profusely and say that when you informed me of those things I was very grateful and said that is what we expected from Italy and that there is no doubt that they are our friends in all matters. We trust no one except first God and then them. . . . As for the British Minister, tell him that we are fully satisfied first with God and then with the British Government. . . .[65]

Yet in spite of additional Italian offers of arms, the Saudis took their time about recognizing their annexation of Ethiopia. On 31 October 1938, they received word from the British that they could do so,[66] and on 29 November, Foreign Minister Faysal informed Rome of Saudi recognition in a laconic, dry letter.[67]

By that time, it seems, Ibn Sa'ud was determined to throw in his lot with the British. He may have assumed that the British were still stronger in the Red Sea arena. In March 1939, the Italian flight trainers were told to leave and the young Saudi pilots left for Egypt. Italy still swallowed its pride and exchanged polite words with Ibn Sa'ud.[68] In late 1939 and early 1940, the Fascists even strengthened their propaganda campaign. More pilgrims from Ethiopia were sent to Mecca. More Islamic personalities were invited to tour Ethiopia, and their positive impressions of Islam there were relayed across the Red Sea.[69] When Italy entered the war in June 1940, Saudi Arabia remained officially neutral. Expressing some interest in Ethiopia, Hafiz Wahba in London told the British that while he understood that they were friends of Haile Selassie, his country expected Britain also to consider the various minorities there. In January 1941, as the British-Italian struggle over Ethiopia began, Wahba added that the Saudi's main concern in Ethiopia was the fate of the Islamic community in Harar.[70]

## Harar and *Wahhabiyya*, 1941–1942: Which Islam?

On 19 January 1941, the British invaded Africa Orientale Italiana. With the Suez Canal in their hands, they enjoyed military superiority in the Red Sea and the Horn of Africa. At that time, that was the only corner of the world where they could gain a victory, and they pushed forward on all fronts. On 27 March, they captured Harar, and they took Asmara four days later. Addis Ababa was liberated on 3 May 1941, and Emperor Haile Selassie—who, with British guidance, had helped to inspire Ethiopian guerrillas—waited two days to enter his capital ceremoniously on exactly the same date on which it had fallen five years earlier. On 4 February 1941, the British government declared it had no territorial claims in Ethiopia and implied that it would restore Haile Selassie's authority within the previous borders. Though not all British military political officers were in agreement, the emperor's government was duly reestablished in all core regions, including the town of Harar.

Apart from Wahba's statement to the British in January 1941, I found no record of any direct Saudi interest in Ethiopia or its Muslims during the entire period discussed in this chapter. But indirect Saudi influence was very much in evidence. The thousands of Ethiopian hajj-makers who crossed the Red Sea courtesy of the Fascists were exposed to Wahhabi ideas and to Islamic political activism in the vein of Arslan and Zabiyan. Since the early nineteenth century, Wahhabi control over the hajj had been instrumental in spreading their influence in various corners of the Muslim world.[71]

Two Harari personalities have already been introduced: Shaikh Yusuf 'Abd al-Rahman and Hajj Hasan Ibrahim, who had spent time in Saudi Arabia in the early 1930s and adopted Wahhabi concepts. Shaikh Yusuf, back in Addis Ababa in 1939, would indeed become the leading figure in spreading the *Wahhabiyya* in Harar and in Ethiopia. Below, we shall follow his activities throughout the period discussed here. In 1976, he would leave Ethiopia and return to Medina where he is still active (in 2005) as a Harari Wahhabi. It is also from his writings—and from those of his anti-Wahhabi Harari rivals—that we can reconstruct the story of the 1940s.[72] A third Harari worth mentioning here was Hajj 'Umar Muhammad 'Abd al-Rahman, another member of the Islamic Welfare Association, which, as mentioned, was rather dormant under the Fascists.

After the British liberated the country, in the early summer of 1941, Shaikh Yusuf traveled from Addis Ababa back to his native Harar. He met with Hajj 'Umar and told him it was time to revive the Harari nation and to do so in the spirit of political Islam. Shaikh 'Umar, who had stayed in Harar under the Italians, was skeptical. He said that the Hararis were divided and too concerned with their own trivial interests. He spoke of their shallow, popular Islam in the same language as Zabiyan. Shaikh Yusuf, to his frustration, now saw firsthand how the better-united Christian Ethiopians had reasserted their governance. He gathered some of the Islamic elders and approached the British provincial adviser in Harar, Colonel Dallas. Their petition for British backing to restore Harar's independence was flatly rejected, with the British not even bothering to invite them to sit down. It was after that offense, Shaikh Yusuf wrote, that he decided to lay down the infrastructure for a long campaign.[73] He began by making speeches in the central mosque, and after three weeks was in a position to gather all those who agreed to work for an Islamic state in Harar, many of whom were graduates of the Jam'iyya school.[74] They declared the establishment of a National Islamic Association (*Al-Jam'iyya al-Wataniyya al-Islamiyya*)—popularly known as *Al-Watani*, the national or the patriot—to replace the old Islamic Welfare Association. A twelve-man secretariat and other bodies were elected. All members of the leading bodies were *hujjaj*, persons who had made the pilgrimage to Mecca. They all swore to free Harar from the yoke of Ethiopian colonialism and to rebuild an Islamic state on the historical model of Ahmad Gragn, centered on Harar and uniting—through the true Islam—its tribal Somali hinterland.[75]

According to Shaikh Yusuf, in that summer of 1941 they all realized that they could not risk a frontal confrontation with the Ethiopians before intensive reeducation of Harar's Muslims. It was therefore decided that the Watani Islamic Association would focus on the revival of the Islamic school that had been established by the old Welfare Association. After three months of fundraising and preparations, Shaikh Yusuf wrote, the school was reopened under the management of Hajj 'Umar. Its curriculum was quite similar to that of the old school—classes in modern sciences combined with Arabic and Islam.[76] However, this time, it was Wahhabi Islam taught by Hajj Ibrahim Hasan.

While Shaikh Yusuf 'Abd al-Rahman was busy running the Watani Association, the moving spirit in the school was Hajj Hasan. As testified to by one of his students, he not only taught the Wahhabi doctrine in school, but also organized evening classes in his home. It was the result of his example and endeavors, Yusuf Isma'il wrote fifty-six years later, that the *Wahhabiyya* spread and that he managed to attract and unite its followers. In preaching against the popular Islam of Harar, Hajj Hasan told his students they had to purify their faith, that they were drowning in superstitions and vanity like followers of grave cults. He told them that what they called Islam verged on polytheism (*shirk*).[77] Instead of worshiping the grave of Abadir, the founder of Harar, the school began educating its students in the Islamic militant spirit of Gragn. Gragn's history as the holy warrior who united all Muslims around Harar and destroyed Christian Ethiopia became one of the school's messages. It was recycled in poems, in the school's hymns, and in parades and ceremonies organized by the Watani Islamic Association.[78] Shaikh Yusuf 'Abd al-Rahman, himself an owner of a bookstore in Addis Ababa, imported Arabic textbooks from Egypt. These included copies of *Al-Qira'a al-Rashida*, the standard elementary Arabic textbook introduced in the 1930s in the core countries of the Middle East, as well as copies of Wahhabi literature.

The initial response of the Ethiopian government was tentative. Though the "Gragn trauma" was now, after the Fascists' work, more relevant than ever, the Christian authorities were still disorganized. Harar, however, remained a focus of the emperor's attention. From his own history, he knew that the town was an important key to all-Ethiopian influence and power. His favorite son, Lij Makonnen, was restored as the "Duke [*leul*] of Harar" (he had been given the title in 1934) and resided in the town. Haile Selassie's son-in-law Ras Andarge Masai was appointed governor of the province. Both busied themselves with rebuilding their administration, this time also answerable to a new Ministry of Interior in the capital.[79] They were also busy reconstructing the old network of economic and commercial monopolies in collaboration with the local upper circles and at the expense of the middle class that the Italians had upgraded. Their men in Harar did pay some attention to the activities of the Watani Association. Shaikh Yusuf wrote of a policeman who removed the sign over the Jam'iyya school. Sometime during the 1941–1942 school year, an education inspector (Kebede Mikael, later minister of education) visited the school. Having listened to translations of the hymns praising Gragn, he forbade the singing of them. He then forced the school to reintroduce Amharic as the principal language.[80] Naturally the Ethiopian government remained most suspicious of and attentive to information regarding Islamic affairs. Haile Selassie's chief adviser on Islamic affairs, Makonnen Habta-Wald, who had long been in touch with the community of Harari merchants and dignitaries in Addis Ababa, coordinated activities aimed at restoring full Christian hegemony throughout the country.

The real confrontation that followed was not between the Ethiopian authorities and the Wahhabi-inspired Watani Association, but between the latter and their local Muslim opponents. The majority of Harar's inhabitants, though resentful of the renewed Ethiopian intrusion, were not ready to begin a costly struggle against Ethiopia, nor were they really inclined to adopt that kind of fundamentalist Islam. As mentioned above, Harari Islam, though it preserved the collective memory of political independence and of anti-Ethiopian jihad, was rather a pragmatic mixture of Sunni moderate orthodoxy and Sufism. It was a flexible, apolitical Islam capable of coexisting with other cultures and, by the 1940s, long-adapted to accepting Christian Ethiopian hegemony. Harar's culture was highly permissive, in many ways revolving around popular cults of grave visitation and ecstatic ceremonies of saint worship, *zikr*. It was strongly based on the Sufi principle of *tawassul*, reaching Allah through intercession. Side by side with a tradition of Sunni orthodox learning and law, Harar was also a producer and exporter of *qat*, the narcotic that influenced and reflected Harar's Sufism as well as the town's leisure life and pragmatic commerce. The *Wahhabiyya* categorically rejected all these. It had developed in the Arabian desert of Najd, not in an intercultural environment like Ethiopia. Imported into Harar from Saudi Arabia, in large part due to the Fascists' enterprise, and feeding also on the resentment of some local middle class circles, *Wahhabiyya* was able to take root by reviving the local legacy of Gragn and giving it a new theological interpretation. But it collided with the equally resilient legacy of Shaikh Abadir—that of Harar's relatively popular, flexible religiosity, adaptability, and pragmatism.

The man who now rose to oppose the *Wahhabiyya* in Harar was Shaikh 'Abdallah ibn Muhammad ibn Yusuf. Born in Harar in the 1910s, he received an orthodox education and became associated with the local *Qadiriyya* Sufi fraternity. Further pursuing his studies, he spent time in Jimma where he became affiliated with the *Tijaniyya* fraternity. 'Abdallah was also said to be visiting Islamic centers in Wallo and other Ethiopian regions.[81] Before and during the Fascist occupation, Shaikh 'Abdallah spent most of his time in Addis Ababa where he integrated into the local Islamic commercial circles led by figures like Hajj Barasu and the agents of the Muhammadali company. These circles, which included strong Harari representation, had cooperated economically and even socially with the imperial regime prior to the Italian conquest. During the Italian occupation, some of them, like Hajj Barasu, remained in contact with Makonnen Habta-Wald and Shaikh 'Umar al-Azhari in Jibuti and Paris. Shaikh 'Abdallah spent considerable time in Addis Ababa's *mercato*, in bookstores, in coffee houses, and at *qat* sessions, gaining fame as a Sunni scholar and widening his circle of admirers. His strong character and charismatic personality indeed paved the way to a long career. He would leave Ethiopia at the end of this period and begin to build his scholarly prominence in the Middle East. In our concluding chapter, we shall return to Shaikh 'Abdallah at the beginning of the twenty-first century when he is the head of an all-Islamic, international association, which is arguably the more effective opponent of the *Wahhabiyya* in the world of Islam.

In Harar of 1941–1948, Shaikh 'Abdallah began his lifetime rivalry with Shaikh Yusuf 'Abd al-Rahman. Upon hearing of the establishment of the Watani Islamic Association, and the activities of the renewed school, Shaikh 'Abdallah organized the opposition to the *Wahhabiyya*. He initiated provocative disturbances during the meetings of the association and met with students of the school to deter them from the Wahhabi doctrine. One of those students, Yusuf Isma'il, testified that the shaikh was, at that time, also critical of the modern aspects of the school's curriculum, including the pictures in the imported textbooks and geography lessons that taught that the world was round.[82] His rivalry with the Wahhabi group soon turned into enmity, and the Harari community split along personal and theological lines. When Hajj Ibrahim Hasan quoted a Wahhabi interpretation of a quranic verse that implied that Allah sat like a human being, Shaikh 'Abdallah made public mockery of it. He made speeches against the Wahhabi's personification of God and their worship of the Quran to the extent of betraying the true spirit of the Sunna. He appealed to the Hararis to define themselves as *Ahl al-sunna wal-jama'a* (the community of orthodox Islamic beliefs) and to declare the Wahhabis infidels. In late 1941, heated discussions in coffee houses and *qat* sessions turned into street fighting. Shaikh 'Abdallah called on the Hararis to boycott the school even after the Ethiopian authorities had modified its curriculum. Sometime in late 1941 or early 1942, following one of his provocative actions against the school, he was even arrested and held in custody for a while.[83] The arrest may have been staged by the government, which undoubtedly supported Shaikh 'Abdallah. Back in Addis Ababa, the shaikh was said to have informed the government about Hajj Ibrahim Hasan's 1935 article in the Arab press that denounced Christian Ethiopia in general, and Haile Selassie in particular. Hajj Hasan and the other Wahhabi teachers in the school were duly arrested and tried. Hajj Hasan was sentenced with others to exile from Harar to another part of Ethiopia, where he died 23 years later.[84] Shaikh 'Abdallah was now appointed the mufti of Harar, and the Wahhabi activists in Harar had to keep a low profile and bide their time. Their next opportunity for organizing would come in 1947.

## The "Fraternal Strife of the Club" and the Fall of Political Islam in Harar, 1947–1948

Throughout 1942–1947, the proponents of political Islam in Harar, like elsewhere in Ethiopia, had to come to terms with the resolidification of

Haile Selassie's regime. The Ethiopian imperial government was now determined to fully revive Christian hegemony and punish Muslims who had collaborated with the Italians.[85] In 1942, the Church's Egyptian connection was resumed, with the return of Abuna Qerilos V from Cairo. In 1946–1948, this ancient church bond underwent modernization when the Egyptian Copts agreed to the appointment of five Ethiopian bishops and declared that the next *abuna* would be an Ethiopian. Meanwhile, the translation of the Bible into Amharic had been completed. The church regained its economic assets and, under the emperor's close control, reasserted much of its traditional influence throughout the country. The swift recuperation of Christianity as the country's hegemonic culture was multidimensional. It also proved helpful in the emperor's new campaign to annex the territories of the fallen Italian empire, those lying outside of Ethiopia's pre-1935 borders. With the end of World War II in 1945, a diplomatic struggle over both Eritrea and Italian Somalia began. The Ogaden region, which according to Anglo-Ethiopian agreements of 1942 and 1944 was to be returned to Ethiopia, was still temporarily in British military hands.

The Ethiopian campaign to regain Eritrea proved successful. The Ethiopians played their international diplomatic cards well, and, with the help of the Church (and through systematic intimidation and manipulation), managed to win most Christian Eritreans over to their cause. In late 1947, the Eritrean Unionist Party was instrumental in persuading the UN's fact-finding commission sent to gauge public opinion in the former Italian colonies. In 1952, Eritrea was federated with Ethiopia and was fully annexed in 1962. I shall return to the Eritrean story in the following chapters.

Ethiopia's aim and methods with regard to Italian Somalia (under British military rule) were similar. At the UN, the emperor demanded the entire former Italian colony, and his diplomatic team included Somalis from Harar and the Ogaden—namely, Hajj 'Umar al-Azhari and Hajj Farah. The Italians countered by requesting restoration of their colony, including the Ogaden. No diplomatic solution was worked out in 1946–1947, and the issue, connected to the Eritrean problem, awaited the same UN fact-finding commission.[86] Meanwhile, a third element had appeared forcefully on the scene. Back in 1943 an authentic Somali nationalist movement, backed by the British and strongly anti-Italian, was established in Mogadishu. Called the Somali Youth Club, it began working for Somali independence and quickly spread through all Somali-inhabited areas.[87] In 1946, the British estimated its membership at over 25,000. In 1947, anticipating the UN commission, the movement changed its name to the Somali Youth League and established branches in the Ogaden. The 1947–1948 momentous rise of Somali nationalism reenergized and added a new dimension to the Ethiopian-Islamic story revolving around Harar.

The Ethiopian government responded to the new developments by trying to use Harar's Somali connection as a springboard to the Ogaden and to the whole of former Italian Somalia. Hajj Farah was sent to establish a new Somali Mutual Relief Association, which was also sponsored by the Harari community in Addis Ababa (headed by Hajj Barasu) and worked openly to mobilize Somalis in support of unification with Ethiopia. Its emblem was a combination of a cross and a crescent, and its membership cards were printed in Amharic. To combat any potential anti-Ethiopian Islamic dynamism, the government announced that no pilgrims from Harar would be allowed to leave for Mecca in the forthcoming Hajj season.[88]

However, in spite of the Ethiopian money distributed in Harar and in the Ogaden, the Somali Mutual Relief Association scored only minor success.[89] No doubt Haile Selassie knew he needed a better Trojan horse among the Somalis, one comparable to the Eritrean Unionist Party. Because some leading Somali tribal leaders in the Ogaden proved ready to benefit from both Somali nationalism and Ethiopian favors[90] (Maqtil Tahir, heading the league's branches in the Ogaden had the imperial Ethiopian honorific title of *Qannazmach*), the plot then weaved in Addis Ababa was to try to convert the anti-Italian Somali Youth Club into an Ethiopian tool.

In early 1947, the Ethiopians enabled the Somali Youth Club (the old name persisted) to open a branch in Harar as well as elsewhere in Ethiopia. According to British reports, the Harari branch was soon a success; 800 members registered in August and over 1,000 in October. Their political and religious energies, however, were not really controlled by the Ethiopians. As the future of the area was being debated, many Hararis began to emphasize their Somali identity and roots, and in return were harassed by the Ethiopian police.[91] In late 1947, the British reported that the Ahmad Gragn spirit in town had been wholly revived. The air was filled with slogans calling for Harar's independence and its annexation to a free Islamic Somali state. Pictures of various Arab kings and drawings of Gragn—the Islamic holy warrior who had united Hararis and Somalis against Ethiopia—were posted on walls,[92] and the rumor spread that Harar would soon become the capital of an Islamic, Somali state.[93] At first most members of the Watani Islamic Association were suspicious of the club. Their agenda was local Harari-Islamic, not

Somali (indeed the modern Arabic term *wataniyya* implies local patriotism rather than ethnic nationalism). But having lost their game in 1941–1942, the renewed Somali momentum of 1947 seemed yet another option to revive Islam's political identity and remove the Ethiopian yoke. By 15 November 1947, all members of the Watani Association, in spite of the wary disapproval of Shaikh Yusuf, then in Addis Ababa, had also joined the Somali Youth Club.[94] With word spreading that the UN fact-finding commission was to visit Mogadishu the following January, tension in Harar grew.

On 24 November 1947, the Ethiopian deputy governor of Harar made his move. He was none other than Blata Ayele Gabru, who back in 1935 led the last Ethiopian mission to Ibn Sa'ud. No doubt he still carried the memory of his humiliation by the Wahhabi state and of the paternalistic way that Ibn Sa'ud ignored Ethiopia in her hour of plight and helped Mussolini. Ayele Gabru had been educated in the Capuchin Mission school in Harar (the one attended by the emperor in his youth) and was most familiar with the new developments and the personalities involved. He now hastened to arrest the club's chairman, Hajj Halil, and replace him with his local agent, Ibrahim 'Abd al-Salam. He then convened a gathering of dignitaries and made them apologize to the emperor for evoking the Gragn spirit and for wishing to secede from Ethiopia.[95] Shaikh Yusuf 'Abd al-Rahman recalled that it was Shaikh 'Abdallah—undoubtedly in close touch with Ayele Gabru—who pulled the strings and tried to manipulate the club.[96] Judging by the ensuing events, however, it is clear that the Ethiopians now had better intelligence on the club's activities, but no real control over it.

In January 1948 it all exploded. Examining the British reports, the recollections of Shaikh Yusuf 'Abd al-Rahman and of Yusuf Isma'il, and papers by Harari students in Addis Ababa University (based on oral testimonies) provide the following picture. When it was established that the UN commission was coming to Mogadishu, the club's leadership talked the Watani Islamic Association members into traveling together to Mogadishu to meet with the international diplomats. A similar call came from the Somali Youth League in Mogadishu. Shaikh Yusuf recalled that he warned against such a move, fearing Ethiopian provocation. A delegation was secretly organized consisting of four original Watani members, eight club members, and one independent person. By mid-January, they managed to cross the lines and reach Mogadishu, where they were enthusiastically received in the streets but managed to receive little attention from the international committee. They were flatly told by its members that Harar, as an Ethiopian town, had nothing to do with the issue of former Italian colonies. After two more months in Mogadishu, the delegates were ordered by the British to leave. They had applied for asylum in various Arab countries and obtained it from Saudi Arabia, most probably through the connections of Shaikh Yusuf. They were then hosted in the Saudi town of Ta'if for two months and enjoyed the hospitality of Prince Faysal. The latter arranged for their transportation to Egypt and for their reception by his old friend 'Abd al-Rahman 'Azzam, now secretary-general of the Arab League. True to his old pro-Ethiopian policy 'Azzam told the Harari delegates that the Arab League, occupied with the war in Palestine, would not deal with the issue of Islamic Harar. However, Hasan al-Banna, the leader of the Muslim Brothers, was ready to take care of their maintenance in Cairo.[97]

Meanwhile, on 21 January 1948, the Ethiopian secret police arrested fifty-two members of the Watani Association and the Somali Youth Club. A general strike was called for the next day, and a delegation of fifty elders approached the governor. They were all arrested. A public gathering was proclaimed under the governor, only to end with more arrests. By February 1948, the number of detainees stood at more than 200 and all were subject to investigation. By March, most of the detainees, after begging for imperial forgiveness, had been released. Haile Selassie was apparently more considerate toward the Youth Club members and their Somali irredentism than toward the Hararis and their Islamic political orientations. Eighty-one members of the Watani Islamic Association, its leadership and backbone, were all sentenced to exile. Divided into three groups, they were sent to other parts of Ethiopia (to Jimma, Gore, and Gojjam). Most were allowed to return after one year.

Simultaneously, in December 1948, the emperor, fearing that the whole issue would ignite anti-Ethiopian sentiments in the Arab East, sent conciliatory messages to those who fled to Egypt, and nearly all returned.[98] Having asked for imperial pardon, most of those activists preferred now to settle humbly in the capital. Meanwhile, on 23 September 1948, Ethiopia regained the Ogaden and thus sealed its full control over Hararge province. However, Haile Selassie's plot to use the Somali Youth League to gain Italian Somalia as well proved illusionary.

The events of January 1948 in Harar marked the end of the Islamic political revival in Ethiopia that began in 1936. They can be viewed together with the simultaneous victory of the Christians over the Muslims in determining the future of Eritrea. Revived Ethiopia regained both the Ogaden and Eritrea and reasserted Christian hegemony over their Islamic communities. Beyond the similarities, there were also significant differences. The Muslims of Eritrea had been integrated into that entity by the Italians in the late nineteenth century. They had hardly ever been under Christian Ethiopian rule and now were not even partially assimilated into the all-Ethiopian fabric. Rather, they would soon associate themselves with revolutionary Middle Eastern pan-Arabism, create a modern liberation front, and from the end of the 1950s, fight for the establishment of an Arab-Eritrean identity.

In comparison, the demise of political Islam in Harar was more significant. Harar was both an integral part of Ethiopia (after 1887) and, for centuries, the capital of Islam in the Horn (most Eritrean Muslims had adopted Islam in the 1820s). No wonder the Fascists considered Harar a springboard to their Middle East–oriented imperial vision. As we have seen, Harar was a center of local, *habashi*, popular, and flexible Islam, but was also a center of learning and hajj, maintaining contact with Mecca and Arabia since Harar's medieval incipience. The town was also the historical capital of Gragn, always carrying the legacy of the anti-Ethiopian jihad. This was a legacy of holy war based on the unification of Somalis, Adaris, and other local groups, as well as on Arabian inspiration and help. It was this Harari-Gragn dimension, indirectly revitalized by the Fascists and more directly through their hajj enterprise, that had the potential of combining with the *Wahhabiyya* and its fundamentals. Moreover, the stricter principles of Wahhabi Islam appealed to some of the local traders, long deprived by the regime-connected leading families, as a potentially suitable ideological platform for local revival. Importing the Wahhabi doctrine and militancy from Saudi Arabia made Harar of the 1940s a challenge to Ethiopian culture, both Christian and Muslim. At the same time, as we have seen, Harar had always had an equally strong, or perhaps even stronger, dimension, that could not coexist with Wahhabism. Forcefully and successfully, it resisted the imported doctrine.

Shaikh Yusuf 'Abd al-Rahman, the leader of the *Wahhabiyya* in Harar, temporarily had to acknowledge defeat.[99] From the beginning he wanted local, Harari fundamentalization, not the overt anti-Ethiopian, Gragn-like militancy of cooperating with non-Hararis. After 1948, with the dismemberment of the Islamic National Association, the school in Harar was put under the direction of Ahmad Kibu, a loyal functionary of the imperial regime. Shaikh Yusuf, who thought that patient education of Hararis was the key to Islamic victory, went on teaching the school's standard Amharic-based (with some Arabic) curriculum. He spent most of his time in his Addis Ababa bookstore and in time would usefully serve the government. He would become a member of Parliament, as well as the head of the imperial Hajj Committee, which regulated the pilgrimage to Mecca under the watchful eye of the regime. Shaikh Yusuf would also find himself helping the emperor with the ultimate stage of the Ethiopianization of the country's Muslims, namely the translation of the Quran into Amharic.[100] As long as Haile Selassie was in power, the country saw no real sign of Wahhabi revival or of any other effective manifestation of political Islam. Only in 1976, after the rise of the communist regime in Ethiopia, did Shaikh Yusuf return to Medina. As we shall discuss below, he stayed in Saudi Arabia until 2004, helping and inspiring the Wahhabi followers of today's Ethiopia. He returned to Harar in the summer of that year.

Also in 1948, Shaikh 'Abdallah left Ethiopia. As one of his younger associates testified, Haile Selassie accused him of foiling the dream of annexing Italian Somalia.[101] He passed through Mecca and then spent time in Jerusalem and in Damascus. In 1950, he moved to Beirut, where in 2006, he was still active. In the 1980s, he established his Association of Islamic Philanthropic Projects *(Al-Ahbash)*, which by the turn of the century had become an important movement in the all-Islamic context, leading Sunni Islam in Lebanon and participating in the moderate Islamic struggle against Wahhabism on all continents. We shall return to this later. The rivalry between Shaikh 'Abdallah al-Harari and Shaikh Yusuf al-Harari has indeed become a dynamic reflection of what troubles Muslims not only in Ethiopia but also in the entire world.

In their current Wahhabi-"Ethiopian" polemics, the two old shaikhs and their followers often return to the formative events in Harar of 1941–1948. Shaikh 'Abdallah and his men claim that the shaikh was an Islamic patriot who hated Haile Selassie and his Christian domination, that he stood for the true, sober, and moderate Islam, the Ethiopian-Islamic version, capable of coexisting and prospering with moderate Christians. They deny that Shaikh 'Abadallah plotted with the imperial government against Harar's independence.[102] It was because of the *Wahhabiyya,* they charge, and because of Shaikh Yusuf and his friends who imported this fanaticism from Saudi Arabia, that such a disaster befell the Islamic community in Harar. Shaikh Yusuf, they claim, was the instigator of the self-destructive strife,[103] and Wahhabi fundamentalism led inevitably to reckless militancy. The Wahhabis in today's Harar, on their part, call their 1941–1948 trauma *fitnat al-kulub* (the *fitna* of the club). *Fitna* in Arabic has various meanings, including a fratricidal war, as well as provocation, temptation, enticement, and heresy. In the eyes of today's Harari followers of Shaikh Yusuf, nearly all those meanings are applicable. They were disastrously tempted to immaturely join an overt, regional anti-Ethiopian cause (and many radical Hararis would be

tempted to repeat this mistake—to the regret of Shaikh Yusuf—in the
late 1970s and as of the 1990s). They were provoked to do so by those
who sought a self-defeating fratricidal strife. It was 'Abdallah, "the
instigator shaikh," they insist, who thus betrayed the Islamic nation of
Harar to his Christian masters.[104] His kind of Islam, maintain the
Wahhabis, is a heretical prescription for Islamic humiliation and defeat.
Only the *Wahhabiyya*, they claim, and persistent spreading of Islamic
fundamentalism, is the key to the salvation of Ethiopia and all of Islam.

## Notes

1. The title "Custodian of the Holy Places" was adopted officially by the
Saudis in 1986 only.
2. For general analyses of Islam in Ethiopia during the Fascists' occupation, see Borruso, *L'Ultimo Impero Cristiano,* pp. 194–197, 229–232; Borruso,
"La crisi politica e religiosa dell'impero etiopico sotto l'occupazione fascista,"
pp. 57–111; Buonasorte, "La politica religiosa italiana in Africa Orientale dopo
la conquista," pp. 53–114. For a succinct summary, see Sbacchi, *Ethiopia Under
Mussolini,* pp. 161–166.
3. FO 401/35, Stonehewer-Bird to Eden, 4 January 1938, "Report on
Events in Ethiopia During 1937."
4. FO 371/20202, "Italian Policy Regarding Arabs in Ethiopia and the
Near East," by Mr. Roberts, Addis Ababa, 18 August 1936.
5. See detailed declaration in "Manifestation of Loyalty," *Giornale di
Addis Ababa,* 12 August 1936, in FO 371/20202. See also FO 371/20200,
Barton to Eden, 17 June 1936.
6. See Erlich, "Identity and Church," pp. 23–46.
7. FO 371/20202, "Italian Policy Regarding Arabs in Ethiopia and the
Near East," by Mr. Roberts, Addis Ababa, 18 August 1936.
8. FO 371/20927, "Italian Regime in Ethiopia: Question of the
Mohammedan Element," by Mr. Roberts, 22 December 1936.
9. FO 371 20940, "Records of Leading Personalities in Abyssinia," 4
May 1937.
10. FO 401/35, Stonehewer-Bird to Eden, 4 January 1938, "Report on
Events in Ethiopia during 1937"; FO 401/35, Roberts to Eden, 3 November
1936.
11. For this effort in Saudi Arabia, see "Annual Report, 1937," *Records of
Saudi Arabia,* vol. 6, pp. 555–560.
12. See Claudio Segre, "Liberal and Fascist Italy in the Middle East," pp.
199–212.
13. *Giornale di Addis Ababa,* 12 August 1936, in FO 371/20202.
14. Ibid.
15. FO 371/20202, "Italian Policy Regarding Arabs," and FO 371/20927,
"Italian Regime in Ethiopia."

16. The reintroduction of Arabic as an official language in Harar was well-received throughout the Arab world and to the credit of Italy. The Italians made an effort to give it wide publicity in the Middle East. See ASMAI, EFG, Busta 113, "La Lingua Araba Ristabilita nell'Harar," Cairo, 18 June 1936. See also FO 371/20056, Calvert to Eden, Jedda, 5 September 1936.

17. FO 371/20928, Report by British Consulate, Harar, Acting Consul T. Wikeley, 11 February 1937.

18. See Ricci, "Cerulli, Enrico," pp. 708–709.

19. Zabiyan, *Al-Habasha al-muslima*, pp. 50–52.

20. Yusuf, *Qissat al-kulub*, pp. 42–45.

21. FO 371/20928, "Extract from *Corriere Hararino* of 15 May 1937—Translation of Speech Made by Shaykh Ibrahim ibn Mohammed Abdurrahman," in Bird to FO, 14 June 1937. See more examples in ASMAI, EFG, Busta 113, Ciano to Pilotti, 25 August 1936; FO 371/20202, "Manifestations of Loyalty," attached to "Italian Policy Regarding Arabs"; FO 401/35, Roberts to Eden, 3 November and 29 November 1936; FO 371/20929, "Marshal Graziani's Tour," in Helm to FO, 6 October 1937.

22. FO 401/35, Wikeley to Bond, 9 February 1937; FO 371/20928, Wikeley to FO, 11 February 1937.

23. FO 371/20928, Bond to Thompson, 1 March 1937.

24. FO 401/35, Wikeley to Stonehewer-Bird, 17 May 1937; FO 371/20929, Ellison to FO, 2 November 1937.

25. FO 401/35, Drummond to Eden, 25 March 1937; Helm to Eden, 14 September 1937.

26. FO 371/20928, Stonehewer-Bird to FO, 9 March 1937.

27. FO 370/1287, Howe to Eden, 5 July 1943.

28. FO 371/35626, "Draft Paper on Ethiopia" (for the Italian Handbook), by Mr. Bernard Wall (Research Department, FO) to Mr. Howard, 4 June 1943.

29. Sbacchi, *Ethiopia Under Mussolini*, p. 165.

30. See Pizzigallo, *La Diplomazia dell'Amicizia*, pp. 94–95.

31. Yusuf Yasin to King, 31 May 1936, *SASIR*, p. 166.

32. "Annual Report, 1937," *Records of Saudi Arabia*, vol. 6, pp. 555–560.

33. FO 371/20056, Calvert to Eden, 28 September 1936.

34. Perisco to Ministero, 10 July 1936, ASMAI, EFG, Busta 115; "Report for October 1937," *JD*, vol. 4, p. 127.

35. FO 371/20056, Ryan to FO, 13 May 1936.

36. For a general analysis of the hajj and its place in Saudi history, see Teitelbaum, "The Saudis and the Hajj."

37. FO 371/20055, "Report on the Pilgrimage of 1936 (A.H. 1354)," in Calvert to Eden, 3 August 1936.

38. "Report for March 1937," *JD*, vol. 4, p. 171; "Annual Report, 1937," *Records of Saudi Arabia*, vol. 6, p. 555–560.

39. "Report for December 1936," *JD*, vol. 4, p. 147; "Report for February 1938," *JD*, vol. 4, p. 264; "Annual Report, 1937," *Records of Saudi Arabia*, vol. 6, pp. 555–560.

40. *Oriente Moderno* (Rome), March 1938, p. 136; FO 401/35,

Stonehewer-Bird to Eden, 4 January 1938, "Report on Events in Ethiopia During 1937."

41. "Annual Report, 1937," *Records of Saudi Arabia*, vol. 6, pp. 555–560.

42. "Report for February 1938," *JD,* vol. 4, p. 265.

43. *Oriente Moderno* (Rome), March 1940, p. 138.

44. "The Pilgrimage, 1946," *Records of Saudi Arabia*, vol. 8, p. 587.

45. Yusuf, *Al-Rasa'il al-thalath,* pp. 60–61.

46. Zabiyan, *Al-Habasha al-muslima.*

47. FO 371/27532, Lampson to Eden, 7 March 1941.

48. At the same time, Zabiyan's brother and closest associate, 'Adnan Zabiyan al-Kaylani, wrote a book entitled *Bloodstained Palestine.* He sent copies to *Umm al-Qura.* See "Report for February 1938," *JD,* vol. 4, p. 259.

49. See also FO 371/20056, Calvert to Eden, 28 July 1936.

50. Report by R. A. Butler, 22 January 1941, in *Records of Saudi Arabia,* vol. 7, pp. 240–241.

51. See "Italy" in "Annual Report, 1937," *Records of Saudi Arabia*, vol. 6, pp. 555–560.

52. "Report for October 1936," *JD*, vol. 4, pp. 127–134; "Annual Report, 1936," *Records of Saudi Arabia,* vol. 6.

53. See Teitelbaum, "The Saudis and the Hajj."

54. See Coury, *The Making of an Egyptian Arab Nationalist,* pp. 22, 292–299, 415–416. Also, Kramer, *Islam Assembled*, pp. 131, 135–136.

55. *Al-Ahram* (Cairo), 23 November 1935.

56. "Report for February 1937," *JD,* vol. 4, pp. 165–166.

57. Ibid.

58. "Report for February 1938," *JD,* vol. 4, p. 266.

59. "Annual Report, 1937," *Records of Saudi Arabia*, vol. 6, pp. 555–560; "Report of April 1937," *JD*, vol. 4, p. 184; "Report of June 1937," *JD,* vol. 4, p. 195.

60. "Annual Report, 1937," *Records of Saudi Arabia*, vol. 6, pp. 555–560.

61. "Annual Report, 1937," *Records of Saudi Arabia*, vol. 6, pp. 555–559; Faisal to King, 6 November 1937, *SASIR,* vol. 7; "Report for December 1937," *JD*, vol. 4, p. 230.

62. Fu'ad Hamza to King, 7 January 1938, *SASIR,* p. 288.

63. See Nallino's report, "Viaggio a Gedda, Relazione al Ministro degli Afari Esteri e appunti sul viaggio nell Arabia Saudiana (1938)"; see also *Oriente Moderno* (Rome), April 1938, p. 174; Nallino, *L'Arabia Saudiana.*

64. King to Faysal, 22 April 1938, *SASIR,* p. 296.

65. King to Faysal, 24 April 1938, *SASIR,* pp. 298–299.

66. FO 371/22415, Bullard to FO, 31 October 1938.

67. ASMAI, EFG, Busta 165, Feysal to Ministro, 22 November 1938, in Sillitti to Ministro, 29 November 1938.

68. Ibn Sulaiman to King, 25 and 27 March 1939, *SASIR,* pp. 306–307.

69. FO 371/24635, British Consulate, Addis Ababa to FO, 26 January 1940.

70. Report by R. A. Butler, 22 January 1941, in *Records of Saudi Arabia,* vol. 7, pp. 240–241.

71. See Peters, *The Hajj*.

72. Our discussion below of the period 1941–1948 focuses on the story of Harar, Wahhabi influence, and the rivalry between the two local shaikhs, Shaikh Yusuf and Shaikh 'Abdallah. Apart from the British reports, it is based mainly on the recent writings of these shaikhs and their followers. See Muhammad Yusuf Isma'il, *Qissat al-Kulub*, p. 126. (The author had been a follower of Shaikh Yusuf and later turned against his Wahhabi tendencies.) Shaikh Yusuf 'Abd al-Rahman Isma'il, *Al-Rasa'il al-Thalath*, p. 148 (written in response to *Qissat al-Kulub*). These books are available at the *Institute of Ethiopian Studies*, Addis Ababa University. We shall return to Shaikh Yusuf and Shaikh 'Abdallah in the conclusion.

73. Yusuf 'Abd al-Rahman, *Al-Rasa'il al-thalath*, pp. 3–4.

74. Rahji Abdella, "The Kulub."

75. Yusuf 'Abd al-Rahman, *Al-Rasa'il*, pp. 4–7. The names of the members are on p. 6.

76. Ibid., pp. 7–8.

77. Yusuf Isma'il, *Qissat al-Kulub*, pp. 14–15.

78. Yusuf 'Abd al-Rahman, *Al-Rasa'il*, p. 9.

79. FO 371/35626, "Ministry of the Interior, Annual Report (for the year ending 10 September 1942)," by D. A. Sandford. For a detailed analysis of the administration of Harar and Ethiopian security in those periods, see Tim Carmichael, "Approaching Ethiopian History."

80. Yusuf 'Abd al-Rahman, *Al-Rasa'il*, pp. 9–10.

81. On 'Abdallah's early life, see also his rival's description in Yusuf 'Abd al-Rahman, *Al-Rasa'il*, pp. 46–52.

82. Yusuf Isma'il, *Qissat al-kulub*, pp. 15–16.

83. Yusuf 'Abd al-Rahman, *Al-Rasa'il*, pp. 10–11, 30–34; Yusuf Isma'il, *Qissat al-kulub*, pp. 7–21, 124.

84. Yusuf 'Abd al-Rahman, *Al-Rasa'il*, p. 53; Yusuf Isma'il, *Qissat al-kulub*, pp. 7–21.

85. See descriptions in Al-Ithyubi, *Al-Islam al-jarih fi al-Habasha*. See a review of this book in Ahmed, "The Historiography of Islam in Ethiopia," pp. 15–46.

86. For background, see also Spencer, *Ethiopia at Bay*, chap. 9.

87. For general background, see Lewis, *The Modern History of Somaliland*, pp. 120–125, 129–131, and Carmichael, "Approaching Ethiopian History," chap. 5.

88. FO 371/63216, Curle to FO, 24 November 1947.

89. FO 371/63216, Curle to FO, 8 October 1947; War Office (hereafter WO) 230/236, Howe to WO, 30 October 1947; FO 371/63216, Curle to FO, 24 November 1947.

90. For an analysis based on documents from Harar's archives and oral evidences, see Carmichael, "Approaching Ethiopian History," chap. 5.

91. Rahji Abdella, "The Kulub." The study was also based on records of Harar's police archives. See more in Carmichael, "Approaching Ethiopian History," chap. 5.

92. FO 371/63216, Curle to FO, 27 August 1947; British Legation, Addis

Ababa to Bevin, 3 September 1947; "Somali Youth League" by British consulate, Harar, 5 September 1947; Curle to FO, 24 November 1947.

93. Rahji Abdella, "The Kulub."

94. Yusuf Isma'il, *Qissat al-kulub*, p. 62.

95. FO 371/63216, Curle to FO, 24 November 1947.

96. See his description in Yusuf 'Abd al-Rahman, *Al-Rasa'il*, pp. 11–17.

97. See details (including names of the delegates) in Rahji, "The Kulub." See also Mahdi Shumburo, "The Hannolato Movement and the Culub Insurrection."

98. FO 371/69423, Lyon, British Consulate, Harar, to British Legation, Addis Ababa, 16 January 1948; WO 230/236, Dolan to GHQ, 20 January 1948; FO 371/69423, H. M. Consul, Harar to Chargé d'Affaires, Addis Ababa, 24 January 1948; Lyon, Harar to Chargé, Addis, 31 January 1948; WO 230/236, Mogadishu to WO, 31 January 1948; FO 371/69423, Lyon, Harar to Chargé, Addis, 7 February 1948, 12 February 1948, 14 February 1948, 15 February 1948; Legation, Addis Ababa to Bevin, 6 March 1948; WO 170/1454, Addis Ababa to FO, 5 April 1948; FO 371/73677 "Treatment of Harari Muslims by the Egyptian Government," an article from *Journal d'Egypte*, 13 December 1948. See also Carmichael, "Approaching Ethiopian History," chap. 5.

99. See Yusuf 'Abd al-Rahman, *Al-Rasa'il*, pp. 20–22.

100. Yusuf Isma'il, *Qissat al-kulub*, pp. 42–49; Yusuf 'Abd al-Rahman, *Al-Rasa'il,* pp. 60–61.

101. Yusuf Isma'il, *Qissat al-kulub*, pp. 68, 122.

102. Ibid., pp. 37, 50–96.

103. "Al-Wahhabiyya ayqazat fitnat Yusuf al-Harari," in *Manar al-Huda* (Lebanon), number 31, annexed to Yusuf 'Abd al-Rahman, *Al-Rasa'il,* pp. 122–123.

104. Yusuf 'Abd al-Rahman, *Al-Rasa'il,* pp. 25–45; also Dimashqiyya, "Al-Ahbash du'at takfir."

# 5

## The Saudis and the End of the Christian Kingdom

WE HAVE SEEN THAT BETWEEN 1935 AND 1948 SAUDI ARABIA AND Wahhabism were relevant to Ethiopian history. In the fateful year of 1935, Ibn Sa'ud chose to ignore Ethiopia's plight and avoided helping Haile Selassie in his last-minute effort to improve the lives of Muslims in Ethiopia and to rebuild Christian-Islamic mutuality. Instead, he supplied camels for Mussolini's invading army. From 1936 to 1941, the fascist occupiers of Ethiopia viewed the Saudis as potential partners in their effort to politicize Islam in the Horn of Africa and to render Ethiopian Christianity isolated and marginal. The Italian-subsidized pilgrimage of Ethiopian Muslims to Mecca had an impact that outlived their occupation. In 1941 to 1948, many of the Ethiopian Muslims who had been subject to Wahhabi influence abandoned their traditional "Ethiopian" Islam. In Harar, their ancient capital, they struggled to implement the newly imported fundamentalist concepts and to revive the local medieval Ahmad Gragn legacy of anti-Christian militancy. The story of those years became a major chapter in the history of Harar. In the 1990s, as Wahhabism reappeared in Ethiopia to challenge Ethiopia's Islam and her religious culture, the Saudi role in the 1936–1948 period retroactively acquired importance.

The period from the 1950s to 1974 seems less dramatic. Saudi-Ethiopian relations during those years were of secondary importance to both. The neighboring countries shared the same stormy regional arena and faced similar challenges, but their strategic agendas ran in parallel more than they met. Both countries continued to recycle and deepen their religious, monarchical political systems. Toward the end of the period under discussion, they both seemed to have successfully stabilized their

97

regimes. Under King Faysal (1964–1975), Ibn Sa'ud's formula, combining Wahhabi fundamentalism with modern statehood, was updated and upgraded. The early 1970s can be regarded as the years during which Saudi Arabia's existence as an Islamic kingdom was secured for the rest of the twentieth century and beyond. The late 1960s also witnessed the apex of Haile Selassie's Ethiopia as a Christian state. However, Ethiopia was not to survive as such. In 1974, the last Christian king was deposed, and church and state in Ethiopia would separate, with all of its consequences, to this day. The Saudis—as we shall see—played a significant role in the 1973–1974 events that led to the collapse of Ethiopia's imperial regime and the abrupt end of Ethiopia's long history as a Christian monarchy.

## Common Enemy: Revolutionary Arabism

The spirit of the times in the Red Sea theater presented Ethiopia and Saudi Arabia with the same formidable challenge. The era of Nasserism and Ba'thism in the Arab Middle East unleashed new energies that threatened both countries. New military regimes in core Middle Eastern countries represented the interests of an educated, urban middle class, which were entirely antagonistic to systems based on absolutist monarchies. As of the mid-1950s and up to the late 1960s, pan-Arab revolutionary ideas and forces seemed successful in their aim to reshape the entire region. They worked to wipe out the old oligarchies and rebuild societies around secular concepts in which religiosity would be rendered apolitical. Arab unity during those years became consonant with revolutionary socialism. Though not based on Marxist materialistic concepts, it combined with the anti-Western heritage of the anticolonial struggle to strategically orient Nasserism and Ba'thism toward the Soviets. The threat to Saudi Arabia on one hand and to Haile Selassie's Ethiopia on the other was multidimensional; it gained momentum from the mid-1950s and culminated in 1962. On the Arab shore of the Red Sea in September 1962, an antimonarchical revolution in Yemen ignited the Yemen War, which enabled Nasser's army to entrench itself in the Saudis' backyard until 1967. The war between the Royalists of Yemen, backed by the Saudis, and the Republicans, supported by the Egyptian army, developed during the 1960s into an all-Arab conflict over the future of the entire peninsula. On the African shore of the Red Sea, the newly created Eritrean Liberation Front (ELF) was already active. Established in 1960 in Nasserite Cairo by young Eritrean Muslims, the ELF resisted the Ethiopian-Eritrean federation arrangement of 1952, and especially Haile Selassie's harsh methods, legitimized also by the local priesthood, aimed at abolishing all aspects of representative politics in Eritrea. The beginning of the ELF mutiny in western Eritrea in late 1961 and the presence of Nasser's army in nearby Yemen moved Haile Selassie to annex Eritrea fully under his imperial absolutism in November 1962. The war that ensued in Eritrea would last until 1991 and would change directions and content. In the period discussed here, it was essentially a conflict between the central government of the Christian kingdom and the predominantly Muslim separatists. It was also, like the war in Yemen, a struggle over the future of the Red Sea basin and of the Horn of Africa. Inspired and directly helped by the pan-Arabs of the Middle East, the new generation of Muslims in Eritrea redefined itself as revolutionary Arab and aspired to spread this new spirit throughout Ethiopia. In the 1960s and beyond, it was no longer political Islam in the vein of Shakib Arslan or Wahhabism that, from the Ethiopian point of view, threatened to undermine the Christian hegemony. It was rather the more secular energy of pan-Arabism that seemed to reunite and galvanize Ethiopia's young Muslims. Nasserism, spreading its revolutionary social and political messages, also had some influence on the new generation of educated Christians, young intellectuals, and army officers.[1]

Facing the same challenge caused the Ethiopian and the Saudi regimes to draw somewhat closer. Occasional American attempts to encourage their mutual interests also bore some fruit. In early 1957, King Saʻud paid a friendly visit to Addis Ababa during which he expressed his warm approval of the state of Islam in Ethiopia and the establishment at that time of diplomatic relations between the two kingdoms.[2] In January 1960, Haile Selassie paid a three-day visit to Riyadh, which yielded a joint statement about pursuing regional stability and the promotion of economic ties.[3]

A vivid example of Saudi acceptance of a stable Ethiopia in the early 1960s was provided by Saudi author ʻUmar Tawfiq. Born in 1918 in Mecca, he can be defined as a typical product of Ibn Saʻud's blending of Islam and statehood. After completing his religious studies in Medina, he began teaching in the local Madrasat Dar al-Aytam,[4] but later moved to the new, modern civil service, first working in the government printing house and then in the royal palace in Mecca. In October 1962, when Crown Prince Faysal became prime minister, Tawfiq was appointed minister of communications and was put in charge of the hajj. During the 1970s, Tawfiq published dozens of articles in the Saudi press as well as a number of books. In 1980, he issued his

*Memoirs of a Traveler,* a reprint of his 1961 series of articles in the *Al-Bilad* (Jedda) newspaper, describing two weeks he spent earlier that year when on business in Eritrea.[5]

The Saudi visitor's impressions of Ethiopian Eritrea in 1961 were generally positive. Asmara, he noted, was a beautiful, clean town where law and order prevailed. He observed striking social injustices, with the privileged upper class composed of a small layer of foreigners, not Ethiopians. In Tawfiq's eyes, the Italians were the enemy. Though they had built Asmara, he viewed them as foreign conquerors who remained as exploiters. In the entire book, there is nothing disapproving about Haile Selassie or his administration. He described Christians, Muslims, and Jews all enjoying civil rights. The Arab community in Asmara, he wrote, prospered. Socially, they were just below the foreigners and much above the deprived masses. The central mosque of Asmara was beautiful and busy; Muslims spoke good Arabic in an accent reminiscent of the Hijaz. The Saudi visitor attended Friday prayers and listened to the chief mufti's sermon on the issue of justice. The speaker referred to the Prophet as "the initiator [owner] of the two hegiras," reminding his audience of the first Muslims' emigration to the *najashi*'s court, and how the Christian king helped to save the pioneers of Islam (pp. 25–28). Two days later Tawfiq admired the serene atmosphere of the Christians' Sunday. He wrote that the Muslims should perhaps watch and learn from them how to rest better on Fridays. The Saudi expressed some concealed criticism when he said that Muslims were sometimes too passively pious to actively resist injustice, and they thus allowed a minority (the Christians) to rule them (pp. 32–39). Harsh words, however, were reserved by Tawfiq for the one Jew he talked to who tried, in vain, to hide his identity (p. 49).

Tawfiq's book can be regarded as a reflection of the attitudes of the Saudi ruling establishment. Ethiopia of the 1960s, conservative and pro-Western, was surely not branded an opponent. In fact, during that period, some affinity did develop on a personal level between the Saudi and Ethiopian princes. Although 1961 was the year when the ELF ignited the war over Eritrea, it did so in the name of the revolutionary Arabism that the Saudis dreaded. Tawfiq's rosy description of Christian-Islamic relations in the land of the negus meant purposely turning a blind eye to a different reality in Ethiopia and Eritrea.

## Ethiopian Christian Hegemony Revitalized

For all intents and purposes, Haile Selassie's post–World War II Ethiopia remained a Christian kingdom that identified the cross with the crown. The church now became an operative branch of the imperial government. A new decree of November 1942 regulated church administration and placed it directly under the emperor. In January 1951, with the death of the last Egyptian *abuna*, an Ethiopian was for the first time consecrated—still in Cairo by the Coptic Patriarch—as the head of the Ethiopian Church. The new *abuna*, Baselyos, the emperor's long-time devotee, and his clergymen in Eritrea proved most efficient in spreading imperial influence among local Christians and guiding them to undermine the 1952 federation. A new constitution enacted in 1955 defined Ethiopia in territorial terms (article 1) and guaranteed religious freedom (provided no politics were involved, article 40), but it also defined the country as a Christian state, forever to be ruled by members of the Ethiopian Orthodox Church (articles 16, 21, 126). In 1959, Abuna Baselyos and the emperor traveled to Cairo to ensure the final break with the Coptic Church and the declaration (on 28 June) of the Ethiopian Church as autocephalous. Soon after, in December 1960, the church's loyalty played an important role in foiling a coup attempt by Nasserite-inspired Ethiopian officers and intellectuals. Abuna Baselyos's call to unite behind the Christian King, while Haile Selassie was still abroad, helped the loyalists to win the day. Throughout the 1960s, the clergy, though having lost much of their earlier influence on education, law, and other aspects, were guardians of the system of which they were an integral part. Christians and Christianity remained hegemonic in all conceivable dimensions: political, social, and spiritual. The Amharization of culture, deeper at that time than ever before, was consonant with the voluntary Christianization of those who wished to participate and be appointed. Up to 1974, Ethiopia's identification with Christianity was such that many observers looked upon the Italians' 1936–1941 attempt at politicizing Islam as illusionary. The country's internal dynamism seemed to stem from ethnic and regional differences as well as from socioeconomic developments rather than from religious issues. Only the revival of Islam in Ethiopia in the 1990s (this time not couched in secular pan-Arabism) would retrospectively render Christian-Islamic relations during the period discussed significant.[6]

Muslims remained deprived and disunited.[7] At first, it seems, Haile Selassie did learn the lesson of 1935. After liberation, Muslims who had cooperated with the Fascists were punished, and in Harar, we have seen, attempts at reviving political Islam were firmly crushed. But no less visible were efforts to appease Islam as long as it did not challenge the political culture. Muslims continued to dominate the capital's commercial life. In his speeches, Haile Selassie tried to enhance an atmosphere of religious tolerance. Prominent Muslims expressed gratitude and proved ready to cooperate.[8] In 1954, for example, in Cairo, the native Harari Sadiq al-Habashi published his book, *Ethiopia in Its Golden Age: The Period of Haile Selassie I*,[9] which praised the emperor as the embodiment of tolerance and enlightenment. The 1955 constitution, as mentioned, contained elements of equal citizenship. Al-Habashi, returning from Egypt, was appointed to the new parliament prescribed by the constitution. In the previous chapter, I mentioned the whereabouts of Shaikh Yusuf 'Abd al-Rahman, who, having led political Islam in Harar between 1941 and 1948, began serving as Haile Selassie's man in charge of administering the hajj, as well as an inspector of the Quran's translation into Amharic. Indeed, the 1940s and the first half of the 1950s were years when the Ethiopianization of the country's Muslims deepened in spite of Christian hegemony.

The rise of Arab revolutionary nationalism in the Middle East, especially after the 1956 Suez War, the destruction in 1958 of the monarchy in Iraq, and its simultaneous threat to undermine Christian hegemony in Lebanon, resulted in a change in Haile Selassie's Islamic policy at home. The revolt in Eritrea, which threatened to turn Ethiopia's apolitical Islam into dynamic Arabism, evoked the old, and recently refreshed, Gragn trauma.[10] From the late 1950s to the end of the decade, Ethiopia's imperial regime made sure that only a few Muslims would be appointed to positions of significance in government, administration, security, and the armed forces. Muslims hired in lesser positions had to rest on Sundays and work full days on Fridays. Old traditions like denying Muslims the right to own land persisted. Education in Amharic continued to practically exclude Arabic in Islamic schools. Arabic journalism was nearly nonexistent.[11] Arabic was taught in Eritrea until 1957 when its official use was abolished in favor of Amharic.[12] In the late 1950s, the issues of inheritance and of matrimonial and family law were publicly debated in Ethiopia's Parliament, and in some drafts, Islamic customs and laws were taken into consideration. However, when the law was finally passed, it included nothing of the sort.[13] Also in 1960, an underground book entitled *The Wounded Islam in Ethiopia*, written by Abu Ahmad al-Ithyubi (a pseudonym), contended that Muslims were a majority in the country and detailed their deprivation and plight. Islamic Shari'a courts, which survived only in Eritrea, were abolished in 1964, two years after the annexation. They were replaced by Islamic judicial councils, which debated and ruled in Amharic only, and a cross was inserted into their official letterhead. The mufti of Eritrea, Ibrahim al-Mukhtar Ahmad 'Umar—the man our Saudi visitor Tawfiq heard delivering a moderate sermon in 1961—died in 1969. No new mufti was appointed and the government cancelled the mufti institution in Eritrea altogether.[14] "Ethiopian Muslims," summarizes Hussein Ahmed, "were, during the imperial era, the subjects of the Christian state and not full citizens enjoying equal rights like their fellow Christians."[15]

The pan-Arabism of the 1960s reactivated the siege mentality of the Ethiopian elite and further strengthened the country's Christian identity. An important dimension of this consciousness was found in the special relations then developing with Israel.[16] The Jewish state, itself under siege, was seeking alliances with Ethiopia and with other non-Arab Middle Eastern countries. After formulating their "periphery strategy" in 1959, the Israelis helped to save the emperor during the 1960 coup, and by the mid-1960s, their experts were involved in Ethiopia in many fields. Israel's crushing victory in June 1967 over combined Arab armies ushered in the rapid demise of revolutionary pan-Arabism in the Middle East and was seen by many members of Ethiopia's elite as heaven-sent. After 1967, Israel invested in Ethiopia, sending experts and know-how, as it did nowhere else throughout its history. Israelis were now entrusted by the regime with the most sensitive tasks. The spectrum of Israeli presence in Ethiopia in practically all spheres of modernization is outside our scope here. It would, however, be no exaggeration to state that Israel's role in the regime's security services and armed forces was central. These special relations were not without strains. While Israel was pushing for a full-fledged, open alliance, the Ethiopians were much more cautious. The views of Haile Selassie's leading advisers, Ras Asrate Kassa (governor of Eritrea, 1964–1970) and Prime Minister Aklilu Habta-Wold (as of 1961), differed. The former supported cementing relations with Israel, while the latter contended that this would lead to a devastating Arab reaction. In practice, the emperor opted for concealing, though not reducing, Israeli involvement. Thus, no Ethiopian embassy was opened in Israel and no official treaty was signed.

Beyond the mutual interests and concrete benefits, there was a very strong religious dimension in Ethiopian-Israeli relations. Ethiopian history leaned, from its inception, toward strong spiritual affiliation with the concept of Israel. Ethiopian Christianity as a state religion was molded early enough to remain oriented toward the centrality of the biblical Holy Land. It also absorbed and retained Hebraic and Judaic customs that influenced pre-Christian cultures in the Horn of Africa. No other branch of Christianity remained as close to biblical Judaism. The Ethiopians persisted for centuries in preserving the custom of circumcision, observing the Sabbath, following similar dietary laws, building all churches after the model of Solomon's temple, and referring to their ancient capital of

Aksum as Zion, Jerusalem. It was not only the cross, but also the crown, that was traditionally connected to historical Israel. The ethos of the "Glory of the Kings," introduced in the fourteenth century, related Ethiopia's ruling emperors, "the kings of Zion," to King Solomon and defined Ethiopian Christians as the "true children of Israel." All these ancient "Israeli" concepts survived until the demise of Haile Selassie, the "Conquering Lion of the Tribe of Judah." Reflective of his approach was the fact that in Beirut, in July 1966, he stated, "That we recognize Israel is a fact. We accord this recognition to Israel not out of any urge to harm our Arab brothers but because of historical factors and national policy." The daily *Voice of Ethiopia* of 12 July 1966, reporting on the emperor's trip and statement, added, "Misunderstandings have cropped up from time to time over Ethiopia's recognition of the state of Israel and occasionally through malicious propaganda by certain enemies of our country. While the Holy Quran itself attests to the fact that this country has been a haven for Islam refugees as early as the 7th century, it is indeed absurd, and even an insult, to accuse Ethiopia of religious intolerance."[17]

In the 1960s, and especially after 1967, the traditional "Zionist" aspects of Ethiopian Christianity blended with reliance on Israel in facing pan-Arabism to constitute a significant dimension of the regime's security. The nonwritten alliance between Haile Selassie's regime and Israel was symbolically sealed by a religious gesture. On 25 April 1970, Israel, having occupied East Jerusalem in 1967, returned the keys to the gate of Jerusalem's ancient Ethiopian monastery of Deir al-Sultan, confiscated in 1838 by neighboring Egyptian monks, to the Ethiopians. This Ethiopian-Israeli connection from 1959 to 1974 would play a significant role in Saudi-Ethiopian relations as of 1971.

## Faysal's Reinforcing of Wahhabism

During the period discussed in this chapter, Saudi Arabia also continued to strengthen its religious character.[18] Ibn Sa'ud, the formidable father figure, was still the only decisionmaker in the country when he died in 1953. Back in 1929, just before the beginning of our Saudi-Ethiopian story, he had crushed the religious-tribal leaderships that challenged his pragmatic autocracy in the name of pure Wahhabism. In facing the Fascist-Ethiopian drama of 1935–1936, we saw that Ibn Sa'ud, though himself a devout Wahhabi, consulted his Lebanese, Syrian, and Egyptian advisers rather than his Saudi scholars. As long as he lived, the more purist among the latter would have had only marginal influence and little concrete, political weight, especially when it came to foreign relations. In any case, after World War II, Ibn Saʿud, as he confessed in March 1950 to the Americans, took little interest in Haile Selassie's Ethiopia.[19]

King Saʿud, who reigned from 1953 to 1964, failed to replace his father as an undisputed ruler. Though his brother Faysal was quick to recognize him as king, their old rivalry (we have already seen them differ regarding the 1935 "Ethiopian crisis") remained. In 1954, Saʿud appointed Crown Prince Faysal as prime minister but never really allowed him a free hand, and the royal family began to split apart. In addition to the rift between the followers of the king and those of Faysal, there appeared a third group of younger princes who, in the late 1950s, came under Nasserite influence. The ensuing internal tensions cannot be presented here. In striving to consolidate his power, King Saʿud opted for strengthening his ties with the tribal chiefs and occasionally with the "free princes" who flirted with constitutional and even Arab nationalist ideas. In the mid-1950s, King Saʿud drew closer to Nasser and for a while supported his increasingly anti-Western policies. Though in later years Saʿud moved against Nasser (and also, as mentioned, drew closer to Haile Selassie), his policy and personality did not help to unite the royal family. Prince Faysal resigned from the government in December 1960, and he and his followers continued to emphasize their differences. Faysal confronted Nasserism and conceived of modernizing the state machinery, as well as remobilizing Islam and Wahhabi scholars as an active wing of Saudi politics. Faysal himself, related through his mother to the Al Shaykh family of Muhammad ibn ʿAbd al-Wahhab, was the embodiment of the Saudi-Wahhabi historical alliance. In working to reintegrate Wahhabi scholars into the state system, Faysal did not aim to restore their fanaticism of the 1920s but rather needed revitalized Wahhabism to help stabilize and further legitimize the regime at home and to stem revolutionary and socialist nationalism in the region. With King Saʿud failing, and with regional threats mounting, Faysal's influence grew within the royal family. Crown Prince Faysal's mounting power was best reflected in May 1962 when he convened a new Islamic International Conference in Mecca. Attended by representatives of Arab and Islamic countries from the region and beyond, the international gathering emphasized resistance to communism and to revolutionary secularism. The conference ended with the establishment of the Muslim World League (*Rabitat al-ʿAlam al-Islami*), with the declared aim "to disseminate Islamic *daʿwa* and expound the teaching of Islam" on all continents. Centered in Mecca and funded, supported, and controlled by the Saudi government,[20] the Muslim World

League (henceforward, MWL) would play an important role in the Islamic revival in the Middle East in the 1970s, and throughout the world in the 1990s. We shall return below to the MWL's role in influencing Saudi policy in Ethiopia.

Not long after this reassertion of Islam as an active political strategy, the September 1962 revolution and the ensuing war in Yemen brought the threat of revolutionary Arabism to the kingdom's very doorstep. The royal family, numbering around 5,000 princes, now proved its ability to close ranks at crucial moments. In October, King Sa'ud was forced to appoint Faysal as prime minister and the actual prime decisionmaker. In November 1964, the internal family dynamic resulted in the deposition of Sa'ud and the crowning of Faysal.

If Ibn Sa'ud built the Saudi-Wahhabi formula that balanced family hegemony, tribal and regional interests, elements of modern state machinery, and Wahhabi Islamic fundamentalism, Faysal restabilized and upgraded this balance. In so doing he was helped by both the external pan-Arab challenge and mounting petrodollars. During Faysal's years, 1964–1975, the kingdom's income from oil revenues grew sixteen-fold. These new, enormous resources enabled the creation of a welfare state in which citizenship assured almost all necessities. The limitless funds also enabled the building of effective state machinery and the modernization of infrastructure and services. Faysal proved ready and able to introduce public education and initiate reforms in communications, employment, and other aspects conducive to social change. A discussion of his various reforms is beyond the scope of this chapter. However, all these significant changes were in harmony with further cementing Wahhabi Islam as the core of identity, state, and culture. Faysal repeatedly stated that he was the leader of the Wahhabi community rather than a king, and that the Shari'a was the law of his country. Wahhabi scholars, who identified with Faysal's "modernization without secularization," were organized in new religious councils. They strengthened the regime's legitimacy and Faysal's pious image, and in return—as a tamed branch of the establishment—were actually put in control of education, culture, and law. The initial Saudi-Wahhabi alliance between rulers and scholars, state and Islam, was thus readapted and reinforced.[21]

## Saudi Policy in the Horn up to 1967

Faysal's formula combining modernization and revitalized Wahhabism was also the basis for Saudi foreign policy. On one hand, the work of the

MWL, which viewed global affairs through rather Wahhabi purist eyes, gained momentum. MWL circles, closely connected with the government but also beginning to develop connections of their own, initiated a wave of attacks on Haile Selassie's Ethiopia. Soon after the establishment of the MWL, in mid-1962, The Voice of Islam radio station in Mecca began an intensive campaign against Ethiopian maltreatment of Muslims and their oppression in Eritrea and Somalia. Eritrean Muslim leaders broadcast from Mecca, and Ethiopian pilgrims to the holy city were reported by the Ethiopian media to be exposed to Wahhabi indoctrination. Articles denouncing Ethiopia's policy toward its Muslims also appeared in the Saudi government press. In late March 1963, the Ethiopian government retaliated by threatening to cut off relations if such propaganda continued. "The Saudis claim they have chosen to champion the cause of freeing Moslems," ran the editorial of the *Ethiopian Herald* of 3 April 1963. "Mecca and Medina have today become the launching pad for subversive propaganda. Is this not contrary to the teachings of the Prophet?" Further alluding to the *najashi*'s saving of Muhammad's followers, the editorial concluded, "The Saudi press is currently preoccupied with trying to pay back this country's hospitality with hostility."[22]

On the other hand, the actual Saudi foreign strategy, though always strongly influenced by religious concepts, stemmed from concrete threats. For Faysal, the stemming of Nasserism was conceived as a matter of survival and the first priority up to 1967 and somewhat beyond. As long as the Egyptian army was entrenched in Yemen and threatening to spread revolutionary Arabism throughout the peninsula, Ethiopia was viewed as a partner. Official Riyadh allowed the MWL to complain, and itself paid lip service to the plight of Muslims in Ethiopia, but in practice it accepted Haile Selassie's empire as a stabilizing factor. In the context of stemming Nasserism, Riyadh was even ready to accept Ethiopian-Israeli cooperation. The Christian-Zionist connection, for awhile, seemed a much lesser evil, even a useful ally against the common enemy. Responding to a British intelligence initiative, Saudi, Ethiopian, and Israeli services joined to help the Royalists in Yemen fight the Egyptians. Israel and Saudi Arabia cooperated in supplying the Royalist warriors, dropping arms and ammunition from Israeli planes. In 1965, agents of the Israeli Mosad built installations on Ethiopian soil to intercept Egyptian army communications in Yemen, and between Yemen and Egypt. The contents of these communications, as agreed by all sides, were routinely transferred to Riyadh through the British.[23]

King Faysal also avoided aiding Haile Selassie's Muslim opponents in the Horn of Africa. In July 1960, newly emancipated British and Italian Somalia united to form the independent Somali Republic and renewed the claim to the Ogaden. The Somali nationalists, whose role in Harar's Islam of the 1940s was discussed above, also adopted the legacies of Gragn and of Muhammad bin 'Abdallah Hasan, the sixteenth- and early-twentieth-century Islamic leaders who managed to unite the Somalis by waging holy wars. However, the new regime in Mogadishu, by working persistently to undermine the Ethiopian hold over the Ogaden, opted rather to join the regional momentum of Nasserism.[24] In 1969, when the parliamentary system in Somalia collapsed, the new authoritarian regime of Siyad Barre allied itself with the Soviets. As a result, during the period discussed here, Saudi identification with the Muslim Somalis under the rule of Christian Ethiopia was little more than lip service.

Perhaps more significant at that time was Saudi policy regarding the Eritrean revolt. The Eritrean secessionists in the period under discussion were also predominantly Muslims. As mentioned, the ELF, even more than the Somalis of the 1960s, chose to express its defiance of Ethiopia's imperial Christianity in Arab revolutionary terms. Led mostly by Muslims from western Eritrea, the ELF political leadership in exile was centered in Nasserite Cairo up to 1963, and then in Ba'thist Damascus. From 1968 and well into the 1980s, the ELF was supported mainly by the new Ba'thist regime in Baghdad, which also developed into the Saudis' archenemy. As a result, no significant aid was rendered by Riyadh to the main core of the ELF leadership. What little there was of a Saudi-Eritrean connection was mainly the work of ELF Secretary General 'Uthman Salih Sabbe, a prominent Eritrean nationalist, yet an outsider in the ELF.[25]

Sabbe was a native of eastern, coastal Eritrea and an Arabic teacher in Massawa. After failing in an effort to build a vital movement among the Muslims of eastern Eritrea, in 1960 he joined the western Eritrean–dominated ELF and was put in charge of fundraising in Arab capitals. Never really accepted as part of the actual leadership, Sabbe also differed with them on what the movement should look like. In his two books and dozens of articles, Sabbe emphasized two main ideas. One was his version of Eritrea's Arabism. Sabbe was undoubtedly the man who contributed more than anyone else to the Arab image that helped to connect Eritrea's Muslims to the pan-Arab momentum in the Middle East. However, Sabbe's Arabism was hardly of the Nasserite and Ba'thist type adopted by the ELF. Rather than being based on revolutionary and socialist ideas, it stemmed from Islamic traditions of Arabic study and use, more relevant to the long history of Massawa and the Red Sea coast than to the Tigre speakers and newly converted Muslims of western Eritrea. Sabbe also consistently spread the notion that the Arab war over Palestine and the Eritrean struggle against what he called the Zionist-Christian regime of Ethiopia were actually the same. The other idea Sabbe held was that Eritrea's Arab-Islamic history had always been centered on the Red Sea coast, "the crucial triangle" of Massawa-Assab-Asmara, rather than on the western part. Eritrea's future, he contended, would also be resolved in connection with the Arab-Islamic effort to preserve the identity of the Red Sea as an Arab lake.[26] While ELF leadership resided in Cairo (until 1963), Sabbe was not a welcome guest in the Nasserite capital. Later, in 1966, his differences with the ELF leadership widened to the extent that he had to flee Damascus for Beirut. As a resident of Beirut, he also felt at home in Saudi Arabia, where he befriended the royal princes. Earlier, in May 1962, Sabbe had participated in the International Islamic Conference, which established the Muslim World League. He managed to put the issue of Eritrea on the conference agenda.[27] As a member of the MWL, he passed a resolution by which Eritrea was declared part of the Islamic world that had been sacrificed by the West to Christian Ethiopia and was now entitled to self-determination. In this position, Sabbe was, to a great extent, the force behind the MWL's anti-Ethiopian campaign of 1962–1963 mentioned above. However, though in Arab capitals he gained the reputation of arguably the most prominent Eritrean Arab, Sabbe was only able to obtain modest financial aid from the Saudi government. He could not conceal from the Saudis the fact that the ELF, with which he was officially affiliated, was sponsored by the Ba'thist enemies of Riyadh, and that his own Muslim followers in eastern Eritrea still carried little weight. Forced to flee Syria after the ELF informed the Syrians about his contacts in Riyadh, Sabbe attempted to gain full Saudi support for these followers. As described by one of his aides, they met with King Faysal on 29 August 1966 and told him that their prime aim was to fight the Zionist-Ethiopian connection. Faysal in return gave them a speech on Islamic piety. He said he was not a king but an imam of an Islamic community. By way of asking questions, he diverted the conversation to the ELF's orientation toward the Ba'th. He said he had been told that the Eritrean revolution was communist, Nasserist, and Ba'thist, but he expressed gratitude for their fighting the Israeli presence in the Red Sea.[28] Beyond that, Faysal indicated that he was ready to increase his support for Sabbe and partially finance his activities. An ELF office was reopened in Jedda enabling Sabbe's men to transfer arms, purchased with Saudi money, to their comrades in the field.[29] Sabbe's Saudi connection was enough to destroy whatever was left of his standing in the ELF. Internal Eritrean differences, thus combining with inter-Arab rivalries, would soon result in a major institutionalized split in the Eritrean movement.

## 1967 as a Watershed

Both Addis Ababa and Riyadh had much more pressing issues than their bilateral relations. Neither, it must be added, had a coherent strategy. Haile Selassie preferred to ignore his major problems, the internal ethnic, religious, economic, and social tensions, as well as the issue of the Eritrean secessionists and the revolutionary Arabism supporting them. Rather, he focused on Africa, where diplomacy assured him continental seniority, and the expedient concept of territorial integrity. In 1963, Addis Ababa was declared the headquarters of the new Organization of African Unity (OAU). Whatever Ethiopian plans existed regarding the Middle East fell victim to the rivalry between Prime Minister Aklilu and Ras Asrate Kassa. Israel's crushing victory of June 1967 seemed at first to strengthen the latter, and the regime, on sensitive matters of security, deepened its trust in the Israelis. However, as we shall see, it was Aklilu's policy of appeasing the Arabs by concealing the Israeli connection that would gradually gain momentum and finally win in 1973.

The Saudis, we have seen, also had no coherent Horn of Africa policy. Faysal needed a stable Ethiopia, a monarchy capable of restraining the region's destabilizing forces. However, as a devout Wahhabi, Faysal allowed the MWL to continue to attack the Christian empire for humiliating Islam. Apparently he was also interested in diverting some of the purists' energy abroad, thus facilitating their co-optation at home. At the same time, apart from some aid to Sabbe, Faysal would not support the Horn's Muslims and their new generation of Arab revolutionaries. The Saudis continued to respond to the changing reality in the region rather than formulating a coherent Ethiopian policy.[30] Like Ibn Sa'ud in the 1930s, Faysal seemed to have little interest in, or consideration for, the Christian African neighbor.

Israel's June 1967 defeat of Egypt, Syria, and Jordan changed the regional status of Saudi Arabia. The Egyptian army pulled back from Yemen and would no longer infringe on Saudi hegemony in the peninsula. In August, an Arab summit in Khartoum adopted the new slogan of "Unity in Defeat," implying inter-Arab solidarity instead of subversion.

Saudi money was now needed to cover the losses, and the broken-down pan-Arab regimes began courting rather than threatening Riyadh. The fall of East Jerusalem to the Jews made the issue of restoring the holy places to Islam a step toward the regional demise of secular pan-Arabism. As the various, separate Arab regimes began to stabilize—a process that began in 1969–1970—a reassured Saudi Arabia, accumulating oil money and emphasizing its historical success in guarding Islam's holy places, began to prosper. From a marginalized and besieged state, Faysal's kingdom emerged in the early 1970s as a main pillar of the post-Nasserite Arab world.

The new reality also brought new threats. With Nasserism failing, the Soviets began to penetrate the region directly. They allied themselves with some of the new regimes in South Yemen, Libya, Sudan, Syria, and Iraq. In 1969, as mentioned, the new regime in Somalia, apparently Soviet-installed, allied itself closely with Moscow. Siyad Barre, who as chief-of-staff had seen to the building, as of 1965, of a new Soviet-equipped army, now deepened his commitment to the Russians and presented a growing threat to Ethiopia. He also added yet another dimension to the pro-Soviet chain of radical regimes surrounding Saudi Arabia. The Eritrean secessionists also grew radical. The ELF came under Iraqi influence and its internal splits, led by a new generation of field commanders, enhanced its militancy. The more the Ethiopian government resorted to naked power in Eritrea, the more the young Christians from the central highlands crossed over to the rebel ranks. In 1969, the Eritrean movement began a long transformation, the analysis of which is outside our scope. The demise of pan-Arabism and the joining of young Christians led to the rise of Marxist orientations. Soviet-inspired slogans and Marxist phraseology served as a natural common ground for the new social and ethnic combination. This was especially true in eastern Eritrea, the region historically connected to the Christian highlands. By 1969, the Muslim fighters in the coastal areas, Sabbe's men, had been joined by enough Christian recruits to enable the formation of a new liberation front, rival to the ELF. In November, Sabbe declared the establishment of what was soon to be called the Eritrean People's Liberation Front (EPLF), the front that would eventually dominate the Eritrean movement and would lead to the establishment of independent Eritrea in 1991. However, when the EPLF was beginning to take shape in late 1969, partnering Muslim and Christian fighters, Sabbe was unable to bring in his Saudi dowry. By that time, the Saudis had been briefed by the Ethiopians on the Eritreans' radicalization[31] and advised by the Americans to warm up their relations with

Ethiopia. In August 1969, the Saudis assured the Americans that they had closed the Eritrean office in Jedda.[32] The frustrated Sabbe, who after fleeing Damascus in 1966 had cultivated close relations with Palestinian leader Yasser Arafat, was introduced by the latter to Libya's new ruler Muammar Qaddafi. After Sabbe declared the establishment of the new liberation front in a Palestine Liberation Organization (PLO) camp in Jordan, he was no longer welcome in Saudi Arabia. He would also lose his influence over his men in the field, who began resorting more strongly to Marxist and revolutionary terminology.

With the Somalis and the Eritreans joining the pro-Soviet camp, the Saudis' interest in the stability and survival of the Ethiopian monarchy grew stronger. After 1967, with the Suez Canal blocked, the Red Sea riparian neighbors cautiously drew closer. American envoys to the region, seeking to stem the pro-Soviet wave, tried to bridge the gap between Riyadh and Addis Ababa. Some economic ties developed. Ethiopia began exporting shoes and vegetables to Saudi Arabia,[33] and the security services of both countries traded information on common enemies. In 1969–1970, however, these ties were still very tentative. The Saudis, like all other Arabs, and indeed more religiously, could hardly ignore the Ethiopian-Israeli connection (even the vegetables they bought were grown on Israeli-advised Ethiopian farms). The Ethiopians remained suspicious that the Saudis sought the victory of Islam over their local Christian hegemony (in fact, Ethiopia continued to buy its oil from Iran).[34] According to a 1969 British assessment, the Americans' toying with enhancing Saudi-Ethiopian cooperation was illusionary.[35]

The Saudi policy toward Ethiopia began to take shape. It was, again, bidimensional. On one hand, Faysal's diplomats began to exert pressure on the Ethiopians to get rid of the Israelis in return for Saudi compensation. On the other hand, after 1967, Faysal's men in the MWL were allowed to intensify their attacks on the Christian empire. On 20 November 1967, to mention one example, the Saudi newspaper *Al-Da'wa* published an article entitled "Ethiopia and Her Defiance, We and Our Tolerance," which described Ethiopia as Islam's worst enemy.

> What Hitler did to the Jews, Haile Selassie is now doing to the Muslims in Eritrea. He has terrorized and frightened them, put them in jails and concentration camps. He has destroyed mosques and holy places and crucified them in the streets and alleys. The model of [Israeli Defense Minister Moshe] Dayan's terrorism on the West Bank of Jordan has been adopted by Haile Selassie and applied against Islam and Muslims in Eritrea. . . . Ethiopia's enmity towards us is a certainty. . . . The tolerance with which we receive Ethiopia's defiance is incom-

patible with our dignity and honor . . . Ethiopia is a tool of imperialism
. . . Islam is suffering in Africa what it did not suffer when it first
appeared. . . . Haile Selassie and his gang are acting against you, the
Arab, and against your religion and your existence. You who are
responsible for the Arabs—beware![36]

On the initiative of the MWL, the Ethiopian underground book
mentioned above, *The Wounded Islam in Ethiopia*, was reprinted in the
late 1960s and distributed by Saudi embassies in various Muslim countries, including in Far East Asia.[37] It described coercive Christianization
in Ethiopia, the destruction of Islamic education, and depriving Muslims
of basic human rights. Haile Selassie planned—the League's journal
later wrote—to turn the Muslims of Ethiopia into a tiny minority, backward and marginal. For this purpose, went the argument, the emperor
and the church resorted to systematic terror. The Saudi press continued
to recycle the contention that Muslims had long constituted the majority
in Ethiopia, ranging from 65 to 70 percent.[38] In the early 1970s, the
MWL became the major channel for converting Saudi petrodollars into
Islamic momentum in Asia and Africa. At its second international conference in Mecca in 1972, the League celebrated the demise of
Nasserism and the success of Faysal's wealthy Islamic state.

The death of Nasser in September 1970 brought no salvation to
Ethiopia. Libyan-sponsored PLO training of the Eritreans upgraded their
guerrilla tactics, and 1970 ended with spectacular Eritrean operations.
Ras Asrate Kassa was consequently removed from governing Eritrea,
and Prime Minister Aklilu was authorized by the emperor to pursue his
policy: unleashing the Ethiopian army to terrorize the province, while
appeasing the Arabs who supported the rebels.[39] The Somalis, meanwhile, continued to build their Soviet-equipped and trained army and
increased their support for a Western Somali Liberation Front in the
Ogaden. By 1973, the threat of a Somali invasion of the Ogaden would
become the most serious external threat to Haile Selassie's regime.

From an Ethiopian point of view, while almost all the Arab regimes
supported their opponents, Saudi Arabia seemed to be a ray of hope.
Riyadh, as mentioned, stopped aiding the Eritreans and was itself suspicious of the Soviet entrenchment in Somalia. Saudi Arabia represented
conservative and pro-Western politics. As reflected in their talks with
Israeli diplomats, leading Ethiopian advisers of the emperor, headed by
Prime Minister Aklilu, were aware of the radical Wahhabism below the
surface but thought they could deal with the Saudis' pragmatic side. In
the Red Sea arena in the 1970s, and on the entire African continent,
another kind of Islam grew in momentum, led by Libya's Qaddafi. His

combination of republican-revolutionary Islam and of pro-Soviet pan-Arabism competed with the Saudis' Islamic campaign, spearheaded by the MWL. Egypt, the eminent Arab country, "the older sister" of Nasser's days, was slowly changing under Anwar Sadat. In his effort to save the devastated economy and regain Israeli-occupied Sinai, by the summer of 1972, Sadat was moving away from the Soviets. On the way to preparing for war, opening up the economy, and reorienting Egypt toward the United States, Sadat's first foreign relations step was to build a strong friendship with Faysal. He was more or less followed by Sudan's Ja'far al-Numayri, who also departed from his secular, Arab-socialist strategy and began courting Faysal, even flirting with political Islam, hoping for Saudi financial help.[40] Haile Selassie, on his part, now seemed more than willing to join them.

### Expel the Israelis, Enhance Islam

In May 1970 the Ethiopian Ministry of Information sent a delegation, headed by a Muslim, to Riyadh with the task of demonstrating Haile Selassie's goodwill toward his Muslim subjects. The delegation paved the way for an official visit by Ethiopia's foreign minister, Katama Yifru, which took place a year later, in the first week of June 1971. The Ethiopian was received by members of the royal family and by his Saudi counterpart, 'Umar al-Saqqaf. The Saudis pointed out to Katama Yifru that they would like to see Ethiopia change in two respects: Muslims should be given full rights, and the Israelis should be expelled. Ethiopia, the Saudis implied, would not regret such steps economically, and certainly not strategically. The Saudis would compensate Ethiopia for the loss of Israeli aid and experts, and the moderate Arabs would restrain the Eritreans and the Somalis. Katama Yifru was authorized by the emperor to take only one step in this direction. A joint Saudi-Ethiopian communiqué issued in Riyadh on 7 June 1971 resorted to Arab terminology and called for Israeli withdrawal from all territories occupied in 1967.[41] The price the Ethiopians were now ready to pay was to continue to conceal the Israeli presence and join the Arab anti-Israeli diplomatic campaign. From that moment onward, Ethiopia endorsed all relevant UN and OAU resolutions, occasionally even leading anti-Israeli rhetoric.[42] To his hosts in Riyadh, Katama Yifru said that Ethiopia kept the Israelis because they were cheap and efficient.[43] In practice, the regime's reliance on the Israelis—with the blessings of the United States[44]—continued to grow, mainly in security, intelligence, and army training experts. In 1971, some thirty Israeli army officers were working with nearly all the battalions of the Ethiopian army.

Throughout 1972, the Saudis and the Ethiopians drew closer. In March, direct flights between Addis Ababa and Jedda were launched.[45] Because the Suez Canal was blocked and the Ethiopians were afraid of a possible Arab air-blockade, the gesture allayed their fears. Moreover, the Saudis initiated a Red Sea Riparian Conference held in Jedda in July with the participation of Saudi Arabia, Egypt, Sudan, North Yemen, and Somalia. Ethiopia was the only non-Islamic country invited. This was symbolically significant, tantamount to recognizing Ethiopian sovereignty over her coast and implicitly denying recognition to the Eritreans. Though officially convened to discuss legal maritime issues and the development of marine resources, the conference had a clear political goal: to reach a consensus over the route that supplied Iranian oil to Israel. The idea of rendering the Red Sea "an Arab lake" rather than an international waterway was resisted by the Ethiopians, whose small navy cooperated with the Israelis.[46] On 27 October 1972, Egypt's *Al-Ahram* newspaper published an article titled "Danger Over the Red Sea," harshly attacking Ethiopia. The author, Muhammad Hasanayn Haykal, a leading Nasserist, stated that all Red Sea riparian countries were Arab and that Ethiopia was a foreign factor, cooperating with the Arabs' enemies. It was a partially disguised threat to block the Ethiopian outlet to the "Arab lake" and to lay siege to its international communications. As *Al-Ahram* would not publish the official Ethiopian response, this appeared on 31 December 1972 in the *Ethiopian Herald*. Ethiopia was a Red Sea country, the response argued, and never an enemy of the Arabs. The country continued to vote with the Arabs in all international forums. In fact, the article added, Saudi Arabia recognized Ethiopia as a Red Sea state.[47]

1973 was a year of mounting tension in the Red Sea, and from our perspective, somewhat reminiscent of the fateful year of 1935. A war, already heralded the previous year, was to break out in October. Though it was Sadat's war to regain Sinai from Israel, Haile Selassie, now old and weary, faced grave concerns. Would he risk continuing his reliance on the Israelis as had been persistently advocated by his most devoted adviser, Ras Asrate Kassa, and now also by the military elite and by the church? Would he not then face a showdown with radical pro-Soviet Arabs, who supported the Eritreans and backed a Somali invasion, already in preparation? In such an eventuality, would Ethiopia's Muslims identify with his Christian empire? Would the United States help him against all his Soviet-armed opponents? Would Ethiopia retain her centrality in African diplomacy? Or would he opt to strengthen relations with the anti-Soviet Arabs, counting on them to prevent an Arab attack and, in the Saudi case, also help him out of his growing economic crisis? The latter option was strongly advocated by Prime Minister Aklilu.[48] With Asrate out of favor (and for most of 1973 also out of the country), the emperor adopted Aklilu's line. Aklilu revealed his approach to the Israelis, stating he was sure that Israel would continue to help Ethiopia in its struggle for survival, understanding that it had to publicly denounce Israel.[49]

During the first months of 1973, the Ethiopian foreign ministry made efforts to arrange an imperial visit to Riyadh, to be reciprocated by Faysal.[50] Foreign Minister Katama Yifru went to Saudi Arabia in April and continued to Egypt. In Cairo, he was assured that Haykal did not represent the Egyptian line. Sadat supported a stable Ethiopia but believed that Ethiopia should cut off relations with Israel.[51] In Riyadh, he had heard the same argument, as well as promises to compensate for Ethiopia's losses by importing meat and grain from Ethiopia and engaging in joint development of Red Sea resources. Meanwhile, Faysal himself, though he traveled to other African countries, would not pay a visit. Rather, he sent missions to Aklilu to stress the need to expel the Israelis. When asked why Ethiopia, of all countries, should be required so strongly to do so, the Saudis replied that Ethiopia was a unique case; it was strategically located and was the spiritual capital of Africa. Though always significant to Islam, Ethiopia had special relations with Israel. It was very important to the Arab world that those relations be terminated.[52]

May 1973 was a crucial month. During the first week, an official Saudi delegation finally came to Addis Ababa. However, rather than the king or a representative of the government, Mecca sent a delegation of the MWL. Headed by the league's secretary-general, Shaikh Muhammad Mahmud al-Sawwaf, the delegation was warmly received by Aklilu and his top ministers in Addis Ababa. It then went on an extensive tour of the country's Muslim centers, and Shaikh al-Sawwaf delivered sermons in the capital's Al-Anwar mosque, and in mosques in Harar, Dire Dawa, and Asmara. He also made donations to Islamic schools and welfare societies. The Ethiopian government and local Muslim leaders went out of their way to convince the Saudi guests that their country was a land of tolerance where Muslims enjoyed equal rights. Shaikh al-Sawwaf said he was satisfied. In an interview with the Ethiopian News Agency, he praised Ethiopia and said that "he had discovered during his visits that allegations by certain quarters of lack of religious freedom in Ethiopia were malicious and unfounded." He stated that upon returning to Saudi Arabia he intended to tell his countrymen more about religious freedom in Ethiopia.[53] Ethiopian officials got the impression that the Saudis would invest in promoting Islam and finance Muslim activities but would also help Ethiopia in general, economically and strategically.[54]

Second, also in the month of May, Haile Selassie experienced a live demonstration of what the radical Arab camp had in store. During an OAU summit in Addis Ababa, Qaddafi attacked Ethiopia as a colonial empire in the service of the United States, South Africa, Portugal, Rhodesia, and Israel. Since Addis Ababa was a center of US and Zionist intelligence, he moved to transfer the OAU headquarters elsewhere.[55] Qaddafi's speech was broadcast live on Ethiopian television. According to some observers, this outright humiliation of the emperor shocked the Ethiopian public and may be regarded as a first step toward the regime's collapse.[56] During the same summit, Haile Selassie met with Sadat, who spelled out clearly that Ethiopia should break off with Israel or be left to the mercy of the radicals.

Third, in late May, the anxious emperor flew to the United States to seek military aid. It was a frustrating trip. President Richard Nixon, although overwhelmed by the Watergate affair, found time for the aging monarch, who, for his part, spent the precious thirty minutes philosophizing (the Ethiopians got a promise of F5-E fighter bombs to be delivered in 1976). US inattention to imperial Ethiopia at that juncture, leaving the Ethiopian army exposed to a modernized, Soviet-advised Somali army (in June 1973 the Somalis were reported to have some 200 Soviet T-34 tanks in the Ogaden facing some 40 old Ethiopian tanks[57]), is outside our scope.[58] "At that point," said American John Spencer, Haile Selassie's life-long adviser on foreign affairs, "Ethiopia had only one friend left to whom she might turn—Israel."[59] But the Ethiopian government made no such overt step. The most the Ethiopians dared to do was to have the army generals talk to their Israeli advisers about Ethiopia's acute military inferiority. Israeli ambassador Hanan Aynor took the initiative. In early July he flew to Israel with a list of the most urgently needed equipment. It was a modest list—US$5 million worth of arms and anti-tank ammunition, mostly obsolete and not in service in Israel. Aynor's papers reveal an angry Israel. Though Aynor, backed by Foreign Minister Abba Eban, quickly persuaded the army chief of staff (and the head of the Mosad) to spare the arms in question, the whole idea was dismissed by Defense Minister Moshe Dayan and Prime Minister Golda Meir. At their meeting, Dayan mocked Aynor's efforts to pacify the Ethiopians. He said that the Ethiopians systematically voted against

Israel but expected favors in return. If they need help, he admonished Aynor, let them ask for it openly and officially. When Aynor began to explain the Ethiopians' dilemmas and that Israel was about to lose all that she had invested in Ethiopia, he was interrupted by Meir.[60] As Israel's foreign minister in the early 1960s, Meir was the architect of Israel's effort in Africa. In large part, she had been responsible for the early stages of the Ethiopian connection. But those were the pre-1967 days when the Jewish state still served as a model for developing countries. Dayan's self-assurance and Golda's self-righteousness combined to create an Israeli policy that was now ready to give up on ungrateful Africa. This same overconfident inflexibility would soon lead Israel to a disastrous war in October 1973.

## Faysal and the Fall of Haile Selassie

While Aynor avoided reporting to the Ethiopians on his aborted initiative, the Saudis seemed forthcoming. Pleased with the report of the MWL, in mid-July Faysal sent his acting foreign minister, 'Umar al-Saqqaf, to Addis Ababa. On leaving Ethiopia, the Saudi told journalists he had had very fruitful talks with Haile Selassie and that Saudi Arabia had decided to triple her investments in the Ethiopian economy and consider generous donations. He also encouraged the emperor to warm up relations with Jordan, Egypt, Kuwait, and other moderate Arab countries. They would work together to block Qaddafi in Africa and help the Ethiopians with their differences with South Yemen over some Red Sea islands. Saudi Arabia, he reassured the Ethiopians, would also restrain the Somalis and continue to refuse aid to the Eritreans. According to Ethiopian diplomats, the Saudi foreign minister persistently conveyed Faysal's message: all was conditional on expelling the Israelis.[61]

Haile Selassie and Faysal finally met in September, at the conference of nonaligned countries in Algeria. According to an Ethiopian source, at the conference Faysal promised a US$200 million package in return for Ethiopia's cutting off relations with Israel. Some of the money would finance the purchase of arms and some was for internal needs. Promises and threats were pouring in from other Arab countries, radical and moderate. Haile Selassie, still hesitant, was still exchanging messages with Sadat when the latter, on 6 October, launched his surprise attack on Israel. During the October War of 1973, sixteen African states, each subjected to a similar version of the Arab-African dialogue, broke off relations with Israel. On 19 October, when Israel still seemed to be struggling, Sadat cabled Haile Selassie that he was losing patience: "It is time to act. No more talking between us. Do what you have to do, but do not only talk."[62]

Haile Selassie's decision of 23 October 1973 to break with Israel was arguably the toughest of his life. He took the step against the advice of Ras Asrate Kassa, the army's chief-of-staff General Assefa Ayene, and the chief priests headed by Abuna Tewoflos, all symbolically representing Ethiopia's long history of imperial Christian independence.[63] The almost 100 Israeli advisers, businessmen, and diplomats, shocked, surprised, and worried about the war in their own country, left within a week, with Ambassador Aynor the last to leave on 3 November. Faysal promptly cabled Haile Selassie congratulating him on getting rid of Zionism "which aims to control the world."[64] He also repeated his promise to compensate them beyond their losses. However, in practice, no real help was to come from across the Red Sea.[65] On the contrary, following the October War, the Saudis created a global oil crisis, which greatly added to Ethiopia's economic plight. Stricken by drought and famine, aggravated by the mishandling of a decaying, corrupt regime, Ethiopia's poor economy could barely cope with an abrupt 50 percent rise in oil prices in January 1974 alone. This was only one dimension of a general deterioration that soon led to the collapse of the entire system. The reasons for the revolution in Ethiopia that began in February 1974 were multidimensional. Our focus here on the Saudi aspect and the impact of the Israelis' abrupt disappearance, while it should be taken in proportion, was by no means marginal.

While Ethiopia itself was falling apart, the emperor found time in January 1974 to pay a visit to the Pope in Rome, together with some other African leaders, in order to discuss the future of Jerusalem. The issue of the Israeli 1967 occupation of the eastern city (which had recently enabled the return of the keys to the Deir al-Sultan monastery to Ethiopian hands) was now a convenient excuse to knock on Faysal's door. Back from Rome on 22 January 1974, this time together with Ras Asrate Kassa, the emperor spent a day in Jedda. As told by the *ras* to his son, it was a very humiliating experience. Faysal was pleased with Haile Selassie's new concern for delivering Jerusalem from the Zionists, but he told the emperor: "You severed diplomatic relations with Israel but retained ties at the Ministries of Interior and Defense." Haile Selassie denied the allegation and said that a PLO delegation had just paid a visit to Addis Ababa (16–18 January, 1973), in spite of PLO aid to the Eritreans. He also added he was ready to consider some concessions to the Eritreans, if they gave up violence. Faysal, on his part, ignored hints regarding his own promises. Nothing was mentioned of the $200 million package. Rather, Faysal talked of a token US$35 million of which a considerable amount should be invested in the construction of an Islamic center in Addis Ababa. He said he would be ready to help Ethiopia with oil and the purchase of arms, implying he would do so after Ethiopia's Muslims obtained their rights. According to another Ethiopian source close to the Emperor, the weary, aging monarch returned from Riyadh overwhelmed. He confined himself to his room and did not appear in public for several days.[66]

The revolution that began in February 1974 did not come as a surprise. Most observers of Ethiopia were of the opinion that Haile Selassie would be the last absolute emperor and that a fundamental change toward political modernization was inevitable. There was also a near consensus among observers that any future change, whether achieved peacefully or following violence, would rest on a formula that combined progressive elements in the elite and representatives of the educated middle class, in uniform and out. From every conceivable angle, both the elite and the intelligentsia were strong enough to work out such a change, introducing representative politics without sacrificing the main cultural aspects of Ethiopian continuity. Very few anticipated the events of 1974. Ethiopia's imperial elite, the layer that for centuries enjoyed full social, economic, and political supremacy couched in religious legitimacy, proved suddenly to be disoriented and paralyzed. The intelligentsia, thought to be spearheaded politically by educated middle- and high-ranking army officers, failed to unite. Instead, there was a protest movement organized in February among the less-educated mid-rank and junior officers in remote field units that, facing the fragmentation of everything above, managed to crystallize into a functioning body, the Derg (the committee). Led by the brutal Major Mangistu Haile Mariam, it slowly destroyed any potential leadership. On 12 September 1974, Ethiopia's New Year, it deposed Haile Selassie. Having executed nearly all representatives of the elite and the better-educated officers, and having stifled the intelligentsia, Mangistu's Derg worked quickly to detach Ethiopia from its traditional roots. Resorting to a new, revolutionary terminology, soon to adopt Marxism, the new leaders declared the end of Christian hegemony. A Stalinist-like regime would persist in a bloody effort to reorient Ethiopia's culture away from messages of local history.

Why did the expected change in Ethiopia go wrong? Why did a protest movement led by junior, half-educated officers meet a paralyzed elite and a disorganized intelligentsia? Again, I cannot give a comprehensive answer, because the perspective of this book has concentrated on the role of the Saudis in this history and I have no pretensions of presenting a balanced picture. Looking at only the abrupt expulsion of the Israelis, it appeared to have a triple impact. First, it must have aggravated the resentment of the junior officers who initiated the protest movement. Second, it most probably deprived the elite, both imperial and military, of basic information about rebellious cells in the army's remote battalions. Third, the betrayal of Israel and succumbing to Arab-Islamic pressure seem to have eroded the confidence of the leading Christian elite at its most fateful hour. Moreover, the effective Saudi pressure to enhance Islam in Ethiopia—a much needed reform in better times—resulted in the sudden surfacing of some religious tensions that only added to the prevailing confusion.

I shall confine myself here merely to quoting some relevant sources. Israel's last ambassador (from 1971), Aynor, wrote an account of the Israeli-Ethiopian connection.[67] He had this to say on the impact the removal of the Israelis had on the army:

> Most political analysts of this period agree that a cause-and-effect relationship existed between the severance of Israel-Ethiopia diplomatic relations and the sudden withdrawal of all Israeli military teams, and the outbreak of mutiny in the remote Ogaden army camps.
>
> I had experienced the complex and often close relations that existed between Ethiopian officers and their efficient, young Israeli counterparts, the products of an egalitarian democratic society and army, who involved themselves deeply in the daily routine of their respective units, even learning to speak some Amharic. These war-experienced officers were loyal to their Ethiopian units and proud of their professional achievements. A problem encountered all too often, was lack of funds available for training. It was well known that corrupt officials frequently channeled divisionary budgets into fake purchases, or monies were simply misappropriated. In an emergency the Israeli adviser would inform the military attaché at our embassy, who in turn would alert the chief of staff or the Minister of Defense, bypassing divisional and regional headquarters. . . . In special or urgent cases, I had to involve the Emperor such as when one of our military teams could not continue serving with a brigade stationed in northern Eritrea, which for weeks had not been supplied with food or fuel and was lacking minimal medical services. On another occasion I had to inform HIM that a long-prepared important divisional maneuver could not take place because promised spare parts, fuel and special ammunition was not forthcoming. . . . The Israeli officers were never afraid to criticize or suggest improvements: they even drew attention to obvious failures in the command structure or to long-term absences of senior officers from their units.

The IDF felt a special responsibility towards two elite units which it had established and trained from the start: the Parachute Battalion and the tank regiment based in the Ogaden desert.

The structure of the Ethiopian army was contradictory, with top positions still awarded by HIM on a hereditary basis to the descendants of the main aristocratic families of the realm. Lower echelon officers, on the whole, spent years training abroad before assuming their military assignments. This situation created strong tensions and animosities, which the Israeli teams serving with various Ethiopian units tried to alleviate, often serving as shock absorbers between the old traditional commanders and the ambitious, professional, young officers. When the Israeli teams were suddenly withdrawn, these tensions and animosities did not find another outlet, and a highly explosive mixture started to evolve. The junior officers who started the mutiny never intended to launch a revolution: they wanted to do away with an antiquated system of promotion and to ensure decent living conditions, proper food and pay for themselves and their men.

On the elite being deprived of information about rebellious cells in the army, Aynor added

While by no means a major cause for the outbreak of the mutiny and the revolution, the withdrawal of Israel's military presence was bitterly resented and unpopular among all ranks and added much to existing explosive tension. It removed an independent, reliable source of information between outlying military posts and headquarters in the capital. . . . The commanding officer of the Israeli mission, worked closely with the Ethiopian chief of staff. . . .

Possibly I will be accused of committing an error of emphasis regarding the impact the severing of relations with Israel had on the Ethiopian revolution. In that case I find myself in good company. The *New York Times* and *Le Monde,* following the Ethiopian revolution in detail through their Addis Ababa–based correspondents, both came to similar conclusions. Over the years I tried to clear up this point with my Ethiopian acquaintances who played important roles in the initial stages of the revolution. All agree, in their distinctive ways, that the break in relations and especially the sudden disappearance of Israeli military teams added considerably to the rebellious ferment in the armed forces.[68]

In the late 1970s, when I interviewed a dozen of those Israeli advisers for my research on the Ethiopian army and the 1974 events, practically all of them repeated the same points—namely, that they indeed were the link between a corrupt elite and the resenting junior and intermediate officers.[69] Some expressed surprise that of all the talented and educated officers they knew—graduates of the Harar Military Academy—it was the hot-headed Major Mangistu and his friends from the nonacademic Huleta Military School who captured power. Many of these advisers were of the opinion that had they stayed, things could have developed much more overtly, and therefore quite differently.

Aynor wrote in November 1973 on the more abstract impact of the break on the elite and the general Christian public, well before the beginning of the revolutionary change:

> The Ethiopian public was taken by surprise and reacted with amazement upon hearing this unexpected news. The roots of historical, religious and emotional ties between Christian Ethiopia and Israel are so deep and rich that they occasionally verge on the irrational. The cutting of relations while Israel is struggling for survival had a stunning effect on many, for on top of all that it had the smack of betrayal and stab in the back. . . . Among the members of the establishment as well as by the masses there was first disbelief, then followed by grief. . . . Soon the issue was added to the growing resentment by the masses against the regime. Ethiopian political humor resorted to double meaning rhymes and the following line was heard all over: "I, Haile Selassie the first, Ethiopia's Emperor, the Lion of Judah, betrayer of Israel."
>
> There is no doubt that the overwhelming majority of Christian Ethiopians, from the royal family, the nobility, down to the peasants in remotest provinces conceive the breaking of relations a matter of great shame and little benefit. The basic [Christian] Ethiopian concept is fundamentally anti-Islamic. What was done is seen as an act of surrender to Arab blackmail, an act for which Ethiopia is soon to pay dearly. In the eyes of the [Christian] Ethiopians Israel has a special status with Providence. Any hurting of Israel cannot but yield the worst of evils.[70]

A week after expelling the Israelis, the British ambassador reported

> Local reactions continue to be completely contrary to what is published here. Ketema Yifru . . . has told me that the church and the army were against it. . . . [He said that] if the government were not to look foolish, it was now necessary to show that they reaped advantage from it. . . . Ato Ketema was skeptical about hopes that the Arabs would switch their line on the Somali question: he said there was a thousand years of history of Muslim/Christian antagonism in this area which was not going to be changed overnight—the appeal of Muslim to Muslim would still, in his view, prevail. But King Faysal had always insisted (for example to Ato Ketema himself when he visited Saudi Arabia two years ago as Foreign Minister) that if Ethiopia would break with Israel he would be interested in seeing that she did not suffer. "If we are going to sell ourselves," Ato Ketema commented, "at least we

should make sure we get a good price." So perhaps the Ethiopians are looking to Saudi gold as their major reward. I wish them luck.[71]

Throughout 1974, the falling regime, either in response to Faysal's demand or out of its growing weakness, enabled the country's Muslims to challenge Christian supremacy. On 19 April 1974, the streets of Addis Ababa saw an unprecedented demonstration of the local Islamic community, in which an estimated 350,000 marchers demanded full equality. There followed a public debate in the press, reflecting the Christians' shock and the Muslims' newly gained confidence. Most of the Muslims who expressed their ideas in writing called to maintain Ethiopia's unity and wished that "the Cross and the Crescent should give way to democracy and equality in matters of politics."[72] As it turned out, these wishes did not materialize. No constructive Christian-Islamic dialogue emerged during these confusing months. In such circumstances, the voice of the deprived Muslims in defiance of a decaying order only added to the disorientation of the crumbling Christian elite. In retrospect, rather, it added to the chaos that led to the emergence of a dictatorship legitimized by antireligious doctrine.

A document that perhaps reveals some of the disorientation that paralyzed the Ethiopian Christian establishment in the aftermath of the break with Israel is the following passage written by the Ethiopian minister of information in the 1974 imperial government. Ahadu Sabure wrote his diary in the Derg prison during 1976–1977 and smuggled it out in parts. On 1 December 1976, after a conversation in the prison yard with former Foreign Minister Katama Yifru on the reasons for Haile Selassie's decision, he wrote,

> King Faysal said in Algiers that if Ethiopia broke off diplomatic relations with Israel, he would try hard for Ethiopia to get significant aid from the Arabs and for the Eritrea problem . . . to be peacefully resolved. However, he did not keep his promise. To please him and the Arabs, Ethiopia canceled in one day the diplomatic relations she had with Israel. In exchange she got nothing. . . . On the contrary, it was confirmed that the amount of aid in arms and money given to the Eritrean bandits after the Algiers Conference was much greater than before.

Blaming the emperor for actually undermining Ethiopia by betraying Israel, Ahadu's words reflect the mixture of rage and frustration that apparently destabilized the regime's elite.

> During the time he ruled in Ethiopia for more than fifty years Haile Selassie used to think that there was no leader who was more sophis-

ticated than he in the art of politics, trickery and cunning. However it is only to be regretted that he died still hoodwinked without understanding that the Arabs were our enemies who for a long time never let up in wounding and bleeding us by looking for opportunities to attack us and injure us, that leaders like Gamal Abd al-Nasser and King Faysal were the uttermost faithless knaves who made their principal work gulling Ethiopia and other black African states with sweet words and promises, whose breath stank, whose pledges were completely untrustworthy, who used prevarication as a major political method and instrument and who, while they turned their face five times a day toward Mecca and prostrated themselves in worship of Allah, were only plotting this swindling action of theirs. The former Emperor's cunning and trickery never went beyond the stage of causing clashes and divisions among his ministers. . . . We ought not judge him if he was unable to cope with foxes like Faysal and his ilk. Even if the pickpockets of downtown Addis Ababa were a thousand times more skillful, there is no one who would wager that they could be considered equals of the hamstrings of Cairo, Baghdad, Damascus, or Riyadh. If God in his subtle wisdom had not confronted the Arabs with a deadly enemy, namely Israel, who would trample them under his feet whenever they get arrogant, the Arabs would be devils who would be good for no one and would be upsetting all creation without letup.[73]

Our effort here to analyze the dialogue between concepts, mainly religious, and political history is by definition impressionistic. How self-defeating in terms of the Christian-Ethiopian identity and self-image was the break with Israel? What was the contribution of the suddenly introduced effort to appease Islam, of the kind represented by the Saudi MWL, to the disorientation and confusion of the royal establishment? Questions like this will never be fully answered. In any case, it would be wrong to conclude that Faysal's policy was intended to undermine Haile Selassie's regime. On the contrary, the facts presented above indicate that the Saudi regime was interested in a stable, antirevolutionary, anticommunist Ethiopia. But the Saudis' strategy was also a Wahhabi strategy—conceptually committed to the victory of Islam and essentially inconsiderate of non-Islamic, indeed non-Wahhabi "others." Though not aimed at Haile Selassie's destruction, Faysal's lack of consideration toward his neighbor's difficulties, in all spheres, contributed most clearly to his downfall. After Haile Selassie expelled the Israelis, he was viewed in Riyadh as a spent card. All his renewed promises never to allow the Israelis to return and to enhance Islam in Ethiopia made no difference. As the imperial Ethiopian regime went on crumbling throughout 1974, and as the Derg exposed its revolutionary tendencies, the Saudis disengaged. Rather—as indicated by Ahadu Sabure—they resumed aid to the Eritrean 'Uthman Salih Sabbe.[74]

King Faysal and the deposed Emperor Haile Selassie were both soon to meet a violent death. On 25 March 1975, the Saudi monarch was assassinated by one of his nephews. It was a matter of a personal grudge, and the murder only confirmed the resilience of the system Faysal had strengthened. He was swiftly succeeded by his brother Khalid. Indeed, the sons of Ibn Sa'ud would remain in power into the twenty-first century, retaining the Saudi-Wahhabi formula of Islam's political supremacy. Their Ethiopian policies will continue to be addressed in this book.

On 12 September 1975, on the first anniversary of his deposition, the eighty-three-year-old emperor was paid a nighttime visit by Mangistu and four of his men. They covered his head with pillows and ensured that he suffocated to death. They then secretly buried his body beneath the sewage system in the yard. This was the end of Ethiopia's last Christian king.

## Notes

1. For the impact of Nasserism on Eritrean and Ethiopian history, the establishment of the ELF and the Arabization of Eritrea's Muslims, see Erlich, *The Struggle over Eritrea*, chap. 2, 3; Erlich, *Ethiopia and the Middle East*, chap. 10, 11, 12; Erlich, *The Cross and the River*, chap. 7, 9.

2. FO 371/131241, Annual Report for 1957, 10 January 1958.

3. *Middle East Record* (Tel Aviv University, Shiloah Center, 1960), p. 381.

4. The same Islamic school, Madrasat Dar al-Aytam, in which our acquaintance Shaikh Yusuf 'Abd al-Rahman of Harar taught in 1935. See Chapter 4.

5. Tawfiq, *Min zikraiyat musafir*.

6. The passage above is derived mainly from Kaplan, "Christianity."

7. The passages below on Islam under Haile Selassie are derived mainly from Ahmed, "The Historiography of Islam in Ethiopia"; Erlich, "Islam and Ethiopia."

8. For example, see "Emperor Receives Islamic Elders at End of Ramadan," *Ethiopian Herald* (Addis Ababa), 15 April 1964.

9. Al-Habashi, *Ithyubya fi 'asriha al-dhahabi, fi 'asr Hayla Silasi al-Awwal*.

10. In 1969, the British ambassador to Addis Ababa thus summarized his impressions: "The phrase 'Arab enemies bent on the dismemberment and destruction of Ethiopia' . . . [is] I believe . . . a view which the Ethiopian ruling

class instinctively share . . . at least in so far as they believe that their Moslem neighbors are basically untrustworthy, that they encourage dissidence where they can, that they covet Ethiopian territories, and that they would try to take advantage of any period of weak government or breakdown of law and order following the Emperor's death to lay hold of parts of the present Ethiopian empire. Ethiopian apprehensions are partly the reflection of the attitudes of mind of a country obsessed with its history and with the facts of its survival over the centuries as a Christian kingdom in conflict with Islamic enemies." See Foreign and Commonwealth Office (hereafter FCO) 31/301, Dorman to FCO, PRO, 12 August 1969.

11. See Ahmed, *"Al-'Alam."*

12. Miran, "A Historical Overview of Islam in Eritrea."

13. Ahmed, "Islam and Islamic Discourse in Ethiopia."

14. Miran, "A Historical Overview of Islam in Eritrea."

15. Ahmed, "Islam and Islamic Discourse in Ethiopia."

16. The passages below on Ethiopian-Israeli relations are partly based on new evidence and partly on Erlich, *Ethiopia and the Middle East*, chap. 13, and on Erlich, *The Cross and the River*, chap. 8.

17. *Voice of Ethiopia*, Radio Addis Ababa, 12 July 1966.

18. The passages below on the periods of King Sa'ud and of King Faysal are also based on Yizraeli, *The Remaking of Saudi Arabia*, pp. 49–98; Rabi, *Saudi Arabia: Islam, Oil, Politics*, chap. 4, 5.

19. "Memorandum of Conversations," by the Ambassador in Saudi Arabia, Jedda, 23 March 1950, *United States Foreign Relations, 1950*, vol. V, Saudi Arabia, p. 1149.

20. On the MWL and on their Saudi charity organizations, see Burr and Collins, *Alms for Jihad*, chap. 2, "Saudi Arabia and Its Islamic Charities." On the first conference of the Muslim World League in 1962, see www.motamer-makkah.net/intro1.php.

21. See Kostiner and Teitelbaum, "State Formation and the Saudi Monarchy," pp. 131–149.

22. See *Ethiopian Herald* (Addis Ababa), 31 March 1963, "Ethiopia Calls on Saudi Arabia to Stop Hostile Propaganda," and the editorial of 3 April 1963, "Hostility for Hospitality." See also *Radio Addis Ababa*, 12 April 1963, *BBC/ME*, 16 April 1963.

23. Bergman, "Israel and Africa: Military and Intelligence Liaisons," p. 259.

24. See analysis of Somali relations with the Arab and Islamic world during 1960–1968 in FCO 31/424, Whitwell, Mogadishu, to Arabian department in Foreign and Commonwealth Office, 11 December 1968: "The Islamic content of Somali foreign policy has been comparatively slight considering that the country is an 'Islamic Republic' in all but formal name. . . . In the first years of their independence the Somalis showed no particular interest in joining the Islamic bandwagon. At that time contact with other Islamic countries was confined to the U.A.R." Later there were some contacts with other Arabs including the Saudis. In 1966 the Somali president visited Riyadh, and an interest-free

loan of $5 million was awarded by King Faysal, who paid a return visit in 1967. See there for more details on the generally insignificant mutual ties between Mogadishu and Riyadh.

25. See Erlich, *The Struggle over Eritrea*, chap. 5, "The Middle East and Eritrea, 1962–1974."

26. For Sabbe's book, *Ta'rikh Irtirya*, see "The Terminology and Literature of Eritrea's Arabism" in Erlich, *Ethiopia and the Middle East*, pp. 157–164.

27. An interview with Sabbe in *Al-'Alam al-Islami* (Mecca), December 1983, pp. 19–22.

28. Hamad, *Al-Ab'ad al-dawliyya li-ma'arakat irtirya*, pp. 177–180.

29. See also FCO 31/301, "The Eritrean Liberation Front," 1969.

30. Long, "Saudi Arabia and the Horn of Africa."

31. FCO 31/305, D. G. Bar, British Consulate in Asmara to FCO, 4 July 1969; FCO 31/301, Dorman, Addis Ababa to FCO, 21 July, 5 August 1969.

32. FCO 31/301, Dorman to FCO, 13 August 1969.

33. FCO 31/305, "Ethiopia—Valedictory Dispatch," Bromley to Stewart, 13 November 1969.

34. FCO 31/1464, "Ethiopia and the Middle East," British Embassy report, 25 October 1973.

35. FCO 31/301, Dorman to FCO, 13 August 1969.

36. *Al-Da'wa*, 20 November 1967.

37. Israel State Archives (henceforward, IGM), 4175/14, Arye Oded to embassy in Addis Ababa: "Saudi Islamic Propaganda Against Ethiopia," 17 July 1969.

38. Samiullah, "Forsaken Muslims of Ethiopia."

39. See Erlich, *The Struggle Over Eritrea*, ch. 3, "Addis Ababa and Eritrea, 1962–1973."

40. The following passage from Warburg's *Islam, Sectarianism, and Politics in Sudan Since the Mahdiyya* (pp. 159–160) reflects Saudi policy at that time (as it can also be applied in the Ethiopian context): "According to Numayri, this so called secular, radical phase came to an end already following the abortive communist coup of July 1971. . . . Following his return to power . . . he performed the Hajj to Mecca. While in the Saudi capital he had long discussions with King Faysal about the new Islamic phase which he now envisaged, probably hoping that this would lead to massive financial help. . . . These meetings paved the way for the new constitution of May 1973. According to one report Numayri had promised King Faysal that his constitution would turn Sudan into an Islamic state, but he was opposed by some of his closest advisers. . . . The amended version of the constitution, which was finally approved, did not satisfy the Saudis, and bankrupt Sudan had to manage without the aid that had been previously promised by King Faysal."

41. See *Al-Bilad* (Jedda), 6, 7, 8 June 1971; FCO 8/1740, Wall to Hall, 21 June, Morris to Acland, 22 June, 1971.

42. IGM 5319/1, Aynor's report "Conclusions and Assessments," 25 May 1972.

43. FCO 8/1740, Morris to Acland, 22 June 1971.

44. Historian Paul Henze, who served as an American official in Ethiopia at that time, adds, "There was a tacit (perhaps even secret) division of responsibility in Ethiopia in the late Haile Selassie period between the US and Israel. The US operated the main military training mission (the MAAG, which had about 125 officers and men at its height) and also had a mapping mission in Ethiopia, while actual work in the field was left up to Israel, so Israelis provided advisers who worked with units in Eritrea, e.g., it was an amicable arrangement —i.e. division of responsibility—and worked well into the early 1970s" (Henze, personal commun.).

45. IGM 5319/11, Shelef to African Department, Foreign Ministry, 14 March 1972.

46. IGM 5319/11, Yafe, Addis Ababa to African Department, 21 September 1972.

47. IGM 5319/11, Yafe to African Department, 28 December 1972, 1 January 1973; "Ethiopia and the Red Sea," by "A Special Correspondent," *Ethiopian Herald* (Addis Ababa), 31 December 1972.

48. IGM 5318/15, Yafe, Addis Ababa to African Department, 20 March 1973.

49. IGM 5318/16, Yafe, Addis Ababa reporting a conversation with PM Aklilu, 12 June 1973.

50. IGM 5318/15, Yafe, Addis Ababa to African Department, 20 March 1973; 5319/11, African Department to Embassy, Addis, 15 March 1973; 5319/11, Aynor's report on conversation with Vice Foreign Minister, Yudith Imru, 10 July 1973.

51. IGM 5318/16, Yafe, Addis to African Department, 25 April 1973.

52. IGM 5318/16, Yafe, Addis Ababa reporting a conversation with PM Aklilu, 12 June 1973.

53. Radio Addis Ababa, 2 May 1973, *Daily Report (DR)*, Foreign Broadcast Information Service, US Government, 4 May 1973.

54. See IGM 5319, Yafe to African Department, 25 April; 4 May, 7 June 1973; Radio Addis Ababa, 2 May, *DR* 4 May 1973.

55. Spencer, *Ethiopia at Bay*, p. 323.

56. IGM 5319/11, Aynor's report: "Changes in Ethiopia's International and Political Standing," July 1973.

57. IGM 5318/16, Yafe, Addis Ababa reporting a conversation with PM Aklilu, 12 June 1973.

58. Spencer, *Ethiopia at Bay*, p. 323–324. Henze adds, "At this time the American Embassy in Addis Ababa had already fallen into a serious decline and the State Department was too preoccupied with other things (Middle East, e.g., collapse in Vietnam) to give much serious attention to Africa. The intelligence people were likewise too preoccupied to give serious consideration to what the Soviets might really be doing in Somalia-Ethiopia-Sudan and the Eritrean situation was judged to be in somewhat of a hold pattern" (Henze, personal commun.).

59. Spencer, *Ethiopia at Bay*, p. 324.

60. Aynor, "Crisis in Africa"; see note 67, below.

61. IGM 5319/11, Yafe, Addis Ababa to African Department, 24, 31 July 1973.

62. Erlich, *Ethiopia and the Middle East*, pp. 172–173.

63. See also FCO 31/1464, "Ethiopia and the Middle East," British Embassy, 1 November 1973; also IGM 5319/11, "A Conversation with Prof. Ephrem Isaac." The Ethiopian American scholar visited Ethiopia in January 1974. Having confirmed that those who opposed the break came mostly from the army and the clergy, Isaac added that the move was received with satisfaction by many members of the young generation. "Many of the students," he said, "saw Israel as a reactionary factor which supported the rotten, feudal Imperial regime." He remembered anti-Israeli songs popular among the students.

64. *Al-Bilad* (Jedda), 25 November 1973.

65. In December 1973, a spokesman of the ELF stated that Ethiopia broke with Israel "after receiving a grant of 20 million dollars from an oil state." See FCO 31/1461 Translation from *Liwa'*, 8 December 1973.

66. The passage is based on interviews with the son of Ras Asrate Kassa, Lij Asfa-Wossen Asserate; an interview with Dadjazmach Zewde Gabre-Sellassie; *Jerusalem Post*, 22 January 1974; Reuters from Beirut as quoted in *Zambia Mail*, 31 January 1974; The Israeli Mosad's report, "Ethiopia—The Emperor's Visit to Saudi Arabia," 25 January 1974 in IGM 5319/11; A report from Paris by Yafe, previously Israeli adviser in Addis Ababa, on his conversation with French journalist Yves Loiseau, 23 September 1974, in IGM 5319/11; PRO FCO 31/1679, Morris to FCO, 25 January 1974; FCO 31/1661, Morris to FCO, 2 February 1974; FCO 31/1657, Murray to FCO, 10 May, 23 May 1974.

67. Aynor, "Crisis in Africa." Hanan Aynor, an intellectual and a diplomat, was the head of the African Department in the Israeli Foreign Ministry prior to his appointment to Ethiopia. Part two of the unpublished manuscript, entitled "Haile Selassie's Ethiopia," is a most detailed, perceptive account of the Israeli-Ethiopian connection throughout 1971–1973.

68. Paul Henze adds, "The collapse of the Nixon Administration did have a serious effect on Ethiopian self-confidence. Combined with the break with Israel later in the year both the Emperor's confidence in himself and the Ethiopian aristocratic establishment's confidence in Haile Selassie began to collapse. . . . Ethiopian aristocrats were so used to Haile Selassie calling all the shots and deciding everything basic that they were incapable of coming together to take responsibility for the direction in which the country was moving. . . . Ethiopia's friends, first and foremost the United States, made no effort to play any role in helping the Emperor or any of the officials he appointed make their way through this period. The weak American embassy, in charge of a third-rate officer (Ambassador Adair had become sick and left; he was not replaced), did nothing significant. No other Western country did anything significant or felt much responsibility for doing so. Israel, which might have played a significant role, had been expelled and was licking its wounds" (Henze, personal commun.).

69. Erlich, *Ethiopia and the Challenge of Independence*, chap. 11, "The Ethiopian Army and the 1974 Revolution," pp. 225–248.

70. Aynor's report of 26 November 1973, in IGM 5319/11.

71. FCO 31/1464, British Embassy, "Ethiopia and the Middle East," 1 November 1973.

72. The quote is from Ahmed Sayed Ali, "What Is an Established Religion of State?" in *Ethiopian Herald* (Addis Ababa), 3 May 1974. This article is a response to Yacob Woldemariam, "In the Name of God . . .," *Ethiopian Herald* (Addis Ababa), 25 April 1974, which strongly expressed a Christian's anger at the Muslims' demonstration of 19 April, reminding them that "one immutable fact of life [is] that the established religion of Ethiopia is Christianity."

73. See more on Ahadu Sabure and this document in Erlich, *Ethiopia and the Middle East,* pp. 176–178.

74. IGM 5319/11, Turgeman, Washington, to African Department, 20 December 1974; Sabbe's interview to the Kuwaiti newspaper *Al-Ray al-'Amm,* 12 September 1974.

# 6

## Wahhabism and Communism: Mutual Demonization, 1974–1991

A S WE HAVE SEEN, HAILE SELASSIE'S CHRISTIAN ETHIOPIA AND THE Wahhabi kingdom of Faysal were able to conduct a dialogue. It was quite a problematic one, never really bridging deep-rooted differences and suspicions, and it eventually contributed to the fall of Ethiopia's old Christian imperial order; however, mutual regional interests, reliance on Western factors, and similar monarchical systems created some common ground and even rare moments of common action. The period discussed in this chapter witnessed what seemed to be a total breakup of any such common ground. The Derg revolution soon evolved into a communist dictatorship allied with the Soviets. In the eyes of many Saudis, Mangistu's Ethiopia turned into the ultimate "other"—the old Christian *habashi* in the new cloak of a pro-Soviet, revolutionary menace. In many Ethiopians' eyes—and certainly in Mangistu's—the Saudis became the embodiment of the historical Islamic-Arab enmity: reactionary, feudal, corrupt neighbors whose aim remained to undermine Ethiopia through subversion and jihad. Yet, beyond the public rhetoric and the realities of a strategic confrontation, neither side was fully monolithic and some elements of mutual pragmatism and respect were preserved. A tentative Ethiopian-Saudi dialogue was resumed in 1987 when the Soviets began losing patience with the failing Mangistu and when the Saudis' main concerns were focused elsewhere.

The period under discussion can be divided into four phases. The first was the early months of the revolution, which were marked with hope for religious equality in Ethiopia and a tentative continuation of the rapprochement between Addis Ababa and Riyadh. The second phase was one of concrete strategic confrontation. With the reopening of the

133

Suez Canal in June 1975, amid soaring oil prices, the Red Sea became the focus of global attention and Soviet-American tension. While Ethiopia joined the local pro-Soviet camp, the Saudis, motivated primarily by their fear of communism, led in building the rival coalition, thereby rendering support to Mangistu's opponents in Ethiopia and the entire Horn. The indirect Ethio-Saudi conflict climaxed in a short-lived Somali invasion of the Ogaden between July 1977 and February 1978 and a battle over Harar, the historic capital of Islam. In this struggle for the Horn, the Saudis and their local supporters were beaten. Islam on the African side of the Red Sea was still, for the most part, too apolitical to replace fading pan-Arabism and compete with trendy Marxism. The more traditional local groups supported by the Saudis proved to be lacking in cohesion, while both Mangistu and his major opponents continued to deepen their hold on society using revolutionary, radical methods. By mid-1978, the Saudis had lost much of the influence they had gained in Ethiopia and Eritrea and failed to fulfill their 1975 anti-Soviet slogan of "Arabization of the Red Sea."

The third phase began after the 1979 Islamic revolution in Iran and the Egyptian-Israeli peace accord. Both events, in combination with other developments, shifted the all-regional strategic focus to the Persian Gulf, a focus that would remain to this day, as the Red Sea was rendered marginal. In the 1980s, the Saudis and Mangistu's Ethiopia disengaged strategically, but they did remain closely connected conceptually. Both were immersed in renewed anxieties that—from our perspective—also recycled old mutual fears and images. With the revolutionary, pro-Soviet Horn at their backs, the Saudis would remind themselves of the Leninist *najashi* and even argue and differ about Ethiopia's past and future. Mangistu and his regime, facing endless problems and the opponents he had systematically created, continued to blame "reactionary Arabs" for all their troubles. Though couched in Marxist terminology, the Derg often returned to the slogans and symbolism of Christian isolation. As in the past, however, the indirect Ethiopian-Saudi dialogue was never unidimensional. Some examples of pragmatism and of demonization, of old dualities in new terms, will be discussed below. In 1987, when the increasingly radical Mangistu began to lose the full support of Moscow, he began to seek friendship with American-oriented Arabs (and with Israel). This fourth phase in his relations with the Saudis (1987–1991), which again attests to fundamental complexities and dualities, will be addressed at the end of this chapter.

One sphere of the relevant Ethiopian duality during the entire period was the regime's attitude toward Ethiopia's Muslims. This wavered between an initial call for Christian-Islamic equality and a Mangistu-style Marxist urge to combat, or at least marginalize, religiosity altogether. Ethiopian Muslims were indeed oppressed, for the most part, on an equal basis with all other groups. They themselves experienced a round of conceptual duality regarding their "Ethiopian-ness." Some of Ethiopia's Muslims, together with other refugees of the revolutionaries' momentum in the Horn, found ways to flee to Saudi Arabia and other Arab countries. There they were paternalized as *habashi* workers but were also inspired by political Islam and Wahhabism. Many would return to participate in the revival of Islam in post-Mangistu Ethiopia.

## Mangistu's Ethiopia: The Marginalization of Religiosity

On the Arab Peninsula, like nearly everywhere else in the Arab world, the late 1970s and the following decades were marked by the deepening of religiosity as a major dimension of politics. We shall refer below to the impact of this phenomenon on Saudi Arabia and her attitudes toward Ethiopia. The situation in Ethiopia, and indeed throughout the entire Horn of Africa during the period under discussion, was very nearly the opposite. Religiosity was rendered secondary as a shaper of history. After 1974, Ethiopian Christianity and the church quite abruptly lost their political significance. In spite of some symbolic gains, Islam made no significant progress toward a political identity. At the center of the new Ethiopian republic, as well as on the periphery, it was the nationalist, ethnic, regionalist, and Marxist movements that competed over reshaping the region. Religious identities, though never entirely abandoned, seemed to play auxiliary roles. Only in the 1990s would both Christianity and Islam in Ethiopia resurface and reclaim concrete significance. Meanwhile the dialogue between the two shores of the Red Sea became more obscure than ever before.

At the initial stage of the revolution through 1974 and somewhat later, the situation was still different. Two factors combined to create a brief moment of Ethiopian openness. First, as already mentioned, the Islamic community of Addis Ababa, sensing the crisis in the imperial-Christian elite, organized and began to actively assert the Muslims' claim to equality. The huge demonstration of 19 April 1974 mentioned above was a memorable event of formative magnitude and was followed by additional steps. While some Christian nationalists and church circles protested, the Ethiopian intelligentsia was supportive. Dozens of articles in leading newspapers urged the rebuilding of the Ethiopian nation on the basis of equality and the separation of religion from politics. "We must appeal to our Moslem brothers," ran the editorial of the *Ethiopian Herald* of 23 April 1974, "who have demonstrated their maturity . . . to eschew mistrust and misapprehension and work hand in hand with their Christian brothers to build this nation—to build a modern Ethiopia where religion will be solely a personal affair and where all Ethiopians will live in equal peace and prosperity."[1] The Derg officers adopted this line. On 23 December 1974, the three major Islamic holidays were included in the twelve annual public holidays declared as national holidays. A new Hajj Coordinating Committee was appointed amid ceremonies, and, with the Derg's blessing, some three thousand pilgrims were helped to make the hajj of late 1974 to early 1975. At a public gathering in Addis Ababa, their leaders were asked by the Derg's chairman to "brief the pilgrims from other parts of the world, whom they would meet in Mecca, on the current changes taking place in the country" and spread the word of the new government's pledge to implement the principle of religious equality.[2]

Second, up to November of 1974, the Derg's young officers were still seemingly being led by their titular chairman, Aman Mikael Andom, a popular old major general on whom they hastened to call to legitimize their revolution. Aman, overconfident in his new leadership, tried to direct the revolution toward decentralization and regional-ethnic pluralism. Aman's main effort was to reach a compromise with the Eritrean nationalists within this decentralized vision, and it was mainly over that issue that his growing differences with the more radical young officers led to his demise. On 23 November 1974, Aman was killed in a shootout, and on the same night, fifty-eight members of the old elite were sentenced to death without trial and machine-gunned by Major Mangistu's men. Still, this radical group opted to work behind another father figure, Brigadier General Tafari Banti, and thus the aura of some open republicanism did not entirely disappear. It would, however, gradually fade throughout 1975–1976, against the background of a series of brutal assassinations within the Derg itself, which cannot be addressed here. Tafari Banti was executed on 3 February 1977, when Mangistu assumed official power as chairman of the ruling Derg.

In the early, fluid stage of 1974–1975, the new regime also tried to open up to the Saudis.[3] Aman was counting on Riyadh to subsidize arms from Washington.[4] His statement that Muslims were a majority in Ethiopia and should enjoy full equality was well-received even in MWL circles in Mecca.[5] Tafari Banti tried to follow suit. In December 1974, he sent a Derg member to Riyadh with a message in the same spirit for

Faysal. The Saudi king responded by confirming that "the historic links between Saudi Arabia and Ethiopia would truly enable the friendship between the two countries to be continued and strengthened . . . [adding that he] would not refrain from giving assistance to Ethiopia in any field. We are pleased to learn that under the new government, Ethiopian Muslims are able to practice their religion freely." Faysal also expressed his wish that "the Ethiopian government find a peaceful and correct solution to the Eritrean problem, so that peace and security would prevail in this region of the Red Sea."[6]

By that time, the Saudis were already suspicious of the Ethiopian revolutionary destroyers of monarchy and resumed their aid to the Eritreans of 'Uthman Salih Sabbe. They would soon witness rapid radicalization under Mangistu and would intensify their intervention in the Horn. From their point of view, Ethiopia was developing into an atheist, communist, pro-Soviet nightmare.

We shall confine ourselves here to a brief summary of the religious aspect of Ethiopia's radicalization. Christianity was soon depoliticized and even blamed for hindering progress. "There is too much fasting and feasting in this country," ran the editorial of the *Ethiopian Herald* of 13 August 1974.[7]

> In fact there are more than 200 days of fast in the year. . . . In the rural areas where the influence of religion is still strong, millions of man-days are lost every month because of the existence of a plethora of saints' days. . . . One of the greatest obstacles to the progress and development of Ethiopia lies in the country's religious practices. We must make these practices amenable to change if Ethiopia is to make any meaningful progress in the future.

The Ethiopian Church quite abruptly lost its historical standing and its economic resources. Religion and state were separated, and land reforms (March and June 1975) deprived the church of its main income source. Abuna Tewoflos, who dared to express some protest, was exposed by the Derg as a corrupt reactionary, and in February 1976, together with three bishops, he was deposed. He was replaced by modest, low-key Abuna Tekla-Haymanot, who had little choice but to cooperate. In March 1979, with the appointment of thirteen new bishops, the reorganization of the Ethiopian Church as a poor, deprived system at the mercy of the regime was completed. Though Christians could continue to celebrate holidays, and in some aspects could go about their lives according to old customs, the regime systematically intruded. When peasant and urban associations were formed in 1975, their lengthy meetings were purposely held on Sunday mornings. Christianity, neverthe-less, was not uprooted. In many ways, it became a sort of anti-Derg protest, and the church, no longer exploitative as in the past, regained some popularity.[8] In difficult moments, even the regime tried to tap the energies of Christian nationalism. It depicted regional opponents as wagers of jihad in the service of foreigners against "Mother Ethiopia." In March 1976, for example, a "Peasant Crusade" was declared by the Derg (and never came to pass), aimed at flooding Eritrea with Oromos. Altogether, Mangistu and his men continued to waver between the lega-cies of ancient Christian-Ethiopian uniqueness and the deep-rooted reli-gious devotion of the country's Christians and Muslims on the one hand, and the universal Marxism they had adopted on the other. They resorted to each terminology according to the status of their struggle for survival and absolutism. In times of weakened opposition, like in the early 1980s, they seemed ready to confront religiosity and were exposed to allegations and condemnation in this spirit.[9] Mangistu himself was seen in church only once, when his benefactor Dejazmach Kebede Tessema was buried, but on revolution day parades, he would have the patriarch and the chief Muslim clerics beside him on the podium. One document that apparently reflected Mangistu's approach was an article in the *Ethiopian Herald* on "Muslims in the Soviet Union." Journalist Tsehaye Debalkew, sent to tour the USSR, returned much impressed:

Since the dawn of Socialism, imperialism has been capitalizing on religion to sow the seeds of discord among the working people. No popular revolution has escaped allegation by imperialist media for suppressing this or that religion. This was the lot of the Great October Socialist Revolution as indeed was the case when some self-styled champions and quarters of religion tried to spit their poison to misrep-resent the Ethiopian revolution. The truth as corroborated by practice in the Soviet Union has been altogether to the dismay of the self-appointed advocates of religion. The picture is clear and unequivocally stated in the constitution of the USSR that 'citizens of the USSR are guaranteed freedom of conscience,' that is, the right to profess or not to profess any religion and to conduct religious worship or atheistic propaganda. Incitement of hostility or hatred on religious grounds is prohibited. In the USSR the church is separated from the state, and the school from the church. . . . The followers of Islam enjoy broad rights guaranteed them by the constitution. . . . The citizens of the USSR belong to a single multi-religious country. . . . [They] fulfill their social obligations in unison, as members of the great family of Soviet peoples and make an active contribution to the construction of a new society and struggle for universal peace precisely because the state and Church are separated.[10]

Islam, though enjoying the new terminology of religious equality, also weakened as a political identity.[11] With the demise of pan-Arabism in the Middle East, the spirit of the 1960s in the Horn, which seemed at the time to be successful at turning young Muslims into revolutionary Arabs, also faded. Pan-Arab, secular ideology practically disappeared, together with the urge to learn Arabic and its modern phrases. The ideas of political Islam, which in most Middle Eastern societies replaced pan-Arabism in the 1970s, were slow to inspire young Muslims in the Horn. After 1974, Ethiopia's Muslims had good reasons to identify even more fully with their Ethiopian-ness. The 1974–1975 official declarations of religious equality were repeated[12] and finally endorsed by the constitution of January 1987. The Derg made meaningful gestures toward Islam. Legally, Muslims were no longer discriminated against; they merely suffered like all others. When they did suffer more, it was not to an extent that would cause them to resist the new system on religious grounds.

Behind the facade of equality—"religion will not divide us" was a slogan voiced on many occasions[13]—very few Muslims were trusted by Mangistu and his men. The Constitution Drafting Commission, appointed in 1975, included only one Muslim, and the 136-man committee appointed in 1984 to organize the regime's party included only three. These figures reflect the picture in practically all political bodies, though a somewhat better balance is discernible in the academic and administrative spheres. As Muslims constituted the overwhelming majority of traders and entrepreneurs, the regime's growing radical socialism inevitably turned against them. In the words of Hussein Ahmed:

> Gradually, however, as the government's proscription of religion became apparent, and as its vast propaganda machine turned to vilifying merchants, it antagonized sections of the Muslim religious elite and the merchant community. . . . Traders became targets of virulent attacks and were denounced as 'exploiters and enemies of the peasantry'. Articles such as 'Plotters against Economy' and 'Reactionary Merchants and the Market' also appeared regularly.[14]

The new secular-revolutionary culture imposed by the regime was only slightly more sensitive to Islamic traditions and law than the previous imperial regime. The old issue of polygamy, which had been ignored by Haile Selassie's constitution, was debated time and again, but the 1987, final version of the new constitution was equally inconsiderate from the Muslim point of view.[15] Muslims were terrorized by the regime, jailed and executed like their fellow Christians. "As much as

there were oppression and wrong doing in the days of the old regime,"
Shaikh Yusuf 'Abd al-Rahman wrote in his memoirs, "the good sense
was to bear with them to avoid the worst, which indeed came after the
introduction of communism. He who shed tears under Haile Selassie
began shedding blood under Mangistu."[16] Still, no significant manifestations of protest stemming from Islamic identity were recorded. "The
reaction of the Muslim community to socialism," summarized Hussein
Ahmed, "which remained mute throughout the Derg years because of
the absence of political freedom, was one of acquiescence with a great
deal of reservation."[17] Muslims actively participated in the opposition
movements based on and inspired by ethnicity and regionalism, chan-
neling their grievances there. Some members of the Islamic elite, mainly
in the center, were manipulated and forced to cooperate with the regime,
even to spread its word on missions abroad. Among those cooperating
were sixteen members of the new Hajj Coordinating Committee
appointed in late 1974. The committee, like in Haile Selassie's days,
was directly answerable to the Ministry of Interior and later to the
Ministry of Public Security. It was often accused by other members of
the Muslim community of corruption and of sharing bribes with the government.[18] Though the Derg, after the initial, more liberal stage, began
to severely restrict the number of pilgrims to Mecca,[19] many, especially
members of the better-connected families, paid their way out. Of those
who made it to Saudi Arabia, through the committee or in other ways,
many preferred to stay, seeking work and gradually creating substantial
Ethiopian Muslim communities in Jedda, Medina, and other Saudi urban
centers. There they also came under the influence of Shaikh Yusuf 'Abd
al-Rahman, who had headed the defunct imperial Hajj Committee and
was dismissed by the Derg. In 1976, after moving to Dire Dawa, Shaikh
Yusuf managed to obtain an exit visa and settled in Medina, where he
has stayed, teaching Wahhabism and spreading the word of fundamentalist Islam among the local Ethiopians.[20]

Among the various "liberation fronts" that opposed the Derg's
regime, Islam remained mostly apolitical. Many of the fronts adopted
Marxist terminology combined with suprareligious ethnic ideology
shared by young Muslims. Christian-Muslim partnership on such a basis
could be found in the Ethiopian People's Revolutionary Party (EPRP, a
leftist opposition movement to Mangistu centered in Addis Ababa); the
Tigrean People's Liberation Front (TPLF); the EPLF; the newly organized (in 1975) ELF; and the Oromo Liberation Front (OLF, a guerrilla
opposition to Mangistu aiming at fulfilling a national ideology of the
Oromo people). In spite of the centrality of Islam in the Oromos' mod-

ern self-awareness, the more prominent leaders of the OLF were Christians, and in any case, both they and their fellow Muslims hardly emphasized the religious aspect of their ethnic nationalism. The liberation fronts of the Afars and the Somalis were, by background and composition, purely Muslim, but in spite of the legacies of their histories— and even though they were supported by the Saudis—they fought against Mangistu's regime more in the name of their regional, linguistic, and ethnic identities, than in the name of Islam. Christianity also played an apolitical role in opposing Mangistu. The more conservative, liberal Ethiopian Democratic Union (EDU), led by members of the old elite (and also supported by the Saudis), fought, until its final defeat in 1978, for the introduction of decentralization and representative politics, not for the restoration of a "Christian empire."

## 1975–1979: The Saudis' Arabization of the Red Sea

The violent death of King Faysal resulted in very little change in Saudi Arabia. King Khalid, aided closely by Prince Fahd, smoothly resumed family control over the kingdom. In the mid-1970s, no opposition of any significance presented a challenge to the prosperous oil empire. Modern educated circles, as well as more purist Islamic leaders in Saudi Arabia, were still well-tamed and had little discernible influence on policymaking. This would change in 1979, in combination with other strategic transformations central to our story. Meanwhile, however, during the crucial years of 1975–1979, the Saudi royal house was quite confident to conduct a foreign policy based on pragmatic, concrete considerations. However, as in the past, even the conceptualization of concrete foreign relations issues was never really detached from Wahhabi fundamentals and from inputs of the MWL. In the years under discussion, the Saudis aimed at blocking the Soviets (and, to distinguish, the Israelis) in the Red Sea, but their relevant involvement in the Horn of Africa cannot be said to have been fully consistent and based on sensitive understanding of the locals. It ended with the Soviets and the Horn revolutionaries more entrenched and with the collapse of the Saudis' potential allies.

The Soviets, we saw, were already present in the area in the 1960s, but the reopening of the Suez Canal in June 1975 aggravated the threat they presented from the Saudi point of view. Until then, the Saudis had done their best to stem the Soviets and scored successes in supporting their opponent in Yemen, and later (in 1972) in helping Sadat of Egypt and Numayri of Sudan to cut themselves off from Moscow. However, by the time the canal was reopened, the Soviets had become entrenched along the Red Sea, in South Yemen and Somalia, and potentially in Ethiopia. Both Mangistu and his major rivals, the various revolutionary liberation fronts, were ideologically, or practically, Marxist- and Soviet-oriented. Though the Americans (until late 1976) and the Israelis (until February 1978) were still hoping to see Mangistu preserve the initial, nationalist promise of 1974, the Saudis, after a short tentative phase, became totally disillusioned. After the murders of Aman Andom and Haile Selassie, and following the reforms and internal terror that deepened in 1975, a clear strategy began crystallizing in Riyadh. It would be called "the Arabization of the Red Sea."

I cannot elaborate here on the more comprehensive aspects of Saudi policy in the mid-1970s. Rich and influential, the kingdom was now a leading factor in the inter-Arab world, allied with Egypt and Sudan and rivaled by Libya, Iraq, and others. Its prime strategic aim, however, was to stem the Soviets and their regional clients, and the focus at that time was on the Red Sea.[21] By mid-1976, Saudi Arabia, Sudan, and Egypt were coordinating their policies. In July, Saudi Arabia joined the Egyptian-Sudanese committee on military coordination, and in November, Saudi Arabia's King Khalid paid a visit to Numayri in Khartoum, where they discussed matters relating to Sudanese-Saudi-Egyptian strategic cooperation in the Red Sea, including Saudi plans to secure a strong naval presence there. Under Saudi auspices, Sudan became the pivotal factor in the making of an Arab Red Sea policy on the African coast. Sudanese-Somali relations improved significantly, and in November 1976, a Sudanese military delegation visited Baghdad and Damascus, apparently to discuss the Saudi-financed transfer of arms from Iraq and Syria to the Eritreans. On 17 January 1977, a Kuwaiti newspaper reported that a Saudi-Sudanese-Egyptian body, aiming to coordinate the defense of the Red Sea, had been established, and that Yemen and Jordan, together with Jibuti and Eritrea once they achieved independence, would be expected to join it. During the coming months, the Saudi-initiated Riyadh-Cairo-Khartoum axis was cemented, and the Egyptians and the Sudanese coordinated their military and naval presence in the Red Sea.[22]

"Arabization of the Red Sea," we recall, was a slogan used by the ELF in the 1960s and by the Nasserites of Egypt until their removal by Sadat. Its initial meaning was revolutionary, namely (from our perspective), turning the Muslims of the Horn of Africa into pan-Arab activists fighting to unite the Horn through an all-regional Arab revolution. The Saudis, though they recycled the same slogan, had no such pan-Arab vision. They aimed at influencing the Muslims of the Horn of Africa to identify with a conservative inter-Arab campaign to stem the Soviets. As things developed, by 1977 this policy would turn into a Saudi effort to undermine a Soviet-allied Ethiopia through aid to Mangistu's opponents in Eritrea, Ethiopia proper, and Somalia. As in the past, their action was never homogenous. It remained a combination of different, sometimes contradictory policies, reflecting the inherent tension between pragmatic considerations and Wahhabi influences and circles. Altogether the Saudi effort ended in failure in northern Ethiopia and with the Eritreans. In Somalia, the Saudi combination yielded a short, self-defeating success in the course of the Ogaden War.

### Saudi Failure in Eritrea

The non-Marxist anti-Derg organizations in northern Ethiopia proved fragile. When the Derg announced the March 1975 land reform, leaders of the Afar people tried to resist but succumbed to the Derg's army. Sultan 'Ali Mirrah fled to Saudi Arabia and was followed in the coming years by thousands of Afars who managed to cross the sea and join the expanding Ethiopian community there. His son, Hanfere 'Ali Mirrah, continued to direct the sporadic, and hardly effective, activities in north-eastern Ethiopia of a Saudi-supported Afar Liberation Front.[23] In north-western Ethiopia, the EDU proved slightly more useful. Led by former generals and ex-princes of the imperial regime, the EDU tried to build on Western support and Saudi help. Consequently, it had enough stamina to survive in the field up to 1978, when, lacking substantial support from the peasantry, and torn by internal rivalries, the EDU finally faded away.

The Saudis expected the Eritreans with their Arabism of the 1960s to be a pillar of their new Red Sea strategy. In fact, they were not. The 1970s saw a significant change in relations between the Eritrean movements and the Arab countries. Though the age of secular, revolutionary pan-Arabism in the Middle East was almost over, the fundamental Islamic-Arab, Saudi-inspired conservative message was no substitute for the new generation of Eritreans. In both the ELF and the EPLF—swelling now, after the death of Aman Andom, due to the mass enlistment of young Christian Eritreans—the actual leadership was taken over by field commanders. In May 1975, the ELF leadership abroad was denounced by an ELF Revolutionary Council congress as "opportunistic and bourgeoisie" and Idris Adam was replaced by Ahmad Nasser. The EPLF was already dominated by Christian Isayas Afeworki and his young Marxist associates who thought of Sabbe and his Arabism in similar—indeed harsher—terms. However, for a while, the development of the Saudi-led Red Sea Arab strategy resulted in Sabbe's becoming relevant again. In late 1974, he had already managed to convince King Faysal that his men in eastern Eritrea's "strategic triangle" would help to ensure that the Red Sea would remain an "Arab lake" and to stem the Soviets on this vital oil route. The Saudis, together with Sadat and Numayri, had no other Eritrean option but to gamble on Sabbe and his promise to integrate the Eritrean struggle into their Arab strategy. Throughout 1975–1977, Sabbe thus managed to procure substantial Saudi funds with which he tried to unite all Eritrean forces. Yet, though he managed to iron out some of his old differences with the ELF, he was totally rejected by the mostly Marxist-oriented Christian core of EPLF fighters. They denounced him as a traitorous bourgeois and a feudal servant of the Saudi Arab reactionaries. Sabbe was indeed deepening his dependence on the more fundamental Wahhabi circles. On 7 December 1976, in the Saudi paper *Al-Madina al-Munawwara*, he published a piece entitled "From the Eritrean Liberation Front to the Muslim World League." The motive underlying his message was that a school had been set up for Eritrean refugee children in Port Sudan and his appeal was to "create Islamic religious awareness among the refugees, to provide religious books to the library. . . . Our objective is to protect the Arabic language, and above all to safeguard the Islamic religion. . . . I humbly present my request to you, hoping that you will as usual respond favorably to my petition."[24] In April 1977, Sabbe established a third organization, Eritrean Liberation Front–Popular Liberation Forces (ELF-PLF), but the symbolic name did not help to promote Eritrean unity.[25] In the early 1980s, when the EPLF achieved hegemony in the field, Sabbe became increasingly irrelevant. Both he and the deposed Idris Adam were not party to the events in the field itself that led to the military demise of the ELF, the victory of the EPLF over Mangistu's Ethiopia, and Eritrea's obtaining independence under Isayas after Mangistu's fall in May 1991.

By the late 1970s, having lost any leverage they had hoped to create in Eritrea, the Saudis' attention shifted away from the Red Sea. Many of the losers in the inner-Eritrean struggle found shelter in the Wahhabi state. Sabbe, upon moving to Saudi Arabia, abandoned his pan-Arab secular vocabulary altogether and, reassociating with MWL circles in Mecca, adopted the language of political Islam. In 1983–1984, he again tried to bring about Eritrean unity, carrying the Saudi assurance of extensive aid and the promise that the Saudis would raise the Eritrean issue in the UN once a united Eritrean front was declared.[26] However, while some joint statements were made in Arab capitals, the EPLF troops in the field engaged in fighting their fellow Eritreans of the ELF. In 1985, Sabbe tried to unify the defeated ELF activists by establishing a new ELF-Unified Organization in Saudi Arabia that would make no significant impact on Eritrean affairs. On 4 April 1987, Sabbe died in a Cairo hospital during surgery. Meanwhile, Idris Adam, his old rival from the days of Eritrea's Arabism, was also fading away. He moved to Mecca, abandoned the secular pan-Arabism he had adopted in the 1960s, and, like Sabbe, turned to political Islam. The founding father of the ELF died in Mecca on 29 August 2003 without setting foot again on Eritrean soil.

### The Saudis and the Ogaden War

The cornerstone of Saudi strategy in the Horn of Africa in the 1970s was the effort to lure Somalia out of the Soviet camp.[27] This effort developed into a multidimensional story leading to short-term success in 1977 and ending in disastrous consequences for the Somalis, from which they have not recovered to this day. The Saudi policy, as in the past, was a combination of pragmatic considerations with a Wahhabi drive, apparently enhanced by the MWL's involvement in foreign affairs. In the Somali case, culminating in the 1977–1978 Ogaden War with Ethiopia, this religious aspect proved decisive.

The Somalis, like all other factors in this multicultural, international analysis, also wavered between different sets of concepts and structures. In the period under discussion, they were polarized between Marxism and a Soviet connection on one hand, and the legacies of Islam on the other. Though united by an ethnic and linguistic nationalist identity— quite a unique phenomenon in all of Africa—the countless Somali clannish divisions prevented their evolvement into a cohesive society. After coming to power in 1969, Siyad Barre opted for secular socialism to encourage supratribal modernization. He deepened his alliance with Moscow and was compensated by receiving more arms to build a mechanized army, strong enough to ensure state superiority. His Marxist policy culminated with the establishment of the Somali Socialist Revolutionary Party whose ideologues were also behind an antireligious campaign. In 1972, Arabic script was abolished and the Latin alphabet was adopted. In 1974, polygamy was outlawed and women were declared legally equal to men. Ten Muslim activists who tried to organize a protest were executed in January 1975.

The history of Islam in Somalia cannot be summarized here, but we do need one general observation in order to make sense of the 1977–1978 story. Throughout the centuries, local Islam, mostly Sufi and oral, contributed only marginally to the cohesion of the clannish Somali social structure. In the post–World War II period, Islam merely played an auxiliary role in the making of modern Somali nationalism. However, at certain junctures throughout its history, Somali Islam did erupt politically. When led by charismatic figures who created *jihadi* movements, it served as a uniting factor. Two cases have remained deeply engraved in the Somali collective awareness. These were the sixteenth-century Ahmad Gragn movement and conquest of Ethiopia, and the two decades of anticolonial struggle led by Islamic leader Muhammad bin 'Abdallah Hassan in the early twentieth century. In both cases, the unifying religious energies were inspired by external challenges and were channeled to the Ogaden region—the Somali-populated area connecting to the Horn, shared with other Islamic peoples, and disputed over with the Ethiopian Christian kingdom, which annexed it in 1887.

The Holy Wars of Gragn and "the Mad Mullah" created moments of Somali unification and inspired other neighboring Muslims. Though both cases ended in costly failure for which local Islamic and Somali speakers paid with dismemberment, the situation created in the area by the time of the 1974 Ethiopian revolution seemed to invite another round. Ethiopia's apparent weakness following the collapse of Haile Selassie's regime made it tempting to revive the struggle for the Ogaden. The Somali leadership faced a problem. In the circumstances thus created, the Soviets favored an accommodation with the radicalizing Derg, and the Soviet-oriented leaders in the Somali establishment, headed by Siyad himself, tended to avoid war. On the other hand, the temptation to regain the Ogaden helped to re-enliven Islam. Marxism and Islam were now competing intensively over the content of Somali nationalism. For their part, during 1975–1977, the Saudis—anti-Soviet Riyadh and fundamentally Wahhabi Mecca—worked to promote the cause of an anti-Mangistu war and the victory of Islam.

Advocates of political Islam in Somalia of the 1960s were relatively weak. Some graduates of the Egyptian Al-Azhar University and of Saudi schools tried to organize. In 1967, the Al-Ahali movement was founded in southern Somalia and a year later Al-Wahda was established in the north, both molded after the Egyptian Muslim Brothers and both soon fragmented. When Siyad came to power, he outlawed such organizations, but their offspring, Al-Salafiyya and Al-Takfir, managed to survive and initiated activities like the translation of the Quran and its interpretations into Somali. These organizations and others were also responsible for a new connection created with the Saudis. With the enormous funds available as of 1973, the Saudis, mainly through the MWL, gave generous scholarships to young Somalis to study in the kingdom and absorb Wahhabi influences. "Tens of thousands of Somalis," summarized Ethiopian researcher Medhane Tadesse, "flocked to Saudi Arabia for employment opportunities. . . . Thousands more were offered scholarships. . . . the majority of them found their way to the Islamic University of Medina. Others studied at Umm al-Qura University in Mecca and the Imam Sa'ud University in Riyadh. . . . The gradual *Wahhabi*zation of Somali Islam and the planting of religious divisions and animosity . . . were part of the project."[28] Back home these graduates strengthened Islamic opposition to Siyad.

Of the ten Islamic activists hanged in early 1975, most were reported to be graduates of Saudi schools, and the anti-Islamic policy of Siyad especially angered MWL circles in Mecca. The editor of *Majallat al-Rabita* reacted strongly to the executions. In January 1975, under the title "The Red Hand That Began Purging Islamic Somalia of Muslim Scholars," he published the names of the ten victims and asked how an Arab and Islamic country could adopt Latin script and Marxist ideology without oppressing the fundamental values of Islam. In April 1976, *Majallat al-Rabita* published another piece mocking Siyad's statements that he could bridge Marxism and Islam. "All I want," asked the author, "is to understand until when will religion be a playing object with which everyone can do what he pleases. Till when will the worshipers of Marxism be allowed to damage Islam? . . . It is socialism which prevents progress."[29]

Siyad, though promoting secular socialism and combating Islam, also had moments of hesitation. As a Somali nationalist and a member of a clan known for its contributions to the historical *jihadi* movements, Siyad began to incline toward forcefully regaining the Ogaden. For this purpose he needed Arab-Islamic backing, and in 1974, after long years of hesitation, Somalia joined the Arab League. In return, Siyad received no financial aid from the Saudis[30]—he still continued to persecute Islamic activists at home—but judging in retrospect, he was beginning to prepare a non-Soviet option. Moscow, indeed, continued to strengthen his army, but the Soviets' regional agenda was hardly compatible with the irredentist legacy of Somali nationalism. The Soviets' vision was to create a Marxist-oriented South Yemen–Somalia–Ethiopia–Eritrea (EPLF) axis that would ensure their control over the Red Sea.[31] In February–March 1977, Fidel Castro toured the region in a last effort to promote this strategy.

To win the Somalis out of the Soviet camp, the Saudis worked to enhance their nationalist, Islamic, and anti-Ethiopian dimensions. Although Riyadh had a difficult dialogue with Mogadishu, the Saudis' main leverage was Somali insurgents in Ethiopian-occupied Ogaden. Soon after Mangistu killed Aman Andom, and together with the renewal of their aid to Eritrean Sabbe, the Saudis, mostly unofficially and through religious organizations, began to help the Ogaden Somali liberation front. This was done directly, not through Siyad, and resulted in successful anti-Derg operations in the desert and around the urban centers of Harar, Dire Dawa, and Jijiga.[32] Mangistu blamed Siyad (in February 1976, Ethiopia published a thirty-nine-page memorandum entitled "War Clouds in the Horn of Africa") and had no difficulty uncovering Saudi fingerprints in the Ogaden. In early February 1977, he accused Saudi Arabia of leading "an international conspiracy of reactionaries intent on creating the kind of coup that destroyed the Allende regime in Chile."[33] Ethiopian-Somali tension continued to grow, culminating in the eruption of open war in July 1977.

Indeed, when this local deterioration triggered the international Ogaden War, it was no longer only over the future of the Ogaden and its Somali inhabitants. Back on 15 January 1976, with Saudi (MWL) support and inspiration, the Western Somali Liberation Front (WSLF) of the Ogaden was reorganized. Some of its Oromo members, headed by the veteran leader of the 1965–1970 Oromo rebellion in the Bale region, Wako Guto, declared the establishment of a sister movement called the Somali Abbo Liberation Front (SALF). Under the guise of a fabricated Somali identity (Wako Guto's father was an Oromo and his mother, a Somali), it was an overtly Oromo-Islamic movement that extended its operations to the provinces of Bale, Arusi, and Sidamo.[34] For all intents and purposes, the Oromos, whether Christian or Muslim, never intended to become Somalis. What was in the making was an all-Islamic movement, complete with the participation of Harari Islamic activists (to whom we shall soon return). Nothing could be more similar to Ahmad Gragn's movement to unite Muslims of all of southeastern Ethiopia.

In the first half of 1977, the more the Derg resorted to crude, brutal methods, the more this anti-Ethiopian, militant Islamic-Somali movement gained momentum in the south. As the new Soviet alliance with Mangistu became clearer, the more apparent Siyad's dilemma grew. The early signs of Soviet rebuilding of the Ethiopian armed forces and the successful operations of the WSLF and the SALF pushed Siyad to make haste and gamble on invasion. His mechanized army crossed the border on 23 July 1977 and with this began a decisive war over the Ogaden and, in fact, over the whole region. Due to massive Soviet, South Yemeni, and Cuban help, the renewed Ethiopian army managed to stem the invasion (in November, Siyad officially broke with the Soviets).[35] Due to Saudi support for Siyad (the Saudis were particularly alarmed by the fact that the Soviets had proved capable of building such a military coalition, sacrificing the Somalis, and winning Ethiopia), the war continued until March 1978. Riyadh pledged Siyad some US$400 million, and supplies at the cost of US$2 million daily,[36] and it was much due to threats by the Saudis and the Egyptians that the Ethiopian army, having defeated the Somalis, was prevented from crossing into Somali territory. Somali defeat and humiliation were complete.

What was the motivation behind the Saudis' involvement? Here again we have to record various Saudi voices, often contradictory. While the strategists in Riyadh aimed at undermining the Soviets, the agents of fundamentalism in Mecca worked for Islam's victory. These aims were not incompatible, but it seems that the fundamentalists' momentum proved more effective than Riyadh may have intended. In March 1978, after the Somalis' defeat, the Saudi undersecretary for political affairs, 'Abd al-Rahman al-Mansuri, confided to an American diplomatic mission:

> I am tired of Somalia. We have wasted a lot of time and money on it and we have nothing to show for it. We do not care about the Ogaden. We would just as well see it belong to Ethiopia. We are only interested in communism in this region. We want the Soviets and the Cubans out of Ethiopia. If Ethiopia could become moderate, we would support her immediately. We would forget about Eritrea. Our strategy is to keep communism from expanding in this region and push it out. Everything else we do is tactics. . . . We will do anything you can convince us makes sense to get communism out of Ethiopia. When Ethiopia is moderate, there will be no difficulty with the Eritreans. We will give them no support. We do not care about Somalia. We do not want to waste more money on it unless we see that you have a strategy for the whole area that will get the Russians and the Cubans out.[37]

In contrast, other Saudi voices, that same month, still viewed it all as a religious, historical conflict with Ethiopia. Radio Riyadh commented:

> The Western Somali Liberation Front, and the Eritrean Liberation Front are waging a liberation war against Ethiopian colonialism, which claims that the region of western Somalia and the region of Eritrea are part of Abyssinia. . . . History and evidence confirm that at no time did these two regions belong to Abyssinia; they are two Arab Muslim peoples.[38]

In practice, it seems that in the case of the Ogaden War, like in many cases discussed in this volume, the Saudis' concrete considerations blended with the motivations of their religious activists. They found themselves initially working to ignite the Somali-Ethiopian hostilities and later, facing total collapse, working to isolate the fire.

These short lines do not render justice to the complexities of the Ogaden War. From our narrow perspective, we shall confine ourselves to quoting the conclusion of Roberto Aliboni's study of the events leading to its outbreak: "In the last analysis, the Soviets never planned the change of alliance between Somalia and Ethiopia. It was provoked solely by the extreme nationalism of the Somalis and the adventurism of Saudi Arabia. The latter, by fomenting the nationalism of Mogadishu, hoped to make use of it to get the Soviets out of the Red Sea area and Somalia itself."[39]

The major battle of the war was the Somali siege on Harar. This strategic springboard to southern Ethiopia was defended by the Ethiopians and their Soviet and Cuban backers, and the Somali failure to capture it determined the outcome of the entire conflict. As both sides were still captives of their Marxist terminology, little was said at the time about the significance of the battle for the historical capital of Islam. According to the Ethiopian press, "the Somali rulers and mass media, to incite and inflame the tribal and religious passions of the jihadist hordes of invaders, narrate and glorify how Imam Ahmed of Harar, nicknamed Gragn, waged the 1527–1543 jihad on the Christians."[40] It is easy to imagine the possible consequences of Harar's potential fall to the Somalis. The late 1970s were soon to witness the momentous emergence of political, militant Islam in the Middle East and in many neighboring societies. The liberation of Harar from Ethiopia by Somalis, Oromo Muslims, Adaris—all supported by the Arabs and the Saudis—could well have turned the Somali-Ethiopian conflict into a religious one. In such an eventuality, the very survival of Ethiopia would have been at stake.

The Ethiopian victory in the Ogaden ensured the continued marginalization of religiosity in the Horn up to the early 1990s. It further ensured the cementing of Mangistu's alliance with the Soviets and the strengthening of Marxist orientations among nearly all significant forces in the Horn of Africa. Unlike the Eritreans, who had rejected the "Arab Red Sea" option and had become stronger, the Somalis, falling prey to Saudi designs, would pay dearly. The connection now built between Somali Islamic radicals and the Wahhabi state would continue to undermine Somali national cohesion in the 1980s. It would also result in the emergence of Islamic international terrorist networks in Somalia in the 1990s.

Of particular interest to us are the implications of the Ogaden War on Harar as an Islamic community. Here again, the public was not united. Like in the days of *fitnat al-kulub*, many of the local Adaris resisted cooperation with Somali nationalism and ambitions. Shaikh Yusuf 'Abd al-Rahman Isma'il (in Medina since 1976) continued, from a distance, to preach for a pure Islamic Harari identity and warned against another round like that of 1948—of disastrous affiliation with the Somalis. On the other hand, there were perhaps no fewer Adaris, together with other local Somalis and Oromos, long associated with the WSLF, who now joined the anti-Mangistu struggle. Yusuf Isma'il testified that some of them, dubbed the "colonels of Harar," took the lead in the pre–July 1977 victories over the Ethiopian third division in the Ogaden. With Somali help, they had been trained by various military academies in the Eastern Bloc and the Arab world. According to this source, the Hararis who collaborated with the Somalis called themselves the "Ahmad Gragn forces," and those who teamed up with the Oromos called themselves *"Tufan"* (flood). Yusuf Isma'il, who back in 1948 had been part of the *kulub* Harari orientation toward the Somalis, in his later correspondence with Shaikh Yusuf praised the bravery of the "colonels of Harar." The latter, in Medina, lamented the futile stupidity of the Hararis' gamble on the Somalis. Both shared the same grief upon witnessing the consequences. Mangistu—they claimed—was revengeful and wanted to flood Harar with emigrants from all over the country. Tens of thousands of members of various linguistic and ethnic groups from all over Ethiopia, they wrote, were settled within its walls, in new neighborhoods outside, and in the now ruined plantations around Harar. Islamic teaching and use of Arabic were now even less tolerated in Harar than elsewhere. The whole social structure of the town, they claimed, was suddenly changed as the nuclear Islamic community was dismembered. Many of the young generation moved to Addis Ababa and integrated into the new communist culture. Many others found their way through Somali territory to Saudi Arabia.[41] There they joined the growing Ethiopian-Islamic community, most employed in domestic service and manual labor, exposed to local old attitudes toward *habashi*s, but also absorbing the values of political Islam. In Harar itself and its surroundings, though local, apolitical, popular Islam continued to flourish throughout, and though the claims about Mangistu's purposeful revenge were obviously exaggerated, the spirit of Gragn, in spite of the new defeat, would survive.

## Mutual Concepts, 1977–1987

*Ethiopian Concepts of Saudi Arabia*

During the months leading to the Ogaden War and during the war itself, in Mangistu's eyes Saudi Arabia began to embody the worst "other." Dozens of articles in the Ethiopian press now depicted the Wahhabi kingdom as backward, corrupt, reactionary, and the enemy of humanity, including of true Islam in general and of Socialist Ethiopia in particular.[42] Under the title, "Symbol of Atrocities of Arab Reaction— Racist History," the *Ethiopian Herald* of 27 January 1978 wrote:

> Even to this day, it has been established by various sources, that the imperial courts of reactionary Arab sheikhdoms are filled with a cortege of slaves and concubines, great-grandchildren of the forcibly abducted and domesticated former African slaves. In spite of the egalitarian teachings of Mohammed and the equality of all children of Allah, the Saudi and other backward Arab ruling cliques have never failed to manifest their arch-reactionary beliefs and tendencies even with regard to the most fundamental of human rights.

Another piece, "Feudalism in the Service of Imperialism," signed by Ethiopian Muslim Salah Ahmed, came with a cartoon depicting fat shaikhs leaning against barrels of petrol, smoking and watching with apathy their oppressed, starving subjects. The text included the following:

> Saudi Arabia is a polity still in the feudal age with all the attributes that expression implies. Its politics is completely dominated by the ruling oligarchy, whose key figures exercise absolute power in the country. . . . The typically feudal oil-rich kingdom openly practiced slavery as recently as 1962. Murderers are still beheaded and people who commit adultery are stoned to death under Islamic law. . . . The extremely conservative political stance of that country, at home, is only matched by its corresponding reactionary policy in foreign affairs. . . . Ever since the masses of Ethiopia threw off the oppressive regime of Haile Selassie and embarked on the socialist path of development, the Saudi regime consciously worked against the over-riding aspirations of the Ethiopian masses to do away with imperialist pressures, sabotage and foreign aggression.[43]

After the Ogaden War, the Saudis, though they diverted their attention to the Persian Gulf and remained only indirectly involved in Horn affairs after 1979, continued to be demonized by Ethiopian shapers of public opinion. It was convenient for the regime in Addis Ababa to blame external forces, like "global imperialism" and "Arab-Islamic" territorial ambitions, for the endless internal wars that Mangistu continued to create. The fact that most opposition bodies in Ethiopia were themselves Marxist, and that Islam was hardly felt politically, made little difference. Justifiably or not, the potential return of Saudi subversion continued to taunt the Derg. Sadat of Egypt, equally condemned in the media (until his October 1981 assassination), was far less demonized. It was apparent that the Egyptian ruler had long abandoned pan-Arabism and was himself fighting political Islam. With the Egyptians, Mangistu could use an old, mythical threat by airing the idea of blocking the Nile, and in any case, Egypt ceased to be actively involved in the Horn as it had been in the past. The Saudis, rich, powerful, fundamentalist, continued to be considered in Addis Ababa the leaders of what was conveniently seen as the Arab undermining of Ethiopia. They also continued to lead the effort to contain Soviet encroachment and combat Marxist regimes of the kind Mangistu was building. After his victory in the Ogaden, for a while Mangistu managed to regain most of Eritrea, and his alliance with the Soviets was further cemented and sealed. (In August 1981, his Soviet connection was further upgraded when he signed a tripartite alliance with South Yemen and Libya.) In January 1981 in Ta'if, the Saudis hosted an Arab summit whose deliberations were only indirectly relevant to Horn affairs. It is mentioned here only as background to the official Ethiopian response, "Ethiopian Foreign Ministry Statement on Ta'if Summit," a document that seems to best reflect Mangistu's basic concepts of Saudi Arabia at that time:

> News from Ta'if has demonstrated that some member countries of the Islamic Conference [Organization] have decided to interfere once again in Ethiopia's internal affairs. . . . With exception of a few progressive members, the conference mainly consisted of reactionaries, oppressors and exploiters of the world, who try to make the world a place where the hegemonistic and expansionist interests of themselves and their like may be fulfilled. . . . The sole purpose of the statements made and positions taken at the Ta'if conference was to divide the oppressed peoples of the world, to develop animosity and ignite wars; and this is masterminded by international imperialism which uses reactionary Arab governments as its instruments.[44]

Depicting Saudi Arabia as the embodiment of immorality, the document went on connecting the kingdom's internal backwardness to its international aggression:

As is well known to the world, the Saudi state, which hosted the summit, is a government that exploits and oppresses the broad masses of Saudi Arabia. While the princes live a life of luxury, the broad masses are condemned to exploitation by the ruling class, in the name of the Islamic religion. The members of the ruling class, as they have betrayed their own people, can not differentiate between an enemy and a friend. Blacks are still serving in their palaces as slaves; women are sold or are bartered as goods; people are either being beheaded or having their hands or legs hacked off. The death of a Saudi princess, who was beheaded,[45] was a demonstration of their barbarism.

As is well known in history, these parasites of society, who accumulated wealth by means of the slave trade, adhering to their old practice, are today promoting an appalling type of slavery in the form of neocolonialism and imperialist hegemony in the Middle East and the Gulf region. While paying lip service to the alienable rights of the heroic Palestinian people, the reactionary ruling class—apart from the huge supply of oil they present to the imperialists—send their petrodollars to their masters. At the expense of the poverty of their people, they involve themselves in the expansion of war industries. Furthermore they try to play the part of defenders of the imperialist interest in the region. . . .

The Saudis' corruption does not represent the true Islam, the statement went on, nor does their imperialist interference in Africa and Ethiopia:

These contemporary imposters of the prophets, had they but a small concern for human welfare, would they have so failed to make a modest contribution to the development effort in Africa instead of pouring into and hoarding their petrodollars millions in imperialist banks and cities? Instead of giving some cheap bribes to some African leaders, who are promoting their unworthy aims and do not stand for the interests of their peoples and thus became the cause of the massacre of thousands of fellow Africans, why do these time-made gods not practice what they preach? . . . Ethiopia and its people in their whole history have stood up and determinedly halted consecutive waves of aggression against them. Today in this age of technology and science they have again rebuffed reactionary Sheikh-emperors who are trying to impose the old and the new slave system in this strategically important part of the world. After failing to disrupt the unity and freedom of our country for centuries, these enemies are trying to achieve this today through their mercenary representatives. . . .

Between 1977 and 1987, dozens of speeches, articles, and official statements expressed similar concepts. They all more or less recycled the same blend of universal communist terminology together with traditional, Ethiopian, and local Christian dimensions of the Ahmad Gragn trauma. The Saudis now seemed to embody the ancient Ethiopian-Christian fears of intrusive Arabism combined with modern Marxist animosity toward "reactionary" political religiosity. The 1981 anti-Saudi statement is indeed harsher and deeper in its demonization of the Saudis than Ahadu Sabure's 1976 words quoted in Chapter 5, which revealed rather traditional attitudes. If there was a modicum of duality in the official voice of Mangistu's Ethiopia, it was between the old sense of Islamic threat on one hand, and the newly adopted communist ideology of apolitical religious equality, on the other. It is doubtful that other voices were raised publicly in Ethiopia in those years.

Ethiopia's Muslims remained mostly silent. We can only guess that the 1977 inner-Harari argument about joining the anti-Mangistu war or resorting to patience reflected a deepening duality among Muslims. Those who expressed themselves in writing had to praise the regime, and time and again they repeated the story of Ethiopian hospitality to the Prophet's first followers as a formative ethos of their own Ethiopian-Islamic identity.[46] During the height of the Somali siege on Harar, for example, Ali Mohamad Nur expressed his Ethiopian-ness and accused the Saudis of deviating from the Prophet's legacy toward his country:

> When the followers of the Prophet Mohammed were being persecuted in Arabia, the Prophet did not send them to Somalia, which did not exist. He sent them to Ethiopia with these words: go to Ethiopia, you will find there a king under whom none are persecuted. It is a land of righteousness where God will give you relief from what you are suffering from. . . . Consequently the Prophet told his followers never to wage a jihad (holy war) on Ethiopia. . . . As a result of the spirit of tolerance preached by the prophet Mohammed, Moslems and Christians have always lived in peace in Ethiopia. . . . His majesty King Khalid of the Kingdom of Saudi Arabia is made by destiny to keep the Holy Cities of Mecca and Medina, and in a sense, also to guard the teaching of the Prophet Mohammed. [Because of his aggressive support for the Somalis] are we to tell millions of Ethiopian Moslems that the Prophet's words "Leave the Habash in Peace" have no value today, as they had 1,400 years ago?[47]

Tens of thousands of Ethiopian and Eritrean Muslims, members of various ethnic groups, now opted to seek refuge in Arabia. Some of them were taken with Wahhabism, others felt humiliated by their new, rich masters. Some even sent contributions to the Derg's various campaigns.[48] Millions in Ethiopia now had a chance to be in direct contact with the Saudis. When Ethiopia was suffering from its terrible drought in the mid-1980s, governments and peoples the world over came to the country's aid. The drought was indeed a challenge to humanity as a whole and the response, overall, was positive. A study of the Saudi response to this challenge exposed quite a narrow approach even toward Ethiopia's Muslims:

> In the Western world, Ethiopia has the image of being a Christian island amongst a sea of Muslims, because the surrounding countries are mostly Muslim majority countries, such as Egypt and the Sudan. In actual fact, however, the population of Ethiopia is largely Muslim. . . . As a result, in the Arab and Muslim world, the media campaign was appreciable, and there was a remarkable outpouring of donations from the public. Organizations like the Muslim World League began their relief efforts. The Saudi Red Crescent, as well as the Kuwaiti Red Crescent, became active in Ethiopia in a way unknown of them before.
>
> Yet, complaints about these organizations were there from the start, mainly because of an overemphasis on religion in the camps where people's main concern was physical survival. These people needed food and clothes to sustain their immediate needs, not religion. To be fair, some of the Christian organizations were not innocent of missionary endeavors, and their proselytization efforts were met with a hue and cry from the Muslim side. . . . The Muslim World League, the largest Muslim charity in the world, the Saudi Red Crescent, and other Saudi charities have a long history of upsetting relief workers, non-Muslims, and Muslims for their callous and arrogant attempts of providing aid. . . . Availing themselves of the opportunity to denigrate non-Muslim relief work, the Islamists then became active campaigners against all relief work with a link to churches. In a fit of hypocrisy, they propagated the idea that the drought was used for Christianization. This propaganda was so fierce, that it interfered with the work of some European relief organizations. . . . It seems as though almost anywhere the Saudis perform relief work, the reactions of the Muslims receiving the "relief" was everywhere more or less the same. The people complained that the Wahhabis concentrated too much on ritual niceties, treating the suffering people as if they were not proper Muslims, whom they had to teach Islam from scratch.[49]

In the years under discussion, Saudi Arabia became, for Ethiopians, the more vivid embodiment of political Islam. Saudi economic strength, Islamic fundamental doctrine, and a new pivotal role in regional strategic affairs combined to render the Wahhabi kingdom centrally relevant to Mangistu's Ethiopia. Ethiopia's Muslims apparently began to waver between the concept of Saudi Arabia as a neighborly power capable of restoring Islamic pride and Islamic politicization and the concept of

Saudi Arabia as a Wahhabi state whose Islam, essentially different from theirs, aimed not only at reforming them, but also at fomenting a conflict with their fellow Christians. For Ethiopia's Christians—or rather for the Derg regime in the years during which it followed rigid revolutionary doctrines—the Saudis seemed to be viewed as the ultimate enemy, incorporating all suspicions, traditional and revolutionary.

### Saudi Concepts of Ethiopia

After the disaster in the Ogaden, Saudi Arabia relinquished its policy of Arabization of the Red Sea. In any event, soon nothing was left of it. In November 1977, Sadat of Egypt made his historic trip to Israel and his peace initiative was soon to end the Saudi-Egyptian-Sudanese alliance. In 1979, the removal of the shah and the emergence of Ruhollah Khomeini's Islamic revolution in Iran ignited a process that transferred the all-regional strategic focus to the Persian Gulf. From the Saudi point of view, the Soviet invasion of Afghanistan in the same year combined the threats of communism and of Shi'ite revolution from that direction. In September 1980, the outbreak of the Iran-Iraq War turned the Gulf into an arena in which the various identities and ambitions of the Middle East were to violently combat each other right up to the present. As the Red Sea area was soon marginalized—its internal wars continued to revolve around local ethnicity and regionalism—the Saudis' external concerns were all diverted to the Gulf. There, the stormy chain of events not only threatened to spill over directly into the heart of the oil kingdom, but also vividly influenced internal developments. From our Ethiopian-Saudi perspective, the more important aspect of Saudi developments in the 1980s was the return of rigid, fundamental Wahhabism to the center of the kingdom's politics and to the Saudi conceptualization of the self and the other.

   The Saudi family, to be sure, remained in full control.[50] When King Khalid died in 1982, he was smoothly succeeded by Crown Prince Fahd, who could safely rely on the loyalty of his close, full brothers. However, the ruling elite was now facing new challenges that required some reemphasis within the old Saudi-Wahhabi formula. In addition to the external threats of Soviets, radical Shi'ites, and Iraqi expansionists, the kingdom was suffering from a drastic decline in oil prices (from US\$40 a barrel to \$15 in the early 1980s). The new need for cuts in the subsidized benefit system left over from the happy Faysal days now combined with the inescapable strategic need to rely more openly on the United States. The facts that the Custodians of the Holy Places now had to depend on non-

Muslims for protection and the urban, educated circles had come under socioeconomic stress created new ideological tensions, which were further fomented by regional storms. On 20 November 1979, a band of Wahhabi extremists led by radical Islamicist Juhayman al-'Utaybi took over the Kaaba Grand Mosque during the pilgrimage. Juhayman proclaimed himself the *mahdi*, or messiah, and was captured within a fortnight and executed. The incident heralded the period of the 1980s as one of growing Islamic radicalism. Graduates of the kingdom's institutions of higher education, which had mushroomed under Faysal, were no longer automatically hired and were discriminated against compared to graduates of Western universities. As many of the latter tended to voice grievances on liberal grounds, the former were mainly inclined to reintroduce Wahhabi puritan fundamentalism as a challenge to the Saudi rulers. (Disturbances by the Shi'ites of the eastern provinces, in November 1979 and February 1980, added to the social and religious tensions.) The new generation of radical Islamicists did not only revive puritan Wahhabism (which had been restrained since Ibn Sa'ud defeated the *Ikhwan* in 1929), it also came under the influence of Muslim Brothers and other radicals who had escaped from Sadat's Egypt, Saddam Hussein's Iraq, and other countries and found shelter and followers in Saudi Arabia. These—together with Saudi growing insecurity following Sadat's 1979 peace with Israel—added new dimensions of Islamic militancy and subversive experience (to which I shall return in the following chapter).

To cope with the new opposition groups, the regime resorted to emphasized religiosity. In line with the old Saudi-Wahhabi formula, established scholars were again encouraged and organized in order to identify and legitimize the system. Islamic leaders loyal to the regime— like those affiliated with MWL circles or members of the *Ifta'* [Islamic jurisprudence] council headed by Shaikh 'Abd al-'Aziz bin 'Abdallah bin Baz—did serve the system loyally but also magnified their own influence, also abroad, through their intercontinental network. Unlike the Horn of the 1980s, the Arab world in general, and Saudi Arabia in particular, deepened their religiosity, politically and culturally. Liberal voices, also challenging the system, were occasionally raised. The Saudi press, richer and more widespread than ever before, enabled some dialogue and arguments. Criticism of the Saudi government, to be sure, was never allowed, but descriptions, analyses of, and debates concerning other societies were tolerated. There, between the lines, in discussing others, some words suggesting self-criticism could be inserted.[51]

During the 1980s, dozens of articles dealing with Mangistu's

Ethiopia and its Muslims appeared in the Saudi press. Most of them resorted to harsh language in describing the plight of Muslims and their overt discrimination by the "Crusade regime" of the Derg.[52] Some were less ideologically oriented, more informative and concrete.[53] Their detailed contents and terminology cannot be analyzed here. I shall confine myself to presenting a debate reflecting a rather liberal approach on one hand, and the voice of fundamental Islamicism on the other.

### A Moderate Voice

Here again, an attempt to follow the main concepts inevitably leads to the various interpretations of the initial, formative episode of the Prophet's relations with the king of Ethiopia. We can try to follow some of the basic Saudi attitudes in the 1980s through the study of an exchange of ideas over *Islam al-najashi* in 1981–1982, in the monthly *Al-Faysal*.

Issued in the mid-1970s in Riyadh by the "Al-Faysal Cultural House," this monthly represented the more modernizing wing of the Saudi elite (which had been led by King Faysal). It hosted writers from other countries and addressed issues of culture, literature, and society, focusing mainly on Islamic affairs. It did so with an air of some openness, and with an emphasis on academic style (most articles, including the two discussed here, have footnotes). The following debate can indeed be seen as reflecting a general tension in Saudi Arabia between moderates and conservatives within the establishment over interpretations of Islam itself, tension that heated up following the "Kaaba incident" of 1979. The year 1979 was also the beginning of the fifteenth Islamic century, an occasion that further energized such principled, historical debates.

In its November 1981 issue (number 55), *Al-Faysal* hosted Iraqi scholar, engineer, and historian 'Abd al-Jabar Mahmud al-Samara'i of Baghdad University. Al-Samara'i can be described as a moderate Islamicist who advocated mutual understanding between Islam and the West. In that light, he published a booklet on Edward Said's famous *Orientalism*, accusing the latter of overcriticizing Western scholarship.[54] Al-Samara'i's article for *Al-Faysal* appeared in a special section devoted to the new Islamic century. It was entitled "The Letters Sent by the Prophet to the Rulers of the Neighboring Countries."[55]

Al-Samara'i's main point is that the Prophet was a great statesman who had the vision to resort to international diplomacy even prior to the solidification of his early Islamic state. The Prophet thus molded Islam's international relations and paved the way for Islam's expansion. Most of the article is indeed a survey of Muhammad's letters to the eight contemporary rulers. The survey is based on various sources, traditional Islamic as well as modern scholarly literature, including the works of modern Arab thinkers, mainly liberal Egyptians. In analyzing the texts of the letters, and after examining some that were alleged to have been preserved, al-Samara'i doubts their authenticity. He repeats the argument, based on scientific examination, that they were actually written at a later period. Al-Samara'i concludes, therefore, that the whole story of Muhammad's letters and the contents of his correspondence are still in need of further research.

Of direct interest to us is how al-Samara'i dealt with the Muhammad-*najashi* exchange. Here again he allowed himself to directly follow the rationality of Western scholarship. After careful scrutiny of the texts—two letters of the Prophet to the *najashi* and the latter's response—he reached the following conclusion:

> From what we are told here [it is clear that] the saying about *Islam al-Najashi* is exaggerated. It is impossible to conclude [anything] from what the *Najashi* did out of courtesy and generosity in responding to the Prophet's call. If *al-Najashi* had indeed converted to Islam at that time, Islam would have spread all over Ethiopia, and her Christianity would have disappeared. But Islam began spreading in Ethiopia only later, and only in her south and east. (p. 74)

Moreover, in footnote 35, referring to the traditional Islamic view that the name of the famous *najashi* of Ethiopia was Ashama, al-Samara'i adds that "modern researchers have shown that the Aksumite king at the time of the Prophet was named Armah II, or Armaha." He thus actually challenged the very validity of the *Islam al-najashi* story. Al-Samara'i's source for this assertion was the Arab-language book of Egyptian Ethiopianist 'Abd al-Majid 'Abidin, *Between the Ethiopians and the Arabs*, published in Cairo in the 1940s. 'Abidin was a student of Murad Kamil, Egypt's leading Ethiopianist and a Christian Copt.[56]

His main source, however, was another Egyptian, Muhammad 'Abdallah 'Inan, and particularly 'Inan's book, *Decisive Junctures in the History of Islam*, first published, in Arabic, in 1929.[57] In fact, an entire chapter of 'Inan's book, entitled "Diplomacy in Islam—the Prophet's Missions" (pp. 202–209), was practically copied by al-Samara'i word for word (the quote above from al-Samara'i is taken directly from 'Inan, p. 207). 'Inan was one of Egypt's leading liberals during the interwar period, a prolific, Western-oriented scholar who worked diligently to free the educated Egyptian public of traditional concepts and instill scholarly rationality instead. He advocated solidarity among all "Eastern peoples" based on inner "Oriental" pluralism and mutual tolerance.[58] 'Inan did more than just challenge the *Islam al-najashi* concept. In 1935, when Mussolini threatened to invade Ethiopia, 'Inan became one of the more prominent Egyptian liberals to identify with Haile Selassie. He strongly denounced Mussolini and refuted the Fascists' propaganda, including its seemingly anti-Ethiopian, pro-Islamic elements. In that, 'Inan at the time found a common cause with Egypt's Islamic modernists, headed by Shaikh Muhammad Rashid Rida, who—as discussed in Chapter 3—worked to persuade Ethiopia's Muslims to unite under their Christian emperor and corresponded with King Ibn Sa'ud trying, in vain, to convince him to join in this effort. The pro-Mussolini camp in Egypt of 1935, on the other hand, included a militant Islamic wing. Many of its members were inspired by the *Islam al-najashi* slogan and the hope that the conquering Italians would politically revive Ethiopia's Islam.[59] By refuting the tradition of *Islam al-najashi* in the Saudi Arabia of 1981, al-Samara'i expressed the voice of those who not only accepted Ethiopia as a non-Islamic, neighborly "other," but also, in the same vein, hoped to enhance the cause of openness in Saudi Arabia.

### The Voice of the Muslim World League

Al-Samara'i's article in the Saudi monthly *Al-Faysal* can be added to the vast Islamic literature that, over the centuries, emitted a spirit of tolerance toward Ethiopia and legitimized her Christian culture. In Saudi Arabia in the early 1980s this voice of moderation was apparently not isolated, and for a while it was even echoed in MWL's circles. For example, in the September 1982 issue of the league's English-language *Muslim World League Journal*, Z. I. Oseni discussed "The Prophet's Contact with Africa." He concluded that "until further research into the religious life of Negus al-Asham brings forth more useful results on this issue, let us, for the time being, be content with the undisputable fact that the Negus al-Asham was well disposed towards the Muslims to such a point as to host some of them in his country, and recognize their leader, Muhammad. . . ."[60] However, the radicals would soon regroup to dictate the MWL's conceptualization of Ethiopia.

In July of 1982, eight months after publishing al-Samara'i's article, *Al-Faysal* published a response—an article entitled "*Islam al-Najashi* and the Reliance on Islamic Sources in Linguistic and Islamic Studies."[61] Its author was Mahmud Shit Khattab (1919–1999), another

Iraqi-born scholar. Khattab graduated from the Iraqi military academy in 1937 and participated in the 1948 war against Israel. In 1958, already a general, he was discharged from the army by the new Iraqi revolutionaries who deemed him overly religious. He then turned to writing and in the same year published his first history book, *The Prophet, the Commander*, on the military dimension of Muhammad's career. He went on to publish some sixty books in Arabic, most on Islamic military history, including *History of the Prophet's Army* and *The Holy War in Islam*. When acting as an editor of the *Arab Military Encyclopedia*, Khattab moved to Cairo. In August 1980, he contributed an article to the *Journal of the Saudi National Guard* on "Collective War in Islam." An article on Khattab, published in July 2000,[62] mentioned that he had joined various Islamic and Arabic Language and Culture Societies in many Arab capitals. More to the point, he was a member of the Founding Council of the MWL in Mecca, where he actually resided. (In the *Al-Faysal* article discussed here, Khattab also lamented the decline of Islamic studies in Hussein's Iraq, which may explain why some Iraqis like himself and al-Samara'i preferred to publish in Saudi Arabia.)

Khattab's article is a harsh attack on al-Samara'i. It contains three major arguments: First, that all those who rely on Western scholarship when addressing Islamic history are no less than traitors. Second, that *Islam al-najashi* is a fundamental truth and that Islam failed to triumph in Ethiopia because of her self-serving priesthood. Third, that when studying the Islamic past, only classical Islamic sources should be consulted. The sources he specifically recommends are those that depict Christian Ethiopia in most negative terms.

The attack on modern scholarship, and on Muslims and Arabs who contribute to it, is in the opening section, *"Masadir* not *maraji'"* (pp. 73–74). Both *masdar* (pl. *masadir*) and *marja'* (pl. *maraji'*) mean "source" in modern Arabic, and in many dictionaries they appear identical. Khattab, following the Islamic fundamentalist line, uses *masdar* in its classical meaning, namely an authentic, early Islamic source, written in a period of direct Godly inspiration. *Marja'* for him is a man-made, much later secondary source, and therefore already contaminated by external interpretation. Scholarship, he argues in the strongest language, must be based on *masadir* only. The early Islamic sources cannot be wrong. Any interpretation contradicting their truth is heresy or a plot. He then goes on to refute the validity of the entire Western scientific approach, stating that Christians and Jews cannot understand Islam and that their relevant scholarly works should be categorically ignored. Not only can they not really understand the essence of Islam and of the

Arabic language, but they are also guided by imperialist and Zionist motives, and their aim is the destruction of Islam. The negation or even the doubting of *Islam al-najashi* by Western historians, he states, is part of the effort to undermine Islam. Muslims and Arabs who resort to such literature, those who go to Western universities and return poisoned with their methods, are even worse than the Christians and the Jews, he says. He checked the footnotes of al-Samara'i's article, he adds, and they are all *maraji'*. He thoroughly checked al-Samara'i's source for refuting the rationality of *Islam al-najashi* (Khattab would not even mention Muhammad 'Abdallah 'Inan by name). He found that "this source" used a mixture of *masadir* and Western historians. To cite such works, he charges al-Samara'i, is to spread the word of Islam's enemies. At the end of his article, Khattab repeats his harsh attack on such "collaborators with imperialism and Zionism," and calls to purge them all from Arab universities and the public media.

The second main theme of the article appears under the section "Disproving the Liars" (pp. 75–76). It contains some arguments from the *masadir* brought to refute the idea that the *najashi* was merely being polite in responding to the Prophet's call. One of Khattab's assertions is that the reply of the Christian ruler of Egypt was no less gentle, yet no Islamic source reported that the Egyptian had accepted Islam. His other contention—repeating an old argument—is that the Ethiopian clergy would not allow their newly converted Muslim king to spread his new religion. To solidify this argument, Khattab describes the Christian priesthood as integrally involved in politics, always in control of material assets and in pursuit of profit. According to his analysis, it was for this reason that Christian states were never really able to separate spiritual religiosity from state politics. In that context, he brings an example from Poland, where forty years of communist government could not uproot the hold of the clergy on the land, implying that Mangistu's Ethiopia combined communism with Christian corruption and heresy. Islam's holy men were never really involved in material affairs, he states, which enabled Islam to remain tolerant toward minorities. Christian states, on the other hand, were always oppressive and Ethiopia was no exception. While the members of the *sahaba* in Ethiopia tried to help the Muslim *najashi*, the priests sided with his enemies and brought about his downfall.

Time and again, Khattab returns to his total negation of Western scholarship on Islam—claiming it is all based on Christian and Jewish twisting of the sources. In a section entitled "On the *masadir* of the *hadith* [tradition] and the *fiqh* [jurisprudence]" (pp. 76–78), he makes his third main point by giving a list of the legitimate, authentic sources for the *Islam al-najashi* issue. The fourteen books he lists, he says, are only a sample of the relevant classical sources. Khattab then quotes them, one after the other, as they all tell the same story about the Prophet praying over the deceased *najashi* like over a departed Muslim. Anyone deviating from the words of those books, he declares, is an enemy.

Of the fourteen books listed by Khattab, two are by Taqi al-Din Ahmad ibn Taymiyya, the medieval, spiritual father of Islamic radicalism, still canonized persistently by the Saudi regime, to whose negative concepts of Christian Ethiopia we referred in Chapter 2. All the traditions regarding Ethiopia quoted by Ibn Taymiyya were naturally recycled from earlier sources. They were reinterpreted as part of his general fundamental militancy.[63] Within that conceptual framework, Christian Ethiopia, when addressed, was the embodiment of evil and danger. Nowhere in Ibn Taymiyya's writings is there a mention of the other Islamic image of Ethiopia, that of a land and a people who saved the *sahaba,* nor a mention of the Ethiopians whom the Prophet ordered to "leave [peacefully] alone."

On 23 January 1983, the MWL's nineteen-member Islamic Jurisprudence Academy (*Al-majma' al-fiqhi al-islami*), headed by the senior Wahhabi scholar of the kingdom, Shaikh 'Abdallah bin Baz, gathered in Mecca for its sixth conference. The seventh meeting was devoted to the exchange discussed above and the moderates were obviously defeated. The meeting ended with a decision (*qarar*) stating that Khattab's article, "an exemplary piece of scholarship [that] should be studied by all researchers" proved *Islam al-najashi* and should serve as a warning for those relying on foreign sources. It was therefore decided "to enact the MWL's endorsement to this article, reprint it and distribute it in Islamic journals to make its important message public."[64] Indeed, a few weeks later, Khattab's article, under the same title but somewhat expanded, reappeared in Mecca as a booklet published and distributed by the MWL.[65]

As of 1986, the MWL would become the umbrella for practically all Saudi-Islamic activities in Ethiopia, and Khattab himself went on to serve in its Islamic Jurisprudence Academy. His writings and general ideas continued to reflect those of the more fundamentalist wing within the kingdom's religious establishment. The MWL persisted in viewing all issues in the Horn—in fact in all of Africa and the world—as a chain of Islamic struggles for survival and victory. The League's *Al-'Alam al-Islami* issue of December 1983 was devoted to Africa and summarized the conflicts in Eritrea, the Ogaden, the Afars, and those of Ethiopia's Muslims in this same spirit.[66] For the Wahhabi fundamentalists, a non-Islamic Ethiopia, in whatever form—imperial, communist, pluralist—was never acceptable. Because Ethiopia's king in the days of the Prophet converted to Islam, they argued, Ethiopia was already a part of *dar al-Islam.* All her Muslims, it follows, should render Islam political and work for the reinstatement of an Islamic government in the "land of the *najashi.*" As Ethiopia turned against Islam, the jihad of Gragn should be revived. "Now when we see the renewed crusade against our brothers by the Ethiopian murderers supported by the Communists . . ." went one article, "we have to stand by them in Eritrea and the Ogaden in order to refute [the idea that] Gragn's was the last Islamic conquest of Ethiopia. . . ."[67] The MWL, it was repeated time and again, should endeavor to mobilize Saudi and other sources for the victory of Islam in Ethiopia. In April 1983, the *Muslim World League Journal* (which, we saw, had just hosted in September 1982 a moderate voice) published an article by Muhammad Saminullah, who had returned from a visit in Ethiopia. The piece, "Forsaken Muslims of Ethiopia," ended thus:

> Ethiopia has the potential of becoming a Muslim State if Muslims of that country are educated and trained on Islamic lines. This will require much hard work, devotion, planning and aid from the world of Islam to enable the Muslims to stand on their own feet and get their rightful position which has been denied to them since long. Says Almighty Allah in the Qur'an: As for those who strive for Us, We surely guide them to Our path.[68]

## 1987–1991: Mangistu Welcomes the MWL

We have followed a complex of dualities in the conceptual worlds of the Saudis, the Somalis, the Eritreans, and Ethiopia's Muslims as they made the histories addressed in this chapter. Only one voice, that of official Ethiopia, seems so far to be unidimensional, at least in one major respect. Mangistu's condemnation of the Saudis was comprehensive and total. However, this seemingly monolithic picture soon faded. When circumstances changed, it was retroactively proven, the Derg's Ethiopia was fully ready to abandon the blunt, Marxist practice and terminology. Within Ethiopia during this final period of declining Derg rule, Muslims, like Christians, became more assertive. The regime's rather confrontational policy toward religiosity in the early 1980s became overtly permissive.[69] The same was true of foreign affairs. Not only was

Mangistu now ready to mend fences with Riyadh, but he was also ready to welcome Mecca to work in Ethiopia and to promote Islam, even on the MWL's terms. For their part, the Saudis, preoccupied with the Gulf area, became less alarmed with Mangistu's Stalinism as he faltered.

In October 1984, after the Saudis gave up on the Eritreans (following the EPLF victory over the ELF), Ethiopia's minister of information visited Jedda and "expressed his pleasure at what he saw in the way of modern construction and the great achievements accomplished by Saudi Arabia under the leadership of King Fahd ibn 'Abd al-'Aziz."[70] In early 1987, when Mangistu, inflicting ever-worsening disasters on his own people, began to lose the Soviets' favor (though massive Soviet military aid continued through 1989), he began to gamble on a new strategy. He opted for renewing relations with Egypt, Israel, and Saudi Arabia, hoping to finally placate the United States. He and his men now had little difficulty courting the Saudis and holding talks "in a brotherly atmosphere on ways to further improve existing ties between the two countries, on the situation in the Red Sea region . . . [and on how to] further strengthen our growing trade relations and reflect the long-standing close ties between our two states."[71] Mangistu was reported to have committed himself not to take any actions concerning the Nile without consulting Egypt, and the Saudis and Egyptians undertook to avoid supporting the Eritreans and the Somalis. After Saddam Hussein's invasion of Kuwait, Mangistu made a special effort to join the international action against him.[72] A grateful King Fahd stated that "he whole-heartedly appreciated the stand taken and the unambiguous support provided by Ethiopia and other peace loving countries and people . . . and expressed a desire to further promote the long-standing relations between his country and Ethiopia."[73]

Mangistu's effort to survive and save his revolution through this strategy proved futile. Throughout 1987–1991, he would be beaten at home by the Eritrean and Ethiopian liberation fronts. Neither the Saudis nor Islam played meaningful roles in these developments, which led to his downfall. It was, however, a period during which direct Saudi-Islamic involvement began in Ethiopia. Back in 1986, the WML, already participating in helping famine-stricken Ethiopia (and in the spirit mentioned above), opened an office in Addis Ababa. On 29 January 1987, as Mangistu's new policy took shape, an agreement was signed between the league and Ethiopia's Relief and Rehabilitation Committee to build a school, an orphanage, and a clinic in Gojjam.[74] In August 1989, the league subsidized a month-long, skill-upgrading course "organized for religious and Arabic language teachers" in various regions, conducted by scholars from Imam Muhammad University in Riyadh.[75] After the warming of relations following the Iraqi invasion of Kuwait, the MWL was welcomed to expand its activities. In November 1990, the league's leadership paid a highly publicized visit to Ethiopia. Hosting the league's secretary-general, 'Abdallah al-Nasif, Mangistu "expressed his gratitude to the MWL for its assistance and pledged that the government would cooperate with the MWL in carrying out its humanitarian endeavors. . . . Recalling that Ethiopia had cherished its long-standing historical relations with the Arab world, President Mangistu noted that Ethiopia has a firm desire to further strengthen its relations with Saudi Arabia."[76]

Before leaving, al-Nasif stated that "his organization is ready to provide aid to Ethiopia in the fields of education, social and humanitarian services as well as for the implementation of various projects in the country. He disclosed that different schools are already being constructed at a cost of 3.75 million US dollars in Wollo, Harar, Addis Ababa and Debre Zeit with aid received from the Islamic Development Bank." After the fall of Mangistu and with the ensuing comprehensive opening of Ethiopia in the 1990s, the Saudi-affiliated and controlled MWL—whose concepts and aims were addressed above—would play an important role in today's redefining of the country.

## Notes

1. *Ethiopian Herald* (Addis Ababa), 23 April 1974. See articles in a similar spirit in *Ethiopian Herald*, 13 August 1974 (editorial: "Religious Reforms"); 25 December 1974 ("In Keeping with Religious Freedom—Id Al Adeha Celebrated Throughout Nation": "At the ceremony in Harar, the chief administrator Ahadu Sabore [whose 1976 anti-Saudi words were quoted in Chapter 4] said that all Ethiopians must rejoice on this occasion because this is the first time that both Ethiopian Christians and Moslems are celebrating a public holiday in unison"); 25 March 1975 ("Mohammed—The Praiseworthy," an article summarizing the Prophet's life on his 1,435th birthday, the *Mawlid*: "Mohammed and Christ and their followers are now on equal footing in a socialist Ethiopia"; and the editorial of the same day, "In God We Believe": "Under the umbrella of Ethiopian Socialism, there is ample room for Christians and Moslems to strive with a singleness of purpose to work for unity. . . . Gone are the days of religious fanaticism. *Melkam Mawlid* [happy *Mawlid*]").

2. Ahmed, "Islam and Islamic Discourse in Ethiopia."

3. IGM 5318/16, Sofer (New York) to Foreign Ministry (FM), 16 October 1974, reporting on a conversation with Ethiopian Foreign Minister Zewde Gabre-Sellasse.

4. IGM 5318/16, Yafe (in Paris) to FM, 23 September 1974.

5. See Muhammad Saminullah, "Forsaken Muslims of Ethiopia," *Muslim World League Journal*, April 1983.

6. Radio Addis Ababa, 14 January 1974, British Broadcasting Corporation (BBC) Summary of World Broadcast (SWB), ME/4805/B/8.

7. See "Religious Reforms," editorial in *Ethiopian Herald*, 13 August 1974.

8. The passage above is also derived from Kaplan, "Christianity—Imperial Religion Between Hegemony and Diversity."

9. A report published in February 1982 claimed to have uncovered a document from the Ethiopian Ministry of Information and National Guidance declaring religious beliefs to be a "dangerous cancer" and outlining a plan to "uproot and destroy completely the anti-revolutionary situation that is prevalent in religious practices." It went on:

> Today, when the Ethiopian revolution is giving hope, it is evident that the places of worship have become tools to frustrate the workers' movement. Since the victory of the masses on land tenure and the eventual redistribution of church property, it was assumed that religious movements would run short of funds and the religious workers would gradually disperse, resulting in the elimination of one source of oppression. This has not happened. . . . Church and mosque workers seem to work with renewed vigor and spirit, the number of believers in both churches and mosques is on the increase. If the revolution is to attain its final goal, it is of the utmost importance to conduct a campaign against religion and to eliminate once and for all this dangerous anti-revolutionary cancer.

See the analysis "Religion" in Legum, *Africa Contemporary Record, Annual Survey,* pp. B165–B167. See more in Moten, "Islam in Ethiopia."

10. Tsehaye Debalkew, "Muslims in the Soviet Union," *Ethiopian Herald*, 8 July 1980.

11. See also Ahmed, "Islam and Islamic Discourse."

12. See, for example, *Ethiopian Herald*, 9 July 1977: "Equality of Faith in Ethiopia"; 16 September 1977: "Id Al-Fitr Celebrated Throughout Ethiopia" and "Religious Equality"; 29 March 1978: "Inter-Faith Seminar Opens at City Hall"; 19 January 1979, editorial: "Full Religious Equality Today"; 11 February 1979: "Prophet Mohammed's 1452nd Birthday Observed Here"; 31 January 1980: "Mawlid Observed Throughout Ethiopia"; 14 August 1980: "Id Al Fitr Celebrated Throughout Nation."

13. See Voice of Revolutionary Ethiopia, "Christian-Muslim Seminar," 29 March 1978, BBC SWB, Middle East (ME)/5776/B/2.

14. Ahmed, "Islam and Islamic Discourse."

15. See two pieces in *The New York Times*, 23 February, 9 March 1987 ("Ethiopians Officially Joining Ranks of Communist Nations" and "Under Marxism, Ethiopia's Christians Abide").

16. Yusuf, *Al-Rasa'il al-thalath*, p. 57.

17. Ahmed, "Islam and Islamic Discourse."

18. Ibid.

19. "Because of the invasion and encirclement of Ethiopia by reactionary enemies, only 671 Ethiopian Moslems were allowed to make the pilgrimage by air this year on account of the country's economic condition" (*Ethiopian Herald*, 22 November 1977).

20. Yusuf, *Al-Rasa'il al-thalath*, p. 118.

21. Paul Henze adds, "Not only were the Saudis alarmed by the turn toward Marxism of both the Eritrean insurgents and Mangistu's Ethiopia itself, they had long before been deeply concerned about Sudan and Somalia, where Soviet maneuvering brought both Siad Barre and Nimeiry to power. Time and again during the early 1970s, the Saudis approached the US with schemes to buy off both Sudan and Somalia with generous aid. They spent a good deal of money trying to do so, but with little basic effect" (Henze, personal commun.).

22. See Erlich, *The Struggle Over Eritrea*, chap. 7, "Arabization of the Red Sea 1975–1977."

23. See *Africa Contemporary Record (ACR)*, 1985–1986, ed. Colin Legum, vol. 18, p. B297.

24. See *Ethiopian Herald*, 9 January 1977, "Making Business in the Name of Refugees and Religion," an article translated from the Ethiopian Arabic newspaper *Addis Zaman* (Addis Ababa) of the previous Friday, which reproduced the text from *Al-Madina al-Munawwara* (Medina).

25. See David Pool's article on Sabbe, "Saudis May Have Backed a Loser," *The Times* (London), 25 August 1978.

26. *Ruz al-Yusuf* (Cairo), 26 December 1983; *Al-Jazira* (Riyadh), 1 January; *Al-Mustaqbal* (Lebanon), 7 January; *Al-Nashra* (Riyadh), 27 February 1984; Riyadh Domestic Service, 19 April 1984; *Daily Report* (FBIS, US Government), 20 April 1984.

27. See a detailed analysis in Aliboni, *The Red Sea Region*, pp. 59–73.

28. For more, see Tadesse, *Al-Ittihad, Political Islam and Black Economy in Somalia*, Chapter 2: "The History of Islamic Movements in Somalia." The quotation is from p. 17.

29. *Majallat al-Rabita* (Mecca), January 1975; 'Abd al 'Aziz Hasan al-Qadi, "What Is Now in Somalia," *Majallat al-Rabita*, April 1976.

30. *ACR*, 1976–1977, p. B333.

31. See Colin Legum, "Russians Make Secret Bid for Power Along Red Sea," *Observer* (London), 8 May 1977.

32. Aliboni, *The Red Sea*, especially p. 62. See also Gorman, *Political Conflict on the Horn of Africa*, mainly pp. 55, 61–66.

33. See Legum, "Saudi Arabia Blamed for Plot," *Observer* (London), 13 February 1977.

34. Aliboni, *The Red Sea*, p. 68; Jalata, *Oromia & Ethiopia*, pp. 126–127, 133; Gorman, *Political Conflict on the Horn of Africa*, pp. 55, 61–65.

35. See more in Henze, *The Horn of Africa*, mainly the section "Consolidation of the Soviet Relationship," pp. 152–154.

36. *Africa Research Bulletin (ARB)*, 1–30 September 1977, pp. 44–58; *ARB*, 1–28 February 1978, p. 4745; *ACR*, 1977–1978, p. B388; *Al-Watan al-'Arabi* (Paris), 23 September 1977.

37. Excerpts from "Notes on Final Phase of Mission to Mogadishu, March 1978," by Paul Henze, a member of an American diplomatic mission to the region headed by David Aaron ["Aaron mission"], which visited Ethiopia, Somalia, and Saudi Arabia in the immediate aftermath of the Ogaden War. I am grateful to Henze for this report and for his extremely valuable information and comments.

38. Riyadh home service, 6 March 1978, BBC SWB/ME, 8 March 1978.

39. Aliboni, *The Red Sea*, p. 73.

40. *Ethiopian Herald*, 28 July 1977, "The Jihad of Siad Barre."

41. Yusuf, *Al-Rasa'il al-thalath*, pp. 40, 92–117.

42. See, for example, "Leitmotif of Egyptian, Sudanese, Saudi Arabian Triumvirate," *Ethiopian Herald*, 1 March 1977; "Motives, Tactics, Agent and Timing of Imperialist Aggression in Ethiopia," *Ethiopian Herald*, 22 April 1977; "Shadows over the Red Sea," *Ethiopian Herald*, 11 May 1977; "Oil: A Tool of Imperialism," *Ethiopian Herald*, 9 June 1977; "Imperialist Plot to Stifle Revolution," *Ethiopian Herald*, 7 July 1977. This last article contained a cartoon depicting King Khalid, Sadat, and Numayri, portrayed with greedy expressions in a typical "elders of Zion" style, redrawing the Red Sea map, with King Khalid saying, "But we decided to re-christen the Red Sea as an Arab lake . . . we can also go ahead and pay in cash to label the Indian Ocean as an Arab Ocean . . . later on, all the lakes and the oceans in the world will be named after us and become ours." More articles in a similar vein: "Behind Current Somali Aggression: Saudi Arabia's Foreign Policy Objectives," *Ethiopian Herald*, 28 July 1977; "Reactionary Arab Designs on Africa," *Ethiopian Herald*, 17 December 1977; "Saudi Plans Expose Imperialists' Plots," *Ethiopian Herald*, 28 February 1978; "Oil Does Not Flow by Itself," *Ethiopian Herald*, 29 September 1978 (on exploitation of the workers in Saudi Arabia).

43. *Ethiopian Herald*, 3 June 1978.

44. Radio Addis Ababa, 31 January 1981, BBC SWB, 3 February 1981, ME/6639/B/2.

45. On 19 April 1980, the Public Broadcasting Service (US) broadcast the program "Death of a Princess," which told the story of a young Saudi princess and her lover who had been publicly beheaded in 1977 for adultery. It created a diplomatic outrage, and the Saudis threatened to break off relations with countries that broadcast it.

46. See "Press Digest," *Ethiopian Herald*, 27 March 1975, summarizing an article in the Arabic paper *'Al-Alam* (Mecca).

47. Ali Mohamad Nur, "Ethiopia and Prophet Mohammed," *Ethiopian Herald*, 9 September 1977.

48. *Ethiopian Herald*, 8 February 1979, 11 January 1980.

49. See Khalid Duran and Josh Devon, "Saudi Relief Hypocrisy—How the Kingdom Uses and Abuses 'Charity,'" 13 May 2003, in www.nationalreview. comment-duran-devon051303.asp. "Khalid Duran, a former chairman of the

Solidarity Committee for the Afghan People, is currently president of the Ibn Khaldun Society, a cultural association and intellectual forum of independent Muslims. Josh Devon is a senior analyst at the SITE Institute, based in Washington, DC" (from website).

50. The passage below is also based on Teitelbaum, *Holier Than Thou*, especially pp. 19–22; Rabi, *Saudi Arabia—Islam, Oil, Politics*, chap. 7; Buchan, "The Return of the Ikhwan."

51. In an article on "Operation Moses," Israel's 1984 action that brought thousands of Ethiopia's Jews to Israel, Saudi writer 'Imad al-Din Adib saved no harsh words in condemning both Ethiopia and Zionism in thus conspiring against the Palestinians in exchange for Israeli military aid to Mangistu. However, the article also contained the following passage: "And what is the reason for this Israeli interest in the Falashas? The answer is to be found in the importance of every Jew in the eyes of his fellow Jew. . . . The value of the individual in their eyes is the source of their strength, while the value of the individual among us is the reason for our weakness." See *Al-Sharq al-Awsat* (London), 5 January 1985. (On 29 January, Ahmad Baha al-Din responded with another piece on "Operation Moses" in the Saudi *Al-Sharq al-Awsat*. He exposed Israel as racist and warlike. Ethiopian non-Jews who penetrated Israel, he wrote, were expelled, and Israel took home only the young, leaving behind Jews unable to become soldiers or farmers.)

52. See *Akhbar al-'Alam al-Islami* (Mecca), 13 February 1984; Muhammad Saminullah, "Forsaken Muslims of Ethiopia," *Muslim World League Journal*, April 1983 ("a report that has been compiled by the author on the basis of his visit to Ethiopia" in September 1982); "The Communist Regime in Ethiopia Continuing Its Genocide of Muslims," in *Akhbar al-'Alam al-Islami*, 10 December 1984.

53. See a series of three articles on "New Ethiopia and the Solution in Eritrea," by 'Amir al-Jabiri, in *Al-Yamama* (Riyadh), 10, 17, 24 October 1984.

54. See the article "Orientalism and Islamic History in the First Centuries of Islam," *Al-Sharq al-Awsat* (London), 18 October 1999, in www.alhramain.com.text.alraseed/950/drasat/4.htm.

> In the conclusion of his book Dr. Samara'i wrote: "Oriental studies are diversified in terms of research and scholarship. Those who treat them in a total, comprehensive way are wrong. They also generalize about persons who devoted themselves to the service of sheer science and pure knowledge. We should not consider Orientalism as a unified trend or as an enemy. . . . Only a small group of Orientalists meant to damage Islam and Arabism in the service of political and imperialist interests."

55. 'Abd al-Jabar Mahmud al-Samara'i, "Al-rasa'il allati ba'atha biha al-Nabi ila muluk al-duwwal al-mujawirah," *Al-Faysal* (Riyadh), no. 55 (November 1981), pp. 71–81.

56. See 'Abidin, *Bayna al-Habasha wa-al-'arab.*

57. 'Inan, *Mawaqif hasima fi ta'rikh al-islam.*

58. For 'Inan, consult Gershoni and Jankowski, *Redefining the Egyptian Nation,* and mainly Gershoni, *Light in the Shade.*

59. See Erlich, *The Cross and the River,* chap. 6, "Stormy Redefinitions," pp. 103–121.

60. See Z. I. Oseni, "The Prophet's Contact with Africa," *Muslim World League Journal,* September 1982, pp. 8–12:

> He [the *najashi*] however, did not openly accept the message of Islam. . . . The more enthusiastic view which is widely held in Islamic circles is that he embraced Islam. This view stemmed obviously from his friendliness to the early Muslims and his display of the time-honoured trait of "African hospitality." . . . Perhaps the acceptance of Islam by the Negus was a matter of mere recognition of the Prophet and admiration of his effort to guide the people, especially the barbarous Arabians, aright. Not much is known of the "Islamic" practices of the Negus and, subsequently, of his successor. Nonetheless, until further research into the religious life of Negus al-Asham brings forth more useful results on this issue, let us, for the time being, be content with the undisputable fact that the Negus al-Asham was well disposed towards the Muslims to such a point as to host some of them in his country, and recognize their leader, Muhammad. . . .

61. Mahmud Shit Khattab, "Islam al-Najashi wal-i'timad 'ala al-masadir al-islamiyya fi al-dirasat al-lughaiyya wal-islamiyya," *Al-Faysal* (Riyadh), July 1982, pp. 73–78.

62. "Scholars of Medical or Engineering Background Who Wrote History" (in Arabic), *Jaridat al-Bayan* (Dubai), 2 July 2000.

63. The following episode attests to the sacredness of Ibn Taymiyya's writings in today's Saudi Arabia. On 22 May 2003, the daily *Al-Watan,* issued in the Saudi town of Abha, published an article signed by Khalid al-Ghanami, denouncing the recent wave of murderous activities by Islamic terrorists in Riyadh. Under the heading "Man and Country Are More Important Than Ibn Taymiyya," it reported that the killers of innocent people were directly inspired by his writings.

> Let us say it openly: our problem today is Ibn Taymiyya himself. Some of our religious men turned his writings into a sacred border one cannot cross. In our times and in our country they give him a standing he did not have in his time and in his own country. . . . They never dispute Ibn Taymiyya's words and would not allow anyone to do so. . . . We the intellectuals who know for certain where the roots of this problem are should raise our voice and declare: man, be he a Muslim or a non-Muslim, is more important for us than the thoughts of a religious thinker. Our country, which might turn into a new Algeria, is a million times more important to us than Ibn Taymiyya.

Five days after the publication of this article, the editor of *Al-Watan*, Jamal Khashuqji, was fired on instructions from the Saudi Ministry of Information. No official reason was given, but the Egyptian weekly *Al-Qahira* reported that it was because of this piece as well as the generally liberal line he followed. See *Al-Qahira*, 10 June 2003.

64. See "Hawla bahth Islam al-Najashi wal-i'timad 'ala al-masadir al-islamiyya," at www.themwl.org/Bodies/Decisions/default.

65. Khattab, *Islam al-Najashi*, pp. 31.

66. See mainly the articles "The Problems of the Muslims in Africa" and "The Movement of Eritrean Struggle," in *Al-'Alam al-Islami* (Mecca), December 1983.

67. See the article by Professor Fahim Muhammad Shaltut, "Fatra mushraqa lil-jihad al-islami fi al-habasha," in *Majallat al-Buhuth al-Islamiyya* (Riyadh), June 1985, pp. 249–268. The author analyzes Arab Faqih's "Futuh al-Habasha"—the history of Ahmad Gragn's sixteenth-century conquest of Ethiopia—as proving that Gragn's holy war was a defensive campaign.

68. Muhammad Saminullah, "Forsaken Muslims of Ethiopia," *Muslim World League Journal*, April 1983.

69. Paul Henze, who keenly toured and observed Mangistu's Ethiopia, adds this about the second part of the 1980s:

> Christian festivals all over the country drew enormous attendance. So did Muslim festivals such as *Mawlid* in Harar and gatherings at Sheikh Hussein. The great Muslim center at Al Kaso in northern Gurageland continued to function without Derg interference. Kulubi, with its manifestation of both Christian and Muslim observance combined, drew hundreds of thousands of pilgrims in the final Derg years. . . . Over time, as he tried to confront the realities of ruling and trying to prevail over all the opposition he had generated, Mangistu modified the strong anti-Christian stance he would have liked to take in imitation of Soviet dogma, but there was little change in the official stance on Islam or in early Derg measures that favored Muslims. In practice prominent Yemeni-origin trading families, such as the Bagershes, were severely dealt with. But Muslim traders in the countryside continued to carry on much as they always had. (Henze, personal commun.)

70. Riyadh Domestic Service, 26 October 1984, *Daily Report*, 29 October 1984.

71. Addis Ababa Domestic Service in Amharic, 25 April 1987, *Daily Report*, 30 April 1987.

72. *Ethiopian Herald*, 25 November 1990.

73. Ibid., 25 November 1990.

74. Ibid., 30 January 1987.

75. Ibid., 7 September 1989.

76. Ibid., 20 November 1990.

# 7

## Wahhabism and
## Ethiopian Identity

THE YEAR 1991 WAS PIVOTAL IN THE HISTORIES OF BOTH ETHIOPIA
and Saudi Arabia. Saddam Hussein's invasion of Kuwait (2 August
1990) and the ensuing Gulf War (16 January through 28 February 1991)
were arguably the most critical events in the annals of the Wahhabi
kingdom. The fact that the proud "custodians of the Holy Places" had to
rely on the American army to ensure their very existence had multidimensional repercussions. The 1990s were marked by growing internal
Saudi tensions that led to religious radicalization of both the established
circles and their various oppositions. A significant part of the fundamentalist and, in contrast, the fanatic energies thus created in Saudi Arabia
of the 1990s was channeled abroad. The global implications of this
Saudi export, and its contribution to today's international terrorism,
need no further mention here. However, a substantial portion of the
Saudi political-religious output, both fundamentalist and radical, was
diverted to the Horn of Africa. In the 1990s, the Wahhabi kingdom
became one of the most important external factors influencing Ethiopian
developments. Islamic militant radicalism, Wahhabi fundamentalism, as
well as diplomatic pragmatism continued to compete over the nature of
this Saudi involvement and over its impact on local Ethiopian forces and
options. Although the multifaceted Saudi momentum in Ethiopia seems
to have slowed after 11 September 2001, the current chapter, for all
intents and purposes, is still unfinished.

The year 1991 was even more pivotal in Ethiopian history.
Following the demise, on 28 May, of Mangistu's regime, the country
began a process of comprehensive redefinition. In many respects, the
new regime ushered in the first real revolution in Ethiopia's long histo-

ry. Led by the ex-fighters of the TPLF, the country was remolded after the Tigrean, not the Amharan, concepts of the Ethiopian world. Instead of the internal centralization of politics and culture, and the ever-recycled notion of external siege, Ethiopia began to open up both to her own diversity and to the neighboring Middle East. The major premise of this redefinition was ethnic, and in 1994 (in practice, as of July 1991), the country was officially divided into nine regional, ethnic "states." But Ethiopia's reopening also revolved around economic, social, and cultural aspects, all of which proved conducive to the reawakening of religions as dynamic identities. Ethiopian Islam and Ethiopia's various Islamic communities were quick to assert themselves as active participants in practically all spheres. The opening up of the culture and the economy and their reconnection with the external world energized major developments in Ethiopia's revitalized religiosity. Christianity was exposed to new influences from the West, and Islam resumed its direct contact with the Middle East. As in the past, the renewed Middle Eastern connection also worked toward the politicization of Islam in Ethiopia. Inspired and aided by the various trends and arms of global Islam, Ethiopia's Muslims, as of the early 1990s, again faced the dual Islamic conceptualization of their own country. Most of them, it seems, chose to identify with their Ethiopian-ness. In the spirit of Muhammad's legitimization of the "land of righteousness," they are now working to promote equality, tolerance, and to advance their new options in the opening economy. Quite a number, however—who are widely referred to in today's Ethiopia as "Wahhabis"—have begun to strive for the political victory of Islam. The intensive Saudi-Wahhabi involvement has had enormous influence over this Ethiopian Islamic revival and its dilemmas. This chapter will address these issues as they shape Ethiopia's redefinition to this day.

## The Resurgence of Ethiopian Islam

The opening of Ethiopia in the 1990s did not stem from developments in the country's center. No resistance by the educated class in the capital brought about the demise of Mangistu's dictatorship. The Amharan and Amharized intelligentsia, in spite of efforts to resist, stood little chance in the face of the crushing brutality of the Derg. Many members of the educated public found themselves—often (though not always) unwillingly—cooperating with the unifying-centralizing ethos of the regime. As in the days of Ras Asrate and Aman Andom, the path to Ethiopia's political opening had to pass through the periphery. It was through the various ethnic-regional "liberation fronts," which revolted against Mangistu, that new molds of representative politics were introduced. And it was through their 1991 victory that the centuries-old imperial unity, centralization of authority, and unification of culture were defeated. Mangistu's crudeness seems to have damaged the ancient Amharan thesis of Ethiopian "one-ness," arguably beyond repair. The Derg's failure to guide the multicultural, diverse country in ways other than centralizing intimidation paved the way for the victory of regionalism and ethnicity.

It was the Tigreans who proved more efficient at both adopting the modern politics of the "liberation front" and at leading the revolt of the periphery. The regime they established in 1991 rests on a premise totally different from almost all previous ones. No Tigrean emperor had ruled the country, except between 1872 and 1889. Under Yohannes IV, Ethiopia was indeed reconstructed as a loose federation of regional kingdoms, held together by recognition of the Tigrean military leadership, as well as by the unification of Christianity and church (in this context, Yohannes' oppression of Islam was briefly mentioned in Chapter 2). In the new version of the Tigrean concept of Ethiopia, regionalism was recycled in the shape of ethnic states, but Christian hegemony was no longer relevant. In the eyes of the new leaders, especially of Meles Zenawi (president from 1991 to 1995, prime minister as of 1995), it was interregional economic interdependence that would hold Ethiopia together. The new regime is based on the opening of a free market economy, local (state) administrative institutions, cultural and linguistic pluralism, as well as on the emancipation of ethnic identities and local historical narratives from centuries of the entrenched exclusivity of the Amharan-Christian hegemony. Though this comprehensive concept and its practical implementation by the ruling party, the Ethiopian People's Revolutionary Democratic Front (EPRDF), have been criticized in various quarters—the whole arrangement revolves around the military power of a victorious minority—it has ushered in a new era. Religions were revived and reenergized; Islam and Muslims began to find an Ethiopia of their own. As traditional Christian occupations—peasantry, soldiery, priesthood, central-state administration, and politics—became marginalized, Muslims began to thrive. The new economy boosted their professions. Local and long-distance trade, commerce, craftsmanship, entrepreneurship, and finances, all traditionally despised by Christians, became the hubs of a new economy. Muslims were quick to benefit from the new liberties and freedom of organization. Their various communities built their own institutions, headed by the Supreme Council of Ethiopian Islamic Affairs, which was connected to the regime. Internal Muslim conflicts and rivalries, which also attested to increasing democratization and to dynamic generational splits, accompanied vibrant progress on many paths.[1] The new freedom of movement abroad enabled the full restoration of the hajj, which had practically halted during the Mangistu period (Ethiopian Airlines now has to lease more planes in the hajj season). Hundreds, if not thousands, of mosques were constructed throughout the country, often with government help (in 2000 in Addis Ababa, there were some thirty mosques, while in 2004, their number was estimated at well over a hundred). They have already changed the very landscape of Ethiopia, challenging, even defying, the old Christian atmosphere. The presence of Muslims in all branches of the federal government (four ministers in 2004), in the governments and administrations of the regional states, in bureaucracy, and in academia seems to be rapidly approaching proper proportions. Clearly Muslims still do not feel or enjoy full equality, and their journals often recycle complaints about girls being mocked for venturing out in public in Islamic dress. However, in general, it seems that for the first time in history, Muslims can compete freely for a place under the Ethiopian sun. In some aspects, they even have an advantage.

Islamic culture is booming. Copies of the Quran, whose import was prohibited under Mangistu, are sold in nearly every bookshop. Islamic publishing houses issue various kinds of religious literature, on morality, law, and history.[2] A large proportion of these are Amharic translations of Arabic books from the Middle East. A glance at a shelf in one of the small bookstores in the *mercato* revealed that not all these translations are compatible with the legacies of local, popular Ethiopian Islam. *The Dependable Adviser for Boys and Girls,* by Saudi religious scholar Muhammad al-Sa'im, attempts to educate the youth in a strict Wahhabi spirit and advises against nearly everything entrenched in local Ethiopian Islamic customs. *The Religion of Godly Revelation Is Islam,* by Saudi 'Abd al-'Aziz bin 'Abdallah al-Hamidi, has been translated into Amharic (1994) by the Al-Da'wa and Islamic Culture Association with warm thanks to Saudi Prince Turki bin Fahd for his help; *With the Hijra to Ethiopia,* by Egyptian scholar Muhammad Shakir, recycles the notion that Ethiopia as a whole was part of the "land of Islam." The writings of Sayyid Qutb, the Egyptian spiritual leader of the Muslim Brothers (hanged by the Nasserite regime in 1966), author of *The Future of this Religion,* included discussions on what he viewed as the eternal enmity of Christians and Jews toward Islam. Qutb called for correcting and defending the true religion from those who have been influenced by the West and have brought upon Islam a new period of ignorance and heresy. He preached that this should be done by small groups of youngsters who should disconnect from society, purify themselves in the periphery, and return to capture power in the center and thus redeem Islam. Recycling and readapting some of Ibn Taymiyya's ideas, Qutb inspired a whole generation of radicals all over the world, including those in Saudi Arabia who, in the 1990s, would spread terrorism around the globe.[3] We shall turn to the influence of these Saudi radicals on Ethiopia's Muslims later in this chapter.

By and large, in spite of such influences, it seems that most Muslims in Ethiopia's capital have remained loyal to their own apolitical traditions. They do their best to channel the new momentum toward redefining Ethiopia as a sphere of religious equality. The new Ethiopian Islamic press reflects this effort, but also its inherent tensions.[4] As restrictions on journalism were removed, newspapers mushroomed in Addis Ababa, numbering nearly a hundred in 1992, many of them private, some even openly oppositional. Muslim entrepreneurs (like the owners of the Al-Najashi publishing house) were quick to enter the field. As analyzed by Hussein Ahmed, in the period of 1996–1998, there were eight local Islamic papers, all with classical Arab-Islamic names, but all printed in Amharic, with some space for Arabic summaries. The issue of the language of Islam is indeed the crux of the matter. Ethiopian Islam, to reiterate, was never united, institutionalized, or persistently political in part because it continued to be conducted in local Ethiopian languages. Islam—observed in Amharic, Orominya, Afar, Sidama, Tigrinya, and Somali—went on popularly combining tenets of orthodoxy, Sufism, and local customs. Arabic was used in some urban centers, notably Harar, Addis Ababa, and Massawa; in regions like Wallo and Jimma; and in the few institutions of higher learning. It was mostly foreign factors, those who had tried throughout history to undermine the Christian hegemony, who worked to introduce and spread Arabic: the Arab Peninsula scholars of Ahmad Gragn, the Italian Arabists of Mussolini, the pan-Arab activists of Nasserism. Conceived as the language of Islamic unity and politicization, Arabic, whenever introduced, was indeed confronted by the champions of the Christian hegemony. The cases in point of Haile Selassie and of Mangistu were discussed earlier.

Most leaders of the established Islamic community in the capital indeed seem quite cautious about the advantages of the new cultural permissiveness regarding Arabic. Nearly all published literature, journals, official statements, judicial sentences, and sermons in mosques are in Amharic. However, Arabic is being systematically introduced through classes in Islamic schools and in mosques, the spread of teach-yourself pamphlets, and imported books. The *mercato* bookstores are full of Saudi, Egyptian, Libyan, Sudanese, and other publications. The young generation of Ethiopian Muslims is apparently attracted to Arabic. For them, it is both the language of deeper piety as well as an avenue to business with and jobs in the richer Arab world. The process of Arabization of Ethiopian Islam, though not necessarily rapid, seems to be steady and perhaps inevitable. The long-term implications on the country's interreligious relations cannot as yet be foreseen.

The vibrant Ethiopian-Islamic press publishes unlimited information on various relevant issues. Here we shall only draw some points from the ongoing discussion of Ethiopia's Islamic history. In line with a major theme of this book, this intra-Islamic discussion always leads to the various interpretations of the "first *hijra*" to Ethiopia, and also reflects the concepts and dilemmas of Ethiopia's Muslims.

Between September 1992 and February 1993, the monthly *Bilal* (named after Bilal ibn Rabbah, the first Ethiopian follower of the Prophet in Mecca, the first *mu'adhdhin*) published a series of six anonymous articles on "Islam in Ethiopia." As analyzed by Tim Carmichael,[5] they were written by at least three different authors. The six articles naturally focused on the formative story of the relations between the *najashi* and the early Muslims. The first three articles hardly mention the classical Islamic contention that the Ethiopian Christian king himself finally adopted Islam. They tell the story in a way that depicts the Ethiopian king as a benevolent, righteous Christian who saved the Muslims from the real villains, the pagans of Mecca. The third article emphasizes the point that the Christian king refused the Meccan mission's demand to extradite the Muslims even before hearing their arguments. The fourth article, apparently by another author, details the dialogue between the Muslim refugees and the *najashi*. Here also the emphasis is on the affinity between benevolent Christians and flexible Muslims. The Muslim spokesman's quotations from the Quran legitimized Jesus as a prophet preceding Muhammad. The enlightened *najashi*—unlike his far less tolerant priests—was happy thus to learn about Muhammad's acceptance of Jesus. Only in the third part of this piece is there a mention of the contention that the *najashi* later converted to Islam. Quotations are brought to prove his Islamization, but there is no further development of the argument. The legacy of that initial dialogue, asserts the article, is the long-standing mutual relevance of

Ethiopia and Islam, and that Islam and Ethiopian-ness are harmoniously compatible.

Articles five and six, observed Carmichael, were written by yet another author and carry a totally different message. It is important to relearn the history of the *najashi*, declares this author, because today's resurgence of Islam in Ethiopia should be inspired by the legacy of its truth. This truth should be openly stated: Ethiopia was the first country outside the Arab Peninsula to embrace Islam. All later rulers of Ethiopia rebelled against the fact that it was the king who accepted Islam and that consequently Ethiopia was an Islamic land. The first to rebel against the *najashi*'s Islam were his priests and opponents, and the article describes their subversive war. After the death of the *najashi*, Ethiopia's Christians gained the upper hand. To this day, the Muslims of the country have responded to their constant oppression by complaining, instead of reviving their glorious history. This is a period of Islamic momentum throughout the world, the sixth article contends, and Ethiopia, with its 65 percent Muslim inhabitants, should join this momentum.

Prior to 1991, it was very rare for an Ethiopian Muslim to mention the concept of *Islam al-najashi*. For example, an Amharic book on the life of the Prophet (first edition 1967, later editions 1987, 1988) by Hajj Muhammad Thani Habib, the imam of the capital's largest mosque, al-Anwar, narrates the story of the "first *hijra*" (pp. 47–56). It includes details on Ethiopian hospitality and a short mention of the Prophet's call to the *najashi* to accept him as God's messenger. It then very briefly and indirectly hints that the *najashi* responded positively but avoids further discussion.[6] In the new Ethiopia, after 1991, *Islam al-najashi* became a principal issue but was given a new, local meaning. Most Ethiopian Muslims mention it as a proof of Islamic-Christian affinity and of the share that Muslims had and should have in Ethiopian life. In this they are often encouraged even by Christians. In December 1997, the government of Tigray Regional State hosted a symposium in the Ahmad Negash mosque in Maqalle. In the presence of the president of Tigray and four foreign ambassadors (from Iran, Turkey, Yemen, and Libya), all discussions revolved around the assumption that the *najashi* was the "first Ethiopian Muslim King." The Islamic journal *Hikma* (Addis Ababa) followed the event, stating that the conversion of the *najashi* to Islam was an established historical fact. The statements made in the Maqalle symposium—for example, a declaration by one participant that Negash, the assumed burial place of the *najashi* and of his first Muslim hosts, was a second Mecca—triggered a stormy debate and harsh Christian responses. An official statement by the Ethiopian Orthodox

Church in April 1998 held that the whole conversion story was a later fabrication intended to create friction in a country known for its religious harmony.[7] Many Christians take *Islam al-najashi* as a slogan coined to help Muslims achieve political victory. This, we have seen time and again, was the interpretation given by Middle Eastern Islamic radicals. Moderate Ethiopian Muslims contend that by mentioning that a Muslim could be the king of the country, they were only working for equality. Nothing better reflects the mutual sensitivity and Ethiopia's Muslims' own dilemmas than the endless debate over this very first, historical Islamic-Christian meeting.[8]

Less abstract and equally reflective of these dilemmas is the figure of Shaikh Muhammad al-'Amudi. The son of a Muslim mother from Wallo, the land of Islamic-Christian coexistence, and a Saudi father from the town of Al-Lith, Muhammad al-'Amudi made a huge fortune in Arabia. After 1991, he began investing in Ethiopia's new, open economy, which he soon dominated. His company, recycling Saudi finances and integrated with Saudi networks, is involved in practically all Ethiopian spheres and monopolizes many major fields. An Ethiopian citizen and a declared Ethiopian moderate,[9] al-'Amudi donates to various charitable and educational enterprises, both Islamic and Christian. Given an honorary degree by Addis Ababa University on 1 August 2003, Muhammad al-'Amudi stated his credo as follows:

> Ethiopia is my homeland. I love this nation very dearly. . . . I also love and cherish my home Saudi Arabia, of which I am proud. That wonderful country is the reason for all my success in the business world. Being a son of both Arab and Ethiopian culture has made it possible for me to see life from different perspectives and to be able to create a bridge between the Arab peninsula and East Africa. I always try to use the opportunity to promote the cultural, social, economic and business relationships between the Arab and Ethiopian communities. I will continue to participate in all efforts to bridge the gap between the two cultures. This relationship has existed for a millennium. This, I believe, is something that I must do, in respect for the two cultures that I am molded from.[10]

Yet for many Christians, al-'Amudi is the embodiment of foreign, Saudi involvement—a new "economic Ahmad Gragn." No conversation on Islam can be conducted in today's Ethiopia without mentioning the Shaikh. On one hand, he built (in 1998) a new Sheraton hotel in the heart of Addis Ababa, which, against the striking poverty surrounding it, stands like a fabulous palace, arguably the most luxurious Sheraton in the world. It is the hub of the busy headquarters of the new economy and the symbol of what entrepreneurship, trade, and Middle Eastern connections can do for Ethiopia. On the other hand, say many Christians, he also built the new mosque over the assumed *najashi* grave in Negash, attesting to his real vision of Ethiopia's future. To this, Ethiopian Muslims respond that building mosques over graves is a reflection of the Ethiopian approach. The Wahhabi doctrine of Ibn Taymiyya and of 'Abd al-Wahhab—they tell their fellow Christians—consider grave cults as the ultimate heresy. A half-joke about the Sheraton, often shared in such conversations, provides a different angle to the meaning of the luxurious hotel. The Sheraton's regular rooms are expensive but affordable to the local business elite and their guests. However, some attached villas in the compound cost $US3,000 to 4,000 per night. They are regularly vacant; who can afford them? "It is all ready for the third *hijra*," I was told with a smile by a local Muslim. "When the corrupt Saudi regime in Riyadh collapses, their princes will fly here seeking asylum in our land of moderation and righteousness. Their rooms are already ready."

## The Saudis and Today's Ethiopia

*Pragmatism, Fundamentalization, and Bin Laden*

In the 1980s, as we have seen, the accumulating internal socioeconomic problems and the aggravated external threats led to the strengthening of religious fundamentalism in Saudi Arabia. Wahhabi purists, whose active participation in the kingdom's daily life had been restrained since 1929, returned to set the tune in various spheres. Their impact was further enhanced by the settling of Islamic radicals from other countries in Saudi Arabia and the emergence of a new generation of religious scholars who defied their elders' cooptation. In the previous chapter, we discussed the impact of this radicalization on Saudi relations with, and concepts of, Mangistu's Ethiopia. The emergence in 1991 of a new Ethiopia, its opening to Islam and to the Middle East, coincided with deepening religious radicalization of the Saudi kingdom. Some general observations about this process are necessary as background to a discussion of Saudi involvement in today's Ethiopian redefinition.

In many ways, Saudi Arabia's regime in general and Wahhabism in particular underwent significant modification in the 1990s.[11] The Iraqi invasion of Kuwait, the need to rely on the US army stationed on Saudi soil, and the dependence on non-Muslims for the removal of an Arab-Muslim threat, put the Saudi system under unprecedented internal pressure. Old socioeconomic and other grievances combined with a new sense of humiliation and energized active resentment in various quarters. The Saudi-Wahhabi formula of Ibn Sa'ud, updated by Faysal, had to be modified once more. The regime responded to the challenges through the March 1992 reforms, which will not be discussed here. Decisionmaking remained exclusively in the hands of the king and his inner circle of relatives, but compromises had to be made with centrifugal interests as well as with forces outside the family. The process of remodifying the Saudi-Wahhabi combination and its reassertion over the various tribal, regional, and social factors has barely been completed as these lines are being written. The stability and prosperity of the 1970s has long been replaced by pressing tensions. Various oppositions emerged to defy the system. Most of their activities had little to do with our Saudi-Ethiopian story. Again, it is the religious dimension of Saudi developments that sheds the most light on the connection between internal affairs and external relations.

The Saudi state continued to cultivate good relations with Ethiopia. The diplomatic rapprochement that began in 1987 has strengthened since the changes that took place in 1991 on both shores of the Red Sea. Focusing even more on the Gulf area, Riyadh was pleased to have friendly relations with Addis Ababa. The Ethiopian regime, for its part, had reason to hope for economic, strategic, and other benefits. When it came to international relations, Saudi-Arabia and Ethiopia began to enjoy reasonably good neighborliness. However, the radicalization of religiosity in the Wahhabi kingdom, and its export, made Saudi relevance to today's Ethiopia far less innocuous.

From the point of view of this study, Wahhabism itself seemed to have been redefined. What has been discussed so far as the kingdom's fundamental doctrine was never stagnant. It underwent change and had its own internal debates (as seen in Chapter 5) throughout its long dialogue with the Saudi state. Yet, though elements of its fundamentalism were long exported to various corners of the world, mostly through the MWL, Wahhabism remained essentially an internal Saudi factor. In the 1990s, this was no longer the case. Still centered on the Saudi kingdom, Wahhabism underwent further radicalization and globalization and became almost synonymous with universal Islamic militancy. Many observers, including Arab intellectuals, began to identify this new Wahhabism with international terrorism.[12]

The radicalization of Wahhabism first in Saudi Arabia seems to have stemmed from the combination of a new generation of local religious scholars who joined forces with representatives of the new urban intelligentsia. In the 1980s, the kingdom's universities dogmatically spread the kind of knowledge exemplified above as prescribed by Mahmud Shit Khattab. Foreign Islamic radicals like Khattab settled in Saudi Arabia and inspired the resentful public to add new, radical, and international dimensions to Wahhabism. The above-mentioned writings of Sayyid Qutb, as well as of other modern militants, further engraved the conceptualization of the West, of Christians, and of Jews, as eternal enemies and defined Muslim rulers who cooperated with non-Muslims as infidels. When, in August 1990, King Fahd announced he would have to rely on US might, voices from both religious circles and the academic campuses insisted that the United States, and not Saddam Hussein, was the enemy. In response, in January 1991 the kingdom's chief mufti, 'Abd al-'Aziz ibn Baz, issued a *fatwa* supporting the regime. In the traditional spirit of loyalty to the Saudi family, he declared that it was up to the rulers to decide on waging war. By justifying resorting to non-Muslims and infidels in such an acute emergency—when fighting more dangerous infidels—Ibn Baz even mentioned the Prophet's order to the first Muslims to seek asylum with the Ethiopian Christian *najashi* ("and he allowed the emigrants among the Muslims to emigrate to Ethiopia in spite of her being a Christian state since this was in the interest of the Muslims to distance themselves from the persecution of the infidels of Mecca").[13] However, the Islamic radicals, for their part, continued to challenge the established scholars and defied their exclusive right to issue *fatwas*. Their camp and their cause were further strengthened with the return in 1989 of some five thousand young activists who in the early 1980s had gone, with the government's blessing, to successfully fight the Soviets in Afghanistan. Led by Osama bin Laden—whose background, doctrine, and later history need not be mentioned here—they came back confident that they could indeed lead Islam to victory, by taking on the powers and the cultures of the West and waging a jihad against them and their partners within Islam. In Afghanistan, Bin Laden and his associates from other Islamic countries built their global network, Al-Qaida. Their aim was not only to topple the Saudi regime, but to lead their version of radical Islam, through terror and holy war, to supremacy throughout the world. In 1992, Bin Laden had to flee Saudi Arabia and found shelter in Sudan. From there, he and his associates would launch their global jihad. In this context, until 1996 the victory of Islam in Ethiopia and the Horn would, for Bin Laden, be a first step toward paving his way back to Arabia.

The facts that Bin Laden was a Saudi citizen (his citizenship was revoked in 1994), that many of his associates were Saudis, and that the Saudi establishment (for reasons outside our scope) did not entirely disconnect from his organization identified Wahhabism, in the eyes of many, with global terrorism. Wahhabism became synonymous with international Islamic militancy and was no longer an internal Saudi feature. Moreover, developments within the kingdom also added to the radicalization of its image. While the leading figures in the royal family remained the sole political decisionmakers (King Fahd, ailing seriously as of the mid-1990s was aided by Crown Prince 'Abdallah), their effort to stabilize the system required compromises. Fundamentalism and fundamentalists, previously restrained, could now dictate their norms. They did so in fields like education and the shaping of public opinion on global affairs, the Ethiopian aspects of which will be discussed soon. While the Saudi royal government continued to conduct relations with other member states of the international community, the MWL—along with other networks of NGOs—was now, more than ever, able to conduct the foreign policy of Wahhabism. In our Ethiopian context, beyond the state-state diplomatic, constructive dialogue, more significant Saudi involvement became bidimensional. The MWL, representing established, now-modified Wahhabism, intensified its dialogue with the Ethiopian Islam of the center. In parallel, Bin Laden's terrorists opened a channel of communication with those Muslims in the Horn who yearned for a victory over, not coexistence with, Christians. As in the past, the borders between these Saudi factors—state, fundamentalists, radicals—remained blurred and volatile.

*The MWL in Ethiopia*

Contemporary state-to-state Ethiopian-Saudi relations, mostly constructive, are hardly significant enough to justify being recorded here. The Saudi government helps Ethiopia financially and trade relations are good. The foreign ministries as well as the security services of both countries often coordinate activities. However, beyond this practical sphere, Saudi deeper involvement in the new Ethiopia, now acquiring central importance, was a field that Riyadh left to the MWL. The Mecca-centered organization and its affiliated associations have been spreading Saudi religious and cultural influence all over Africa and the rest of the world since the 1960s. Its Ethiopian concepts in the 1970s through 1980s were discussed above. In 1983, to reiterate, the MWL's weekly, *Al-'Alam al-Islami,* stated that "Ethiopia has the potential to become a Muslim state if Muslims of that country are educated and trained along Islamic lines." In 1986–1987, we saw that Mangistu invited the MWL to open a branch in Addis Ababa and coordinate Saudi help in various aspects. Under Mangistu's religious policy, this connection seemed little more than a curious episode. However, after the change of 1991, MWL operations added a whole new dimension to the resurgence of Ethiopian Islam.

The religious policy of the EPRDF government—an integral aspect of its decentralist strategy—opened new horizons for the MWL. As reflected in many articles in *Al-'Alam al-Islami,* the new Ethiopian regime and the league were happy to accept one another. The Saudis were given free hand to become involved in, and even control, central aspects of Ethiopia's new Islamic life. In return, the MWL often praised the new system and presented its own aims as merely promoting local progress and helping Islam to defend itself. In a series of five articles published in the MWL weekly between 21 February and 11 April 1993 and entitled, "Days in Makkale and Tigre's Town," Shaikh Babikr Darwish, the new head of the league's office in Addis Ababa, described a tour he conducted in northern Ethiopia in late 1992.[14] He told his readers that Tigre had been brutally ruined by Mangistu, and systematically deprived by Haile Selassie. In Tigre, a more tolerant land than the Amharan provinces, he wrote, Muslims had developed a higher level of religiosity and their mosques were often in much better shape than elsewhere in Ethiopia. In all the Tigrean towns he toured, he witnessed spontaneous, harmonious Christian-Islamic coexistence, even in Aksum. "The new government," he quoted a local Muslim, "won the confidence of the people, succeeded in making peace all over the country. . . . It does not discriminate against, or favor, one group over the other. . . . We, Muslims and Christians, have already resolved to work together and our unity will not be destroyed by extremists."[15] The latter, the extremists, Shaikh Darwish hinted time and again, were representatives of the now-defeated Amharan culture. Haile Selassie used to build churches in high places to overshadow the mosques, he wrote; Mangistu actively desecrated those mosques. A good part of the series is devoted to the issue of the mosque in Aksum. In 1992, the local Muslim community obtained permission from the Tigray Regional State government to build a mosque in the ancient capital. When construction began, Christians burned it down and violence followed. A committee of investigation sent from Addis Ababa arrested the Christian perpetrators. The issue galvanized public opinion. Abuna Paulos stated that Aksum was as sacred to Christianity as Mecca was for Islam. No Christian would dare to propose building a church next to the Kaaba. It was unthinkable, the *abuna* added, to build mosques on land in Aksum that covered ancient Christian churches.[16] Shaikh Darwish—formerly a Saudi journalist—quoted Muslim responses at length, especially from a Tigrinya paper. It was wrong to compare Aksum to Mecca, for Aksum was the city of all Ethiopians and was also the home of the *najashi*. Aksum should be compared with Jerusalem, shared by Muslims and Christians even when ruled by the former. The new Ethiopian government, Shaikh Darwish assured his readers, fully supported equality and justice for Muslims. Not far from Aksum, he described, a new mosque was being built—with Saudi money [Shaikh al-'Amudi's]—over the *najashi*'s grave. He reported that he proceeded to Wallo where he witnessed Islam thriving everywhere. Islamic schools of higher learning were open and busy. The Ethiopia he saw, he concluded, was true to the Prophet's description of the righteous *najashi*'s kingdom: "a land of justice in which there lives a king who oppresses no-one."

Throughout the 1990s, dozens of articles on Ethiopia and Islam were published in the Meccan weekly of the MWL, which left the strong impression that a policy of verbal restraint had been adopted. Statements about the urge to make Ethiopia an Islamic state were quite rarely made in *Al-'Alam al-Islami* (one will be mentioned below). Two relevant themes were developed time and again. First, that *Islam al-najashi* was an undisputed historical fact and that Aksum was the second place after Mecca where Islam was initially accepted. Though the Muslim *najashi* was murdered by traitorous Christians, Islam continued to spread in Ethiopia. Second, that Muslims were already an overwhelming majority in "the land of the *najashi*." Various articles contended that Muslims composed between 55 to 65 percent of Ethiopia's population, with the higher figure quoted more often.[17] Muslims were already a majority in the 1920s, the argument went on, but had always been excluded from the state's active life. Though the combined implication was clearly the need to work to redeem Ethiopia as a land of Islamic government, the air of most of the articles was rather defensive. The MWL was there to defend Muslim rights from the old Christian oppression that threatened to be revived. Africa as a whole, it was reiterated, was facing a Christian-colonialist assault, inspired by a statement the Pope was said to have made in 1992, interpreted to mean that the continent should be Christian by the year 2000. In the league's effort to stem the Christian assault on Africa,[18] Ethiopia, because of its significance to Islam, had a special place. Various articles focused on the activities of foreign missionaries in Ethiopia, their exploitation of poverty to spread Christianity with the help of Western wealth, targeting mainly Muslim orphans.[19] Islam, it was argued in *Al-'Alam al-Islami,* was not the religion of Western colonialism but rather of true democracy and justice. In spreading their word in Ethiopia, the MWL emphasized that Islam stood for political liberty and for representative systems, for full freedom of speech, and for religious tolerance. No one should be coerced to convert; there should be mutual Christian-Islamic dialogue. Freedom of debate, of argument, and of interpretation was an integral part of Islam. In one article, analyzing the Prophet-*najashi* story, it was argued that few Jews ("no more than ten") but many Christians could be righteous people.[20] Indeed, when it came to Ethiopia in the 1990s, league spokesmen rarely mentioned Wahhabi concepts of Islam.

The MWL office in Addis Ababa coordinated Saudi involvement, which was operated by various NGOs. The Saudi Islamic World Salvation Association and Al-Haramayn were in charge of welfare activities, and according to *Al-'Alam al-Islami,* by 1994 the Salvation Association had become the biggest foreign NGO functioning in Ethiopia.[21] It initiated enterprises like drilling wells, opening clinics, and distributing food on occasions such as the end of Ramadan. It also built orphanages that cared especially, though not exclusively, for Muslim boys and girls and made sure that they were educated in quranic schools and even adopted by Saudi families.[22] The MWL donated money to the construction of new mosques throughout the country, their renovation, maintenance, and salaries for the staff. It organized and financed seminars for Islamic preachers,[23] and subsidized the establishment of Islamic institutions of social, religious, and educational activities. *Al-'Alam al-Islami* and other Saudi papers often described such enterprises in Ethiopia in articles accompanied by pictures illustrating a new Ethiopian landscape: towering mosques, their minarets dominating the scene, and gatherings of Ethiopian Muslims, praying and proudly demonstrating their new status. (No mosque, however, has been built to date in Aksum.)[24]

Education was undoubtedly the sphere that the Saudis most desired to influence. The MWL subsidized countless quranic schools, classes in mosques, the publication and importation of Islamic textbooks, and so forth. Its major achievement, embodying its entire mission, was obtaining control over Addis Ababa's central Islamic school, Al-Awliya'. Established in 1958 by a Yemeni immigrant, by 1973 the comprehensive elementary, intermediate, and high school was sufficiently important to be noticed by the MWL's mission to Ethiopia of that year. During Mangistu's rule, the school was under strict governmental control, but after 1991 it began to expand rapidly. Numbering some three thousand students, Al-Awliya' became the biggest Islamic school in the Horn of Africa. In late 1991, the MWL secretary-general, 'Abdallah 'Umar Nasif, visited the school. A newly appointed management (the previous one had been accused of lowering standards) reached an agreement with the Saudis that Al-Awliya' would come under the direct auspices of the MWL. In early 1993, this agreement was endorsed by the Ethiopian Ministry of Education. At the signing ceremony, Shaikh Darwish stated that the MWL was committed to developing Al-Awliya' in a balanced way, focusing on both Islamic and general studies. Teachers were then sent from Saudi Arabia and new buildings were constructed. According to *Al-'Alam al-Islami,* not only did young Muslims enjoy the new facilities, but also a good number of Christian students, eager to learn Arabic, joined the school's classes. In 1994, the MWL's deputy secretary-general, Adnan Basha, headed a mission to Ethiopia and Eritrea. He examined the establishment of a new managing council for Al-Awliya'. He also formed another council tasked with preparing a unified curriculum for Islamic studies and Arabic language in all Islamic schools in Ethiopia.[25]

The spread of Arabic in Ethiopia was a major aim of the MWL. The Saudis subsidized publications, translations, and journals; they organized seminars for teachers and brought in experts from their country.[26] The process of the Arabization of Ethiopian Islam, to reiterate, is still in an initial phase, but its potential significance is enormous. Combined with their interest in deepening and institutionalizing Ethiopian Islam through Islam's canonic language, the Saudis also seemed to be motivated by a somewhat vague concept of Ethiopia's Arabism. We shall discuss this concept below. In practice, the MWL made a special effort to spread Arabic among Ethiopia's largest population group, the Oromos.

In 1991, the Saudis, through the MWL, began a comprehensive campaign to spread Arabic script throughout Africa. The Latin script, it was argued, twisted and colonized the continent's languages, and Africa's Islamic cultures should adopt the Arabic script, modified to suit their languages.[27] One of the languages chosen to pilot the enterprise was Orominya. *Al-'Alam al-Islami* explained as follows:

> As for the Oromo language . . . the Oromos are one of the biggest peoples in Ethiopia, they number over 20 million people. The Oromos were connected to the Arabs from the earliest phases of history. Prior to the emergence of Islam in Africa, the Oromos were among the first peoples in East Africa to host the Muslim emigrants in the days of the Prophet. They were the first Africans to follow the Holy Quran. They were the ones who undertook spreading Islam in Africa after the

Prophet's companions returned from Ethiopia to the Arab Peninsula and made their way to Medina. Their language was oral not written. Its rendering as a written language is attributed to an Arab scholar named Yusuf al-Kunayn who died in the early fifth Islamic century. . . . The Oromos adopted Islam already in the first Islamic century, their Islamic identity originates from the year 65 H. The Oromos consider themselves Arabs. Their scriptures emphasize that their great ancestor came from the Arab Peninsula and that their Arab roots stem from the two Yemeni tribes of al-Azd and al-Zaydiyya. . . . Islam has granted the Oromo defense against colonialization of their tradition and language. . . . Orominya and Arabic share the same linguistic meanings. . . . Oral traditions prove that Oromo has Arabic roots. . . . The Oromo refused to use the Latin script . . . and the Ethiopian authorities forbade using the Arabic one until 1972. The Oromo . . . are still devoted to their Islamic identity, and to the Arabism of their African language which they wish to preserve.[28]

Besides spreading pseudo-scholarship of this kind,[29] MWL activities in Ethiopia from 1991 included subsidizing the hajj and everything that would enhance Islamic awareness and cohesion. Saudi money is behind the momentous spread in Ethiopia of literature calling to adopt fundamental, Wahhabi Islam. For example, the Al-Da'wa and Islamic Culture Association in Addis Ababa is sponsored by Saudi Prince Turki bin Fahd and publishes a series of translated books like the above-mentioned *The Religion of Godly Revelation Is Islam* by Saudi 'Abd al-'Aziz bin 'Abdallah al-Hamidi (1994) and *The Fundamentals of Islam and Faith, from The Book and the True Sunna* prepared by Muhammad bin Jamil Zinu (2002). Saudi-produced books that spread Wahhabi concepts are widely distributed in Addis Ababa. One example: Ahmed al-Sowayan, *Methods of Learning & Evidential Deduction Between Sunnites & Heterodoxists,* [sic] (in English, Riyadh, 2000).

Many in Ethiopia accuse the Saudis of paying Christians, bribing them, to convert to Islam. One hears countless stories to this effect. Here I confine myself to quoting a newly converted Ethiopian Muslim interviewed in *Al-'Alam al-Islami.* "My father and grandfather were senior priests," testified the newly named Muhammad al-Iman, "they were known for their religious leadership." They were considered the most important priests who worked to help missionaries and spread Christianity, reported the MWL weekly. Now that Muhammad saw the light of Islam, he had this to tell his countrymen:

You all live in chaos and disorientation as long as you are not Muslims. Return to Islam in which you will find remedies to all your miseries. In Islam you will find peace of the spirit and of the mind. Islam is the religion of the future for all mankind. I tell you, I saw in Islam what I did not see in other religions: friendship and mutual help, mercy and compassion which exist nowhere but in Islam.

## Saudi Contemporary Concepts of Ethiopia

*School Textbooks*

The fact that the central Islamic school of Ethiopia was put under direct Saudi control, and that the Saudis were actively involved in standardizing curricula in the country's Islamic schools, necessitates a glance at the contents of the Saudi education system. The Saudi establishment's tendency in the early 1980s to compromise with hardcore fundamentalists and to allow them practically to dictate their moral and cultural norms yielded results on all levels of Saudi education. Recent studies analyzing Saudi school textbooks in the 1990s revealed systematic dissemination of hatred of Christians and Jews and the teaching of a radical Islam that aims to rule the world.[30] An eighth-grade textbook, for example, explains why Jews and Christians were cursed by Allah and turned into apes and pigs. A schoolbook for fifth graders instructs the students: "The religions which people follow on this earth are many, but the only true religion is the religion of Islam. As for the other religions, they are false as mentioned in the Koran (the *Sura of Aal 'Umran* Verse 85): 'And whoever follows a religion that is not Islam, it will not be accepted and in the Hereafter he will be among the losers.'" It went on: "The whole world should convert to Islam and leave its false religions lest their fate be hell. As mentioned in the Koran (the *Sura of Al-Nihal* Verse 125): '[I swear] by Him who holds Muhammad's soul in his hand that not one Jew or Christian who heard me and did not believe in the message that I was sent with shall die without being one of those whose fate is hell.'" The Saudi curriculum educates students on the importance of "propagating Islam in all areas of our globe, with wisdom and sound preaching." According to a Saudi weekly, the royal government invested billions of Saudi riyals to spread this kind of Islam throughout the world. The article states that "in terms of Islamic institutions, the result is some 210 Islamic centers wholly or partly financed by Saudi Arabia, more than 1,500 mosques and 202 colleges and almost 2,000 schools for educating Muslim children in non-Islamic countries in Europe, North and South America, Australia, Africa and Asia."[31]

In the 1980s and 1990s, to reiterate, the more the Saudi regime relied on Western military power, the more the radicals were allowed to educate the young. The radical graduates, who defied the system and were often diverted abroad, even indirectly helped to spread their ideas and promote their cause elsewhere. After 11 September 2001, this disastrous combination began to backfire, to the extent that even voices in Saudi Arabia began to criticize the education system and its rigid, hate-spreading messages. Here, however, in this Saudi-Ethiopian context, I shall only reemphasize that Saudi textbooks, teachers, and managers have been partially but directly shaping dimensions of Islamic education in Ethiopia since 1991, and that the Saudi "export" of radicals, headed by Osama bin Laden, had, from another angle, direct consequences on Ethiopia and its Islam.

The mention of Ethiopia itself in Saudi school textbooks was never central. Yet, as all Saudi history books begin with the emergence of Islam—earlier history is mainly discussed by way of an introduction to the great revelation—Ethiopia is often mentioned in the context of the "first *hijra*." In many of the elementary, intermediate, and secondary school textbooks, the story of the Prophet and the *najashi* is mentioned. Some books do so briefly, merely mentioning the Ethiopian's hospitality and his saving of the first Muslims. Though they never mention the Prophet's message of grace toward Ethiopia, the air of these texts is positive.[32] In a fourth-grade book on the life of the Prophet, a father explains to his son why Muhammad told the first Muslims to emigrate to Ethiopia: "The reason he chose Ethiopia was because there was a righteous and merciful Christian king in Ethiopia, and the Christians are the closest people to the Muslims in terms of love . . . and the king respected the Muslims greatly, allowing them to follow their religion."[33] An Arabic reader for the first year of intermediate schools has a chapter on jihad. It summarizes Muhammad's correspondence with the kings of Persia, Byzantium, and Ethiopia and then mentions the jihad waged against those who refused the Prophet's call—the Persians and the Byzantines, not the Ethiopians.[34] A first-year intermediate school geography textbook on the Arab Peninsula reflects some duality. On one hand, it praises the Ethiopian Christian king for saving the first Muslims, on the other hand it devotes two pages to the Ethiopians' earlier conquest of Yemen and their plot to destroy the Kaaba in the name of Christianity (in "the year of the elephant").[35] Quite a number of books continue the story of the first *hijra* to tell about the Ethiopian king's conversion to Islam, implicitly claiming that Ethiopia is a Muslim country.[36] A second-year high-school geography textbook, for example, states that 60 percent of Africans are Muslims and defines Africa as a Muslim continent. The history of Africa's Islamization, it explains, began in Ethiopia:

> The first Muslims to enter Africa were those from Mecca who were oppressed by Quraysh and whom the Prophet told to emigrate to Ethiopia. Later, with the passing of time, their number increased. They mixed and intermingled with the locals who were thus introduced to Islam, were fascinated by it, and adopted Islam faithfully, for it is the true religion of God. Thus, after the entry of Islam into Ethiopia, the number of Ethiopian Muslims continued to grow, and this was Islam's first victory on the continent.

A map attached to the text indicates the initial penetration of Islam to Africa with an arrow from Mecca to Addis Ababa.[37] The story of the first *hijra* is often discussed in Saudi academic circles. In 2002, for example, the new website of the Islamic University of Medina recycled the article "Why Was the First Hegira to Ethiopia?" by Shaikh 'Abd al-Karim 'Abd al-Salam (first published in the university's bulletin in April 1983). Its answer was that by sending the first Muslims to Ethiopia the Prophet wanted to spread the notion of Islam's universality, and that by successfully spreading it outside Arabia, and by the conversion of the *najashi*, the campaign for Islam's global victory was initiated. That the Prophet had known the *najashi* as a righteous king and that he was initially a Christian—and therefore less hostile than the Jews and the other infidels—helped the cause of Islam. No hint was made in the article about gratitude to Ethiopia, and the *hijra* to the land of the *najashi* was presented solely as a revolutionary step on the road to Islam's victory.[38] What is taught in universities and mosques can be learned indirectly from the general Saudi literature.

### General Literature

Judging by the number of newspaper articles, booklets, and books printed in the Wahhabi kingdom and circulating in Ethiopia (most of its Ethiopian-related products circulate in Ethiopia itself), the Saudis' interest in Ethiopia has grown significantly. A survey of relevant Saudi books clearly indicates comprehensive radicalization. Saudi literature since the 1990s barely contains the voices of moderation we discerned in the 1980s. It rather recycles and magnifies the voices that delegitimized Ethiopia's Christian history.

*The Characteristics of the Two Hegiras to Ethiopia* was written by

'Ali al-Shaykh Ahmad Bakr, a member of the teaching staff in the Faculty of Education, Department of Islamic Studies, King Sa'ud University, Riyadh, and published in Riyadh in 1993.[39] The purpose of the study is stated by the author in the introduction. The first *hijra* to Ethiopia, he wrote, is an understudied issue. It should be researched and raised in order to enable the deprived Muslims of Ethiopia to regain their initial glory. The 258-page book makes the following points:

*Because of the najashi's conversion to Islam, Ethiopia has always been a part of the land of Islam (dar al-Islam).* Bakr reconstructs the story of the two-part *hijra* to Ethiopia in detail. This *hijra*, argues the author, was a major victory for Islam. It was the beginning of its history as a universal message, and the beginning of Islam's presence in Ethiopia and Africa. Though the initial reason for the hegira to Ethiopia was to escape the Meccan oppressors, the main aim was to spread Islam among all nations. The *hijra* to Ethiopia ended with a great victory for Islam, because the *najashi* and some of his men were Islamized by Ja'far ibn Abi Talib, the leader of the emigrants. "It was Allah's idea to send the Muslims to Ethiopia to bring about this victory. . . . [p. 43] The *hijra* of the *sahaba* and the Islamization of the *Najashi* succeeded in breaking all mental blocks on the road to Islam's spreading in all directions. Ever since then, through all the centuries since the time of the *Najashi*, Ethiopia and the Red Sea regions of the Horn of Africa have been considered a Land of Islam [p. 181]." Ethiopia knew Islam even before most of the Arabian Peninsula knew it. The *najashi* and his men knew Arabic and were closely connected to Arabian Peninsula affairs (pp. 169–170).

*The initial victory of Islam in Ethiopia has not been properly pursued.* The book contains lengthy explanations for the fact that Islam, as an empire, turned elsewhere and neglected Ethiopia. In the early stages, Bakr explains, history gives no evidence of comprehensive Islamization in Ethiopia after the death of the *najashi*, or of a significant social change at that time compared to what happened on the Arabian Peninsula. "The *da'wa* movement in Ethiopia [after the return of the *sahaba*] was slow and weak . . . [and] Islam did not sweep Ethiopia. Later Ethiopia became isolated from the Islamic world until the emergence of the emirates to the south" (p. 246). After surveying relations between Ethiopia and the greater Islamic world, he concludes, "The attention to Ethiopia on the part of the [Middle Eastern] Muslims was too marginal. . . . Historical circumstances did not enable much attention. The result was neglect of Ethiopia's Muslims" (p. 250).

*Christianity, an oppressing religion, humiliated Islam in Ethiopia.* Throughout history the Christians denied *Islam al-najashi*. Their hatred for Islam is beyond rationality, but their denial of *Islam al-najashi* caused the local Muslims to hesitate (pp. 5–6). The righteous *najashi* chose Islam even when the *da'wa* was still in its infancy. The *najashi*, who until meeting with the *sahaba* followed Christianity, a creed of an oppressive nature, decided to leave Christianity and oppose it (p. 47). The Ethiopian Church, however, went on to implement that oppressive creed. The priests resisted and fought the *najashi* because of his humanistic ideas. Their power persisted. In modern times, the Christians did the same to Lij Iyasu, cooperating with Western powers to remove the new Muslim king. "In these two cases [the *najashi* and Iyasu] we can see the power of the priesthood. . . . They are hateful and intolerant. This is typical of all churchmen, anywhere" (p. 256).

While the 1993 *Characteristics of the Two Hegiras to Ethiopia* claimed Ethiopia for Islam on the basis of *Islam al-najashi*, the 1996 book *Ethiopia, Arabism, and Islam in History* deepened the argument.[40] Written by Muhammad al-Tayyib bin Yusuf al-Yusuf, a judge, an Islamic scholar, and a preacher in Mecca, its main premise is that Ethiopia was both Muslim and Arab.

The two-volume, 700-page book, issued by the prestigious Meccan Publishing House, is perhaps the most comprehensive study of Ethiopia produced in Saudi Arabia during the period under discussion. As it arguably best reflects the conceptualization of Ethiopia by the core fundamentalists of the Wahhabi kingdom, it is worth presenting some of al-Yusuf's major themes:

*Ethiopia is a Muslim country.* Islam, unlike other religions, is a system of justice and tolerance, introduced into Ethiopia by the Prophet's companions. The book details the story of the first *hijra* over 107 pages (vol. 1, pp. 182–289), quoting all sources attesting to *Islam al-najashi* and discussing all due implications. The Islam of the Ethiopians, it hints indirectly, is in need of more devotion and improvement, and in the introduction, the author calls on Muslims of the core countries to teach their Ethiopian fellows the fundamentals of their religion. However, the Wahhabi author makes no harsh statements in this respect. The only two pages he devotes to Sufism in Ethiopia are merely informative, even sympathetic (vol. 2, pp. 310–311). There is, on the other hand, a clear effort to show the scope and depth of Islamic piety in Ethiopia over the centuries. Twenty-seven pages are devoted to short biographies of seventy-two Islamic scholars in Ethiopia, or scholars of Ethiopian origin, who made their names in the Arab world (vol. 2, pp. 283–310). Muslims, states the author, today number 80 percent of Ethiopia's population. A 1935 book by a famous Egyptian Islamic anti-Ethiopian militant is quoted as stating that the number was then 70 percent; a book in the same vein published in the 1960s is quoted as stating that the number was 75 percent.[41]

*The Muslims of Ethiopia are Arabs.* Large portions of the book are devoted to proving that the overwhelming majority of Ethiopians are Arabs, closely related to their neighbors in the Arabian Peninsula not only by Islam but also by origin and history. The word "*al-habasha*" (Abyssinia), states the author, is an Arab term connoting a group of Arab tribes who migrated to the Horn of Africa in ancient times. He would not, therefore, use the Greek term "Ethiopia," and principally calls the country by its Arab name (vol. 1, p. 14). The aim is stated in the introduction:

> We therefore decided to write a book on the history of this country which was one of the Arab spheres, to which Arabs migrated in great waves and in various stages, and upon which they had formative impact even prior to the development of Arabic and surely after. Our book is an answer to the imperialists' plots and the Orientalists hostile to Arabism, whose arrogance is irrational. They ignored the obvious tide of Arabs which has swept the Nile valley and East Africa from ancient times, after the rise of Islam, and to this very day, uninterruptedly. . . . The imperialists try, no doubt, to separate the history of the Nile valley and East Africa from that of the Arab race. They do so in order to engrave in the consciousness of the local peoples a concept of separateness between them and the original, pure Arabism, and to think that the Arabs came to this country under the banner of Islam, and as invaders who resorted to military force. This book amends and corrects this history and proves the continuity of the Arabism of these lands for tens of centuries. It also proves that the Arabs spread their culture and urbanization in Ethiopia, molded its characteristics, and have done so since the dawn of ancient history. . . . (vol. 1, p. 11)
>
> We are therefore committed to stemming and exposing this propaganda so that it will stop harming the unity of the Arab and Islamic nation in the Arab Peninsula, North Africa and East Africa. It is for this purpose that I opened by describing the glorious past and the present connections of Arabism with the countries to which Arabs migrated in the past and in modern times. The connections between Ethiopia and the Arabs are historical and deep-rooted. These are blood connections and the sharing of common history, as you will find them detailed in this book. Historians and archeologists determined that

Arab and Ethiopian blood has mixed together in the veins of the peoples of the coast, of Ethiopia, Eritrea, Eastern Sudan and Somalia,
down to Zanzibar. (vol. 1, p. 18)

Various aspects that connect Ethiopia to Arabism are discussed
throughout. The linguistic connection is analyzed in volume 1, pp.
130–142. The ethnic connection is presented in volume 1, pp. 68–94. It
is summarized as follows:

Ethiopia's peoples are divided into three races. First, mixed, non-pure
Arab, whose color is somewhat dark. Their noses are narrow, faces
round, bodies proportional, narrow lips, smooth and long hair, medium
height. Most scholars agree that these are descendants of migrants who
came from Arabia prior to Islam. They are the majority. Second, pure
Arabs in language and origin, those who migrated after the rise of
Islam. Third, the blacks of the blacks, crooked noses, heavy lips, wide
eyes, tall, curly hair. They are descendants of the ancient Africans.
They are a minority in Ethiopia, found only in her southwest, near
Sudan, called Shanqala. (vol. 1, p. 77)

Altogether, Arabism and Islam are often mentioned inseparably, but
the general message seems to be that Arabism was the base. It preceded
Islam in laying the cultural infrastructure for Ethiopia. Islam and its
adoption came later to complete the integral connection of Ethiopia to
the Arabian Peninsula.

*The Amharas' Christianity is part of a universal plot against Islam and Arabism.*
Though Islam is a religion of tolerance, Christianity and Judaism always
plotted against it:

Islam's tolerance towards 'the people of the book' did not soften their
hostility. Their only aim is to annihilate Islam, the destruction of its
culture and mosques, and the derailing of its followers to the road of
infidelity. . . . The Jews and the Christians inherited an ancient hatred
between them, as mentioned in the Quran, but they forget their mutual
enmity when it comes to uniting in fighting Islam, its annihilation and
the dispersal of its followers. (vol. 1, pp. 6–7)

Ethiopia was one of the important theaters for such Christian-Jewish
cooperation, manifested in both the Solomonian heritage of the Amhara
kings (vol. 1, p. 135) and Jewish influence over American policy in the
region (vol. 2, p. 262). Indeed Saudi defamation of Judaism and
Zionism in today's Ethiopia resorts to the more radical terms and con-

cepts of anti-Semitism.[42] Al-Yusuf's book contains lengthy descriptions of Ethiopia's Christian kings persecuting Muslims from early medieval times to Mangistu. A good portion is devoted to Haile Selassie, the embodiment of imperial Amhara Christianity and its international plot: "After its restoration in the aftermath of World War II the Ethiopian government of Haile Selassie planned carefully, with the help of the crusading nations, enemies of Islam, a war against Islam, in order to wipe it out in Ethiopia and Christianize all Muslims there" (vol. 2, p. 275). Moreover, though nothing was said against the regime that came to power in 1991—in one context it is mentioned that the Tigreans never enjoyed the Amharas' domination—the international plot against Islam in Ethiopia only gained further momentum:

> In recent years the Christianization campaign is no longer only verbal but also by the sword. . . . The enemies of Islam are racing with time to annihilate it in Ethiopia and Christianize its followers. They resort to all means available. They are trying new ways now. They are attempting to disconnect the Muslims of Africa, and specifically of Ethiopia, from the Muslim Arabs. They spread the false lie that the Arabs are not interested in them and would not hurry to save them from hunger, while the crusades' organizations do care and help as part of general humanism. (vol. 1, p. 9)

*Ahmad Gragn's jihad was the true model of facing Islam's enemies.* What the Christians of Ethiopia consider their deepest trauma was indeed a glorious page in the history of Ethiopia:

> Responding to the Christians' persecution of the Muslims, their burning of mosques and holy books, the Muslims rose up to defend their religion. They fought until they ruled all of Ethiopia in the 16th century. The [Muslim] oppressed said: an eye for an eye, a tooth for a tooth. History wrote a golden page for them, a page of pure glory, of hard and true jihad. . . . As for the Imam Ahmad bin Ibrahim who rose up against the Christians' hatred, he responded forcefully and conquered Ethiopia for sixteen years. He was not a foreign invader, but an Ethiopian. His father was from Yeju in Wallo, and he later joined the Muslims in Adal from where he launched his defensive campaign responding to the crusades' aggression. . . . This book testifies to what the Muslims did, an act of holy jihad, of spreading Islam and of persistence lasting for centuries. (vol. 1, pp. 7, 8)

Today's defensive holy war by Islam in Ethiopia has to be aided by the greater Muslim world:

[As] the enemies of Islam are racing against time in working to annihilate it in Ethiopia and Christianize its followers . . . it is urgently vital that Arab governments and organizations step forward and help. . . . When this help comes, the Muslims will rise up with the *da'wa*, and oppose the crusaders. . . . I see that any compromise with this duty exposes Islam to danger. . . . I hereby urge Muslims to face that danger, wake up and save Islam from the claws of the missionaries. (vol. 1, p. 9)

*Ethiopian Islam should be reformed—but it should be done secretly.* The last section of the book, "Islamic Activities at the Present Time" (vol. 2, pp. 343–365), is devoted to surveying the current situation of Islam and Muslims in Ethiopia's various regions. According to the author, the situation is chaotic. Harar, for example (pp. 350–352), is a pale shadow of its past glory. Of the countless mosques and institutions of learning, only one *madrasa* was left in the town (called the Awbidal Institute).

The development and strengthening of this institute is possible if the following is executed:
- Training/reeducating [*tadrib*] the local scholars, who lack teaching qualifications because even the greatest local scholars of Ethiopia never studied in a modern way.
- Training the students in proper methods to raise their standards, so that they are able to resist all temptations [i.e., local customs, Sufi ceremonies, etc.] which so far local scholars proved unable to remove.
- *Financing the various Madrasas in secret ways [turuq khafiyya] so that the enemy is unable to discern them. These ways can be found in coordination with those who guide the local loyal believers and manage their affairs.* (vol. 1, p. 350, italics added)

We shall not discuss here the countless items published on Ethiopia in the press during the 1990s. The majority reflect the same spirit—an exposure of historical Christian Ethiopia, indeed the very concept of Ethiopia, as Islam's enemy. Even the MWL's weekly, *Al-'Alam al-Islami,* which, as mentioned, usually exercised restraint toward Ethiopia and praised the EPRDF regime for its tolerance, occasionally joined in taking this line. On 20 July 1998, for example, it published a long article by Mahmud Bayumi under the headline: "The Biggest Campaign of Christianizing Muslims in East Africa: Christianizing Camps for the Liquidation of Muslims' Faith in Ethiopia. Twisted Translations into Amharic of the Holy Koran and Its Meanings." It opens with the narrative of Ethiopian history from the sixth-century, abortive Ethiopian attempt to destroy the Kaaba and their ensuing betrayal of the Muslim *najashi*, through their hostile strategy of uniting with the medieval Crusades and then with modern Western imperialism against Islam in both the Middle East and the Horn of Africa. The article then details accusations against the current regime of what was summarized in the headlines. It ends with a survey of Ethiopia's oppression of the Ogaden and of the Afar Islamic peoples, calling for the victory of Muslims over a government that is behind a campaign to Christianize the Islamic majority in Ethiopia.

## Radicalization and Peripheries

### Bin Laden and the Horn of Africa

While the MWL, representing Saudi fundamentalism and its methods, worked to influence Ethiopia's Islam mainly through Ethiopian institutions, "Saudi-exported" Islamic militancy worked mostly on Ethiopia's periphery. In 1992, as mentioned, Osama bin Laden left Saudi Arabia (his citizenship was revoked in 1994) and moved to Sudan. He and his men made Khartoum their main base and the headquarters of their international operations and would remain there until May 1996, when they were forced, following American and Saudi pressure on Sudan, to move to Afghanistan. In Khartoum, Bin Laden joined with Hasan al-Turabi, the leader of Sudan's Islamic militancy and the closest associate at the time of Sudan's ruler, General 'Umar al-Bashir. Al-Turabi, an intellectual and a theoretician, had developed a comprehensive ideology that derived from Sunni, Shi'i, and Sufi philosophies to combine liberal aspects of Islamic democracy (such as women's rights and social planning) with a violent anti-Western approach in the vein of Sayyid Qutb and the Muslim Brothers. A rival to what he considered Wahhabi rigidity and Saudi cooperation with the Western enemy, in 1991 al-Turabi, the leader in Sudan of the National Islamic Front, initiated the establishment of the international Popular Arab and Islamic Conference as a radical alternative to both the Arab League and the Saudi-led Organization of the Islamic Conference. Al-Turabi and Bin Laden found common ground in their anti-Western global vision and in their aim of gaining Islamic victory through terrorism. Sudanese involvement in promoting Islamic militancy in Ethiopia climaxed on 26 June 1995 when Sudan assisted an Egyptian terrorist group in a failed assassination attempt against Egyptian President Husni Mubarak when he visited Addis Ababa. This event resulted in the sharp deterioration of relations

between Ethiopia and Sudan, which continued to deepen up to the outbreak of the Eritréan-Ethiopian war in May 1998 when Addis Ababa and
Khartoum drew closer (and even more so a year later when al-Turabi
broke with Bashir and was arrested). The Sudanese input in Ethiopia in
the 1990s was arguably no less meaningful than the Saudis'. Khartoum
became the main source of external, militant Islamic interference,
including Al-Qaida.[43]

An important element of the ideology behind Al-Qaida should have
led to an emphasis on Ethiopia's role in Islam. The concept of *hijra*, as
reinterpreted by Sayyid Qutb—namely, leaving one's motherland to
regroup elsewhere in the service of the global victory of pure Islam—is
central to their theory and practice. Praising ideological emigrants is a
recurring theme on their websites. However, mentioning the "first *hijra*"
to Ethiopia is quite rare. This cannot be explained other than by the wish
to avoid any mention of a righteous, non-Islamic other. One exception
was the description of the *najashi* rescuing the *sahaba* by Al-Qaida
activist and thinker Faris al-Shawil al-Zaharani, alias Abu Jandal al-
Azdi (arrested in Saudi Arabia in August 2004). On the "Forum of
*tawhid* and jihad" website, he told the story of the *hijra* to Ethiopia
(spanning eight pages).[44] He only indirectly alludes to the fact that the
*najashi* was Christian. His emphasis is on the bravery and resolve of the
Muslim emigrants. He then quotes Sayyid Qutb's words on the first
*hijra* (from his book *Under the Shade of the Koran*, 1954), praising the
self-sacrificing pioneer Muslims, with no mention of non-Muslims. The
same "Forum of *tawhid* and jihad" published a summary of a book by
Muhammad Qutb (Sayyid's brother), *On the Implementation of the
Shari'a*, published in Mecca in 2000. Muhammad Qutb had moved from
Egypt to Saudi Arabia, where he became a professor of Islamic studies
and an inspiration for Ayman al-Zawahiri, Bin Laden's mentor. The
"Forum of *tawhid* and jihad" quotes Muhammad Qutb depicting
Ethiopia as still being a land of oppressive Christianity, resorting to the
same negative, harsh terminology used by Islamic radicals when they
referred to pre-1991 Ethiopia.[45] In Al-Qaida's eyes, today's redefinition
of Ethiopia is indeed meaningless. Nothing short of an Islamic victory is
acceptable.

Bin Laden's concept of Ethiopia is part of his philosophy that Islam
needs to be actively defended globally. In 1996 he stated,

> The people of Islam suffered from aggression, iniquity, and injustice
> imposed on them by the Zionist-Crusader alliance and their collabora-
> tors; to the extent that the Muslims' blood became the cheapest and

their wealth was loot in the hands of their enemies. Their blood was spilled in Palestine and Iraq. The horrifying pictures of the massacre of Qana in Lebanon are still fresh in our memory. Massacres in Tajikistan, Burma, Cashmere, Assam, the Philippines, Fatani, Ogaden, Somalia, Eritrea, Chechnya, and in Bosnia Herzegovina took place. . . . All this, and the world watches and listens, and not only did they not respond to these atrocities, but also, through a clear conspiracy between the USA and its allies, . . . the dispossessed people were even prevented from obtaining arms to defend themselves.[46]

Of the fourteen places he chose to illustrate the global picture, the inclusion of three areas in the Horn of Africa reflects its importance in Bin Laden's eyes at that stage. It was rooted more in practicality than principle. As long as he was based in Sudan, he viewed the Horn of Africa as the way back to Saudi Arabia. This area is still considered a "soft underbelly," suitable for harboring his international terrorism.

The Turabi–Bin Laden common effort of 1991–1996 cannot be discussed here. In the Horn of Africa, they worked together to help, directly and indirectly, those movements that identified with their vision of Islamic victory. The three main movements were the Eritrean Islamic Jihad, the Somali al-Ittihad al-Islami, and the Islamic Oromo Liberation Front. Representatives of the three movements often visited Khartoum to participate in the advisory council of the National Islamic Front and Al-Qaida.[47]

### The Failure of Eritrean Islamic Jihad

Eritrea, as we have seen throughout, was never at the head of the Saudi agenda. The Islam of the Eritreans was too Sufi-oriented and, later, overly influenced by Arab secular revolutionaries to suit the purposes of the Wahhabis. When the Marxist- and Christian-dominated EPLF defeated the more Arab revolutionary–inclined ELF in 1981, remnants of the latter moved to Egypt, Sudan, and Saudi Arabia and were exposed to more fundamental Islamic trends. Like 'Uthman Salih Sabbe and Idris Adam who, when in Saudi exile, had abandoned the terminology of Eritrean Arabism and adopted that of political Islam, quite a number of ex-ELF activists followed this pattern, trying to fill the void created by the demise of their secular, socialist, and Arab ideology. In 1981, an Eritrean Pioneer Muslims Organization (*Munazamt Arwad al-Muslimin*) was founded by ELF dissidents, and in 1983, an Eritrean Islamic Liberation Front (*Jabhat Tahrir Itiriya al-Islamiyya*) was established in Sudan. In 1988, they united, merging with three other smaller movements (whose origins can be traced to the mid-1970s), to establish the Eritrean Islamic Jihad (EIJ) and proceeded to work to fan the grievances of eastern Eritrean Muslims said to be discriminated against by the "minority Christian regime," established by Isayas Afeworki in 1991. Declaring their aim to be the establishment of an Islamic state in Eritrea, the EIJ began to perpetrate active subversion in late 1992, mainly after the arrival of Bin Laden in Khartoum. Their 1992–1996 Al-Qaida–assisted activities will not be recorded here. In Bin Laden's eyes at that time, Eritrea was an immediate target, a potential springboard to both the greater Horn of Africa and to Yemen, on his way back to winning Saudi Arabia. However, in the final analysis, Eritrea's Muslims proved less committed to *jihadi* radicalism and they were hardly a serious threat to Isayas's mobilized state. In 1993, a militant faction led by Muhammad Ahmad, said to be more closely connected to Al-Qaida than the central group of Arafa Ahmad, broke away. After 1996, however, EIJ operations began to fade away. In 1998, it changed its name to the Islamic Salvation Front and joined with other opposition movements, which have so far failed to challenge the regime or even to upset the relatively stable Christian-Islamic relations in Eritrea.

*The Somalis and the Union of Islamic Courts*

I have to be equally brief about the Somalis, although the history of their Saudi-related Islamic radicalization as of the early 1990s has a more direct impact on Ethiopian affairs. While 1991 in Eritrea ushered in independence and the establishment of a highly centralized system, in Somalia it brought about the final collapse of Siyad Barre. His ousting in January, by a coalition of warlords, ended his twenty-two-year authoritarian regime. Somali society began to fall apart, fragmented by clannish rivalries and warring militias. Somalia became an ideal environment for international terrorist networks and foreign interference, as well as for local centrifugal tendencies that soon led, de facto, to the creation of three Somali entities. It was against the background of the inherent weakness of Somali sociopolitical institutions, exposed in a deepening crisis, that Islam was readdressed as a source of potential cohesion. As in the past, politicization of Islam among the Somalis went through an external, *jihadi* campaign. As in the days of Ahmad Gragn in the sixteenth century, the "Mawla" of 1899–1921, and the Ogaden War of 1977–1978, the effort to reunite the Somalis through religious militancy had to center on the areas disputed with the Ethiopians.

With the exception of these periods of *jihadi* dynamism, Somali

Islam had never been fundamental. The old mixture of flexible ortho-doxy and Sufism was adapted to reflect, and even to strengthen, clan-nish, individualistic Somali politics. After the fall of Siyad, intermilitia warfare continued to dominate the scene. Governments that were formed in Mogadishu and other places were in no position to stabilize their authority. US, UN, and later Ethiopian interference proved inca-pable of preventing chaos. Movements aimed at re-enlivening political Islam were now given another try at providing cohesion. The reopening of Ethiopia on one hand, and Saudi involvement on the other—from Mecca as well as from Khartoum-based Al-Qaida—gave the revived Somali jihadism a new chance and added energy. There emerged a num-ber of renewed, radical movements of Islamic militancy, like al-Takfir wal-Hijra ("Excommunication and Hegira," a group of extremists who considered Bin Laden too moderate); al-Islah ("Reform, Reconciliation"), and al-Tabligh ("Making Known," linked to Afghanistan).

The leading relevant Somali movement was Al-Ittihad al-Islami, the Islamic Union. Initially established in 1978 on Saudi soil by exiles frus-trated by Siyad's regime and by the Somali defeat in the Ogaden, Al-Ittihad adopted a Somali-Wahhabi platform. It called for the establish-ment of a greater Somali state and a caliphate that would implement strict fundamentalism. As the movement swelled with graduates of Saudi and other Arab universities, and as it came under the strong influ-ence of the Muslim Brothers, Al-Ittihad connected Somali resurgent rad-icalism to international Islamicism. In the early 1980s, it was involved in sending a few hundred Somali youngsters to join the *mujahidun* in Afghanistan, and in 1984, it absorbed a number of other Somali Islamic movements. Al-Ittihad was supported throughout by Saudi NGOs affili-ated with the MWL—mainly Al-Haramayn, which, as of the early 1990s, also aided Bin Laden's Al-Qaida in Khartoum. After the 1991 ousting of Siyad Barre, Al-Ittihad led by Shaikh Dahir Aweys, an ex-colonel in Siyad's national army and a veteran of the Ogaden War, sur-faced in September to officially declare its existence and aims. Though lacking official religious training, Aweys adopted Wahhabism and gave it an even more rigid interpretation. Under his leadership, the revitalized movement strove to reform and unite all Somalis through Islamic radi-calization and to feed this momentum through a jihad in Ethiopia.

At home, Al-Ittihad declared all Sufi customs and traditions to be heretical. It forbade smoking, chewing *qat,* and performing various cults and ceremonies. Beards for men and full Islamic dress for women were enforced. Using Saudi money, Al-Ittihad built mosques, schools, and orphanages and worked to spread Arabic. At the center of these activities was the movement's effort to build a chain of local Islamic courts throughout the country. Backed by their own armed militias, these Shari'a courts enforced strict Hanbali-Wahhabi law, inflicting severe punishments: stoning for adultery, mutilation for theft. Where Siyad's state had failed and local, traditional, clannish law, revolving around blood revenge, was never able to enhance unity, the Al-Ittihad effort to replace popular Islam with puritan legalism aimed at a comprehensive religious-national revolution.

In 1993, Al-Ittihad began its threefold campaign in Ethiopia. First, it waged war on the newly established Somali Regional State of Ethiopia. Cooperating with the local underground, the Ogaden National Liberation Front, Al-Ittihad managed to perpetrate some spectacular terrorist strikes, including an attempt on the life of the Ethiopian-Somali leader, 'Abd al-Majid Husayn. Second, Al-Ittihad cooperated with the radical Muslims of the Oromos, who will be mentioned below. As in the previous historical bursts of Somali jihadism (the last occurring in 1976–1978), this was another effort to unite all the Muslim peoples of southern Ethiopia in the spirit of Ahmad Gragn. Third, they carried out terrorist actions in Ethiopia's center, culminating in the 1995–1996 explosions in Addis Ababa. All these actions were said to be supported, at least indirectly, by Al-Haramayn working under the MWL umbrella, as well as by Al-Qaida from Khartoum (the connection with Bin Laden had been made in Afghanistan).

In an effort to stem Al-Ittihad and its allies, in 1996 Ethiopia moved the action to Somalia. Its army scored a victory in a battle around the province of Luk and went on to destroy several Al-Ittihad bases. Intensive Ethiopian intervention, coordinated with the United States, influenced Somali internal affairs (which are outside our scope). The combined effect of this intervention and of Ethiopia's efficiency in stemming Al-Ittihad in Ethiopia, as well as the organization's loss of the proximity of Bin Laden's Khartoum headquarters in the same year, weakened it militarily. Shaikh Aweys had to retreat to his home region and immersed himself in studies and in further radicalizing his doctrine. In 1997, Al-Ittihad declared its transformation into a political Islamic party and came to be known as the Union of Islamic Courts (UIC). It now diverted more energy to the solidification of its hold on Somali society, focusing mainly on increasing its social and economic activities and getting support for its Shari'a courts. At the same time, it continued to perpetrate subversion in Ethiopia and support Al-Qaida activities in East Africa. Shaikh Aweys was said to be connected to the 1998 bombing of US embassies in Kenya and Tanzania and entered the US list of individuals wanted for international terrorism. In March 2002, the United States and Saudi Arabia blocked funds to Al-Haramayn's Somalia branch because of its support for Al-Ittihad and its links to Bin Laden's Al-Qaida network.

As these lines are about to go to press, in the summer of 2006, the struggle for the Wahhabization of Somali society is entering a new stage. On June 5, Mogadishu fell into the hands of the Islamic militants. The UIC had united with the other Islamic movements mentioned above and managed to oust the US- and Ethiopian-backed Somali interim government. At first the UIC showed a moderate face, presenting Shaikh Sharif Ahmad—an ideological, somewhat less anti-Western rival to Shaikh Aweys—as its leader. However, as in the past, political Islam appears to be influencing the Somalis mainly in a militant version and through *jihadi* momentum. A few weeks after capturing the capital, Shaikh Aweys was declared the leader of the ruling UIC. He proceeded to praise Osama bin Laden, to call for the redemption from Ethiopia of the Ogaden as a part of an Islamic caliphate, and to enforce a rigid Wahhabi, puritan fundamentalism that rejects and harshly punishes any indirect contact with Western culture (including watching football on television). Ethiopian forces, in a preventive step, again crossed into Somali territory in what threatens to become yet another round in an old local war, this time with a connection to international terrorism that has global consequences.

### The Oromos and the Islamic Oromo Liberation Front

While *jihadi* movements in Eritrea and Somalia could indirectly revolutionize Ethiopia's Islam, the political Islam of the Oromos threatens to dismember Ethiopia altogether. The Oromos, who number some 40 percent of Ethiopia's population, are spread throughout its core regions. Their regional state, by far the biggest in Ethiopia, has stretched over the whole center since 1991 and encircles the two federal political entities of Addis Ababa and Harar. Some of their clans had already penetrated the northern highlands in the sixteenth century, settled in Wallo, adopted Islam, and integrated well into Ethiopian history. Most of the Oromos and their southern territories were conquered in the days of Menelik II, in the last quarter of the nineteenth century. By that time, many of the Oromos were completing a sociocultural and political transformation that revolved around the adoption of Islam. Absorbed by the Ethiopian empire and integrated into its multifaceted fabrics, about half of the Oromos (estimations remain controversial) converted to Christianity.

The modern integration of the Oromos was one of the most important processes in twentieth-century Ethiopia. Its history gained heated controversial dimensions, especially after the 1974 fall of the imperial regime and the reawakening of the Oromo political identity. The Oromo Liberation Front was established in the early days of Mangistu's regime, and its leadership was mainly Christian, reflecting the Oromo elite. Though other rival organizations tried to compete, the OLF remained dominant. It led the Oromo guerrilla warfare against the Derg and then for two years participated in the new regime, established in 1991, only to break with the EPRDF government and resume the struggle for an independent Oromia. Throughout, the OLF and most of the intellectual or political representatives of Oromo nationalism downplayed the religious dimensions. They defined their Oromo identity in ethnic, linguistic, and historical terms. Though Islam, in popular local versions, was an important chapter in their history, especially in the history of their crucial meeting with the Christian empire, it has barely been readdressed in the contemporary anti-Ethiopian context. In fact, the Christian-Islamic division had more to do with inter-Oromo affairs, as Islamic activists tried to win the Oromo movement for their cause.

In 1975, Hajj 'Abd al-Karim Ibrahim Hamid, known as Shaikh Jarra Abba Gada, a native of the Harar region and a veteran of the Oromo rebellion in Bale of the 1960s, joined the newly established OLF. In charge of the eastern areas in 1982, he eliminated, and was said to have killed, a senior fellow Christian. He then established the Islamic Oromo Liberation Front (IOLF) which, until the fall of Mangistu, hardly had any impact. In 1988, he unified other Islamic factions, including the SALF, under the name of "The United Command of Oromo Jihad." However, the name of the IOLF persisted and has gained significance since 1991. While the OLF flirted with the EPRDF government (1991–1992), the IOLF accused it of betraying the Oromos' cause. The Islamic *jihadi* organization would now be boosted from all sides. The Saudi religious establishment targeted the Oromos as a main vehicle for the Islamization, and indeed for the Arabization, of Ethiopia. Saudi literature began to develop the argument that the Oromos were Arabs by origin, and in the early 1990s the MWL tried to promote a campaign for the adoption of Arabic script for Orominya. In March 1992, *Al-'Alam al-Islami* interviewed Shaikh Jarra's deputy, Shaikh Muhammad Qitta. Relaying the shaikh's message under the headline, "The Islamic People of Oromo—Historical Facts and Their Purposeful Ignoring,"[48] the weekly of the MWL told its readers that Oromos constituted 70 percent of Ethiopia's population, and that 80 percent of the Oromos were Muslims. Saudi-financed NGOs, under the umbrella of the MWL, invested in promoting their kind of Islam and its infrastructure, especially among the Oromos. Hundreds of young Oromos who had escaped Mangistu's regime and obtained scholarships to Saudi universities were now encouraged to return to Ethiopia. With the help of the Saudi NGOs, as preachers, teachers, social workers, and imams, they worked to spread Wahhabi Islam. They denounced Sufi customs, and destroyed old-styled Oromo tombstones, replacing them with orthodox, Arabic-engraved ones.[49] Ethiopian graduates of the Saudi educational system, not only Oromos, became agents of Wahhabism all over the country. In Ethiopia of the 1990s, *Wahhabiyya* became a term that described observers of strict Islamic orthodoxy who were activists for its political victory. It acquired a negative connotation among Muslims who insisted on retaining their Ethiopian-ness.

The declared aim of the IOLF was the establishment of an Islamic Oromo state. In practice, it seems to have put Islam before the Oromo identity. After 1992, it engaged in clashes with both Ethiopian authorities and with the OLF, closely coordinating its actions with the Somali Al-Ittihad al-Islami,[50] through which it was indirectly helped by Al-Haramayn. In fact, like in the days of the Ogaden War and of the WSLF and the SALF, the common jihad seems to have diminished ethnic differences. The two movements were also helped at the time by Sudan, mainly through Al-Qaida in Khartoum and its agents in Somalia and Ethiopia. The IOLF made a special, symbolic effort to unify and politicize Islam in Harar. As mentioned, by 1991 Mangistu had seen to the changing of Harar's social structure. Of some 120,000 citizens, only 7 percent remained authentic Adaris; most of the others were Oromos, Somalis, and new immigrants from the center and north. The EPRDF Ethiopian regime helped to introduce a representative system through parties and bodies reflecting Harar's new status as an administrative entity. However, the real internal struggle over the capital of Islam actually became religious. Local Oromo Wahhabi activists, most associated with the IOLF, now launched an extensive campaign against Harar's popular Islam. Targeting grave cults, *qat* chewing, youth festivities where boys and girls mingled, ceremonies like feeding hyenas, and so forth, they declared such old Sufi-inspired Harari customs heretical. Their message appealed to many Oromo natives who had socioeconomic grievances against Harar's elite. Much of Harar's land and commerce was still in the hands of the dwindling Adari community; most of their employees and the town's lower classes were Oromos. Though some of the Adaris, as we have seen, were themselves Wahhabi-inclined, most Adaris felt threatened and exposed to *takfir*—being charged as heretics.[51] It was only in 1996, in circumstances I shall mention in Chapter 8, that Harar's flexible, pragmatic Islam regrouped to begin to stem the Wahhabi-Oromo momentum. The struggle for the essence of Islam in Harar is still heated as these lines are being written.

By 1996, the initial IOLF momentum began to slow. With Ethiopian forces taking the action into Somali territory and Bin Laden ousted from Sudan, the radical Islam of the Oromos gradually lost its military sting. It was definitely losing the battle over the character of Oromo nationalism. For all intents and purposes the effort to render it militantly Islamic was overwhelmingly defeated. The process of reconstructing the Oromo collective identity that had begun in the 1970s gained momentum in the 1990s. Some half-dozen liberation fronts contributed to the political modernization of what remained strongly ethnic nationalism. The process saw the revival and reinvention of various cultural aspects and the readdressing of history as a counternarrative to the Ethiopian account. This topic is beyond our scope, with the exception of two aspects. First, the linguistic revival of Oromifa ran counter to the Saudi-Islamicist design to connect the Oromos' language to Arabic. On the contrary, in an effort to separate their history from that of "Christian-Amharic Ethiopia," the more African origins of Oromifa were emphasized. Second, the overwhelming majority of active Oromos, judging by what is reflected in their literature, websites, and so forth, conceive religious differences to be politically irrelevant. Moreover, to emphasize a common religious heritage, some spiritual leaders of Oromo nationalism work to revive awareness of *Waqqia*, their own, traditional religion.[52] The IOLF attempt to mobilize Oromo nationalism for the cause of political Islam seems to have reached a dead end. In 1999, in any case, it was practically routed by Ethiopian forces,[53] and in September 2000, the IOLF accepted the hegemony of the OLF, joining a new United Front for the Liberation of Oromifa, with the aging Shaikh Jarra agreeing to serve as deputy chairman.[54]

## Ethiopian Responses

A chain of developments has led to the apparent marginalization of the Islamicist movements described above. The 1966 ouster of Bin Laden from Sudan; the 1999 arrest of Al-Turabi in Khartoum; Ethiopian policy and the successes of the security forces in southern Ethiopia; the victory of territorial and ethnic nationalism over political Islam among Eritreans and Oromos; the global trauma of 11 September, which also shocked the Saudi establishment; the international effort against Al-Qaida; the focus of Islamic terrorism on other spots on other continents—all these combined to create the appearance that terrorist jihadism in Ethiopia is in retreat.[55] Viewed from our perspective, the momentum of militant subversive Islam in the Horn of Africa is still too fresh to be dismissed.

The challenge of fundamental Islam is surely here to stay. The resurgence of Islam in Ethiopia and the external influences analyzed above created three types of local Islam. One just mentioned is radical *jihadi* Islam. Another, fundamental Islam, can be defined as an Islam striving to redefine Ethiopian culture and working systematically, gradually, and persistently for Islam's political victory in the land of the *najashi*. In Ethiopia, followers of these aims, organized or not, are popularly called "Wahhabists." The third category is Ethiopian Muslims, those who are proud to be equal partners in a pluralist, multireligious Ethiopia, maintaining a balance between local traditions on one hand and innovations stemming from reconnecting to global Islam on the other. From every conceivable angle, it seems that these are the overwhelming majority.

Islam in Ethiopia is no longer the religion of the deprived, the marginal, and the dispersed. It is in many ways reuniting and gaining an integral share in the all-Ethiopian world. It now faces not only the surviving aspects of the old Christian hegemony, but also a struggle among its own, new versions. The same seems to be true of Christianity, whose internal transformations and splits are arguably generating more energy than the Christian-Islamic dialogues.[56]

The revolution of Ethiopia's redefinition has naturally created a most vibrant public debate involving voices from all quarters. This discussion confines itself to addressing some contemporary responses to the challenges of Ethiopian, fundamental, and radical Islam, as well as to the role of the Saudis in today's Ethiopia.

Of the dozens of relevant expressions by individuals who can be labeled moderate intellectuals, we shall quote the words of Solomon Kebede, an expert on international relations, ethnic conflicts, and globalization at the Ethiopian Institute for Peace and Development, a government-supported think tank closely affiliated with the Foreign Ministry in Addis Ababa. In February 2001, on his own initiative, Kebede published a small booklet entitled "Religion, Civilization, and

Human Rights: The Case of Islam."[57] Aiming "to serve as a baseline information for further study on the subject," it makes little mention of Ethiopia itself but is clearly designed to educate the local public about Islam. Its main message is that Islam is progressive:

> The paper is divided into three parts. The first part analyzes human rights and Islam. It states that human rights in Islam maximize the good for all, based on a proper perspective of the self. There is no room for right that encourages or allows evil and harm, or rights that pretend to confer special privileges or status to some above the other. Equity, fairness and justice are the hallmarks of Islamic human rights. . . .
>
> The second part deals with Islam and civilization. In this part analysis is made of the role Islam played in development of world civilization. It shows that during the first part of the Middle Ages, no other people made as important contribution to human progress as did the Muslims.
>
> The third part analyzes why Islam is allegedly portrayed as the enemy of Western Civilization and the Islamic world as the source of violence. . . . It indicates that there are dangerous signs that the process of creating a monolithic threat out of isolated events and trends in the Muslim world is already getting momentum. It also shows that painting Islam as anti-Western . . . is political naivete and an illogical claim charged with paranoia.

Strongly making the point that Islam should not be confused with Arabism, Solomon Kebede had few good words for Saudi Arabia. After a short discussion of its socioeconomic situation, he writes, "As the economy stagnates, resentment over corruption and wealth disparities has become more acute. . . . Saudi Arabia has far more oil wealth . . . but the tiny non-oil sector of its economy is doing poorly. . . . Significant disparities in the allocation of wealth and power in society cause another social grievance. When coupled with growing political awareness, such disparities lead individuals [in Saudi Arabia] to see the government as corrupt or as the servant of a small sector of its citizens." Altogether the message is clear: Saudi Arabia is not the model to be followed; Islam is moderate, progressive, and constructive.

In contrast to Solomon Kebede's moderation, Ethiopian journalist Alem Zelalem, residing in the United States, wrote a harsh attack on the role of the Saudis in radicalizing Islam. His article, "Saudi Arabia's Wahabism and the Threat to Ethiopia's National Security," published in September 2003 by ethiomedia.com, can be regarded as representing views of what is widely labeled as "Amhara-centrists," who oppose both the EPRDF regime and the resurgence of assertive Islam.[58] After opening with the habitual reminder of Ethiopia's grace toward early Islam, Zelalem states:

> Since there is religious tolerance in the country, Ethiopians have man-
> aged to escape destructive religious conflicts which have become
> prevalent in many parts of the world. Lately, however, there has been a
> new development in the country, which, unless timely measures are
> taken to check it, could ultimately be a destabilizing factor in the
> region. This destabilizing factor, which, next to oil, has become the
> major export item of Saudi Arabia—is called Wahabism. . . .
> Wahabism [is a] terrorist and violent form of Islam, that is responsible
> for the slaughter of thousands of innocent lives throughout the world.
> Despite this, hundreds of mosques have been built in Ethiopia in the
> last seven years with Saudi finance with all the paraphernalia of
> madrassas—supposedly Muslim religious seminaries where students
> seat cross-legged on the floor to memorize the Koran. But in actual
> fact, madrassas are brain washing sessions and jihad factories nurtur-
> ing potential Bin Ladens, where students are taught not to live under
> "infidels", and to hate Christians and Jews as a matter of religious
> duty. All the Saudi financed Mullahs—the directors of the madrassas
> are anti-American, anti-Christian and anti-Jewish. . . . Planting the
> seeds of hatred in the minds of our youth, goes contrary to our national
> cultural values and principles. After the madrassas, innocent Ethiopian
> kids are taken to various countries in the Middle East for military
> training, and then return home to participate in the meticulously
> planned and widely coordinated jihad. So far, some 5,000 have already
> been trained, . . .we need to bring an end to it, before it takes deep
> roots. . . .

In Zelalem's eyes, the Saudis' involvement renders Islam a religion of subversion and hatred. Wahhabism stands against moderation, against flexible religiosity, and therefore against the very existence of Ethiopia. He explains as follows:

> The history of Wahabism has been a history of jihad, plunder, con-
> quest, intolerance and violence. One has only to read the history of
> Wahabism and to investigate what its followers like Bin Laden are
> doing throughout the world. Their cruelty and barbarism, and their lies
> and hypocrisy, know no bounds. Historically, Wahabism is associated
> with the removal of head stones from the graves of the members of the
> family of the Prophet Muhammed. . . . Once its followers took power,
> they did whatever they could to destroy Ethiopia. Every Ethiopian
> knows this. . . . Despite what our country had done to save Islam from
> extinction, our fate became provocation, subversion, terrorism, out-
> right aggression and economic blockade, as a way of expressing their

"gratitude" to us. Let us note that these horrendous acts of barbarism have all been done against Ethiopia, in violation of the teachings and instructions of the Prophet Muhammed. Yet, they call themselves followers of the Prophet, and "custodians of the Holy Places of Islam." . . . The Wahabists know that they will never defeat Ethiopia militarily. Since they recognize that their aggression will be fiercely resisted by the people of Ethiopia, they have now changed their tactics and want to conquer us through deceit, or so they hope, without even firing a single bullet. . . .

For Wahabists, a secular state like Ethiopia that strives to create the conditions where Christians and Muslims live in peace and equality is not acceptable. Why? Because Wahabism is a religion of power. Its adherents believe that they have a command from Allah to rule the entire world and to lord every nation on earth, and to force the rest of mankind to submit to them. To that end, they use the jihad to overthrow the system of any non-Muslim country in order to establish Wahhabi authority. . . . For example, by taking advantage of the unfortunate economic conditions of the downtrodden Ethiopian masses, the Saudi Embassy in Addis Ababa is busy bribing people to convert to Islam. The usual amount that they pay is 5,000 birr, which is some $600.00.

Echoing voices that oppose the regime, he puts much of the blame on the EPRDF government:

However, the question is: who opened the doors of Ethiopia to Wahabism? Who authorized Saudi Arabia to do what it is doing today in Addis Ababa, and in the provinces of Shoa, Wollo, Gondar, Arusi, Wollega, Jimma, Harar, Sidamo, and indeed in the entire south? How much bribe did the Saudis have to pay to the corrupt and criminal authorities, who were brought to power with Saudi finance? . . . Our present economic difficulties, which will surely pass, cannot be exploited by Wahhabists to distort and to pervert our cultural values. Saudi Arabia will be strongly advised to keep its hands off Ethiopia. We did not struggle against every conceivable colonialist and imperialist power in the past, and to come thus far, only to succumb to Saudi Arabian Wahabism. That would be an insult to our history and culture. The system that prevails in Saudi Arabia may be good for Saudi Arabia, but not for Ethiopia. We find it offensive to human freedom and dignity. It is absolutely unacceptable to our way of life. Wahabism has no place in our society. The sooner the ruling circles in Saudi Arabia realize this fact and leave us alone, the better.

Here we can only quote two responses representing the public discussion energized by Zelalem's provocative piece. Under the title

"Ethiopian-ness On Trial: In the Name of Wahhabism," a Muslim by the name of Chissu wrote the following on 25 December 2003:[59]

> I am an Ethiopian and proud to be so. I belong to a nation of magnetic beauty and glorious history. I was born Muslim and proud to be so. I admire and harbor the teachings of Prophet Mohammed in one half of my heart and that of Jesus in the other. For they both preach love and tolerance: "love thy neighbor like you love thyself." . . . I am an Ethiopian, first and foremost, and wish to die so. For this reason, I condemn anyone who doubts or undermines my Ethiopian-ness, consciously or unconsciously, with a blue pen, as much as I fight all enemies of Ethiopian sovereignty, security and unity, with a red one.

Accusing Zelalem of intolerance toward Muslims' newly gained equality in Ethiopia and of wholly defaming Islam, he added:

> He holds responsible the Arabs (particularly Saudi Arabians, also Egyptians and Iranians) for financing these mosques and the "treacherous" Ethiopian government for "collaborating with international terrorists." The ultimate culprits being Ethiopian Muslims, (a) for demanding and using these mosques, (b) for betraying their Sunni religion and their country (or for selling themselves out into the "new" *Wahhabi* doctrine). . . . He unequivocally states that Ethiopia is a "non-Muslim country." This is an insult to Ethiopian-ness. . . . The whole article paints Islam as an adopted religion and "Muslims living in Ethiopia" as aliens who are only tolerated thanks to the altruism and hospitality of "Ethiopians."

As a representative of Ethiopian Islam, Chissu blames Zelalem for failing to see the positive aspects of local, authentic religious pluralism.

> The flourishing of mosques has nothing to do with Wahhabism, and every Ethiopian knows that, unlike what Alem wants us to believe. (For the benefit of those who do not know Ethiopian Islam, no mosque belongs to a particular school of Islam.) Nor are Madrassas! . . . Alem also tries, in vain, to make us believe Wahhabism is a new development in Ethiopia, the central plot of the article. The fact is it has always been there side by side with other schools of Islam. Wahhabis . . . or no Wahhabis, Ethiopian Muslims have always condemned any one who use the Qur'an to their malice political ends. They disdain Christian fundamentalists who manipulate the Bible in the name of freedom or unity or security, just as much. . . . Ethiopian Muslims are always Ethiopians, no matter what! . . . Wahhabism is just the latest, but perhaps the most dangerous, political tool of indoctrination against Islam, and is enthusiastically adopted by extreme right-wing pro-

Israeli henchmen in the Bush administration. They are very keen to convince the world that terrorism is intrinsic to Islam in general and Wahhabism in particular. . . . This is why Wahhabism squirmed under the US media spot light "like a maggot revealed under a cold light." This is why Saudi Arabians are relentlessly portrayed as potential terrorists. . . . This is why, dear readers, I am led to believe that Alem's article fits well into a pattern of Orthodox fundamentalists in Ethiopia who have always been antithetic to religious tolerance, primarily because they are obsessed with the illusory vision of "one religion, one people, one Ethiopia.". . . . It is rather sad that the only future "Alemists" foresee for Ethiopia is her past.

Under the title, "Proof of Wahhabi Activities in Ethiopia," Christian Ethiopian Hibret Selamu wrote on 15 July 2004:[60]

Erudite writers such as Alem Zelalem and Chisu have expressed various interesting and, at times, diametrically opposite views and suggestions. However, no direct and concrete evidence was provided to the readers on the evolving Wahhabi fundamentalist mischief in Ethiopia. Assumptions, however plausible, were made based on circumstantial evidence such as the mushrooming of mosques, and the mimicking of Wahhabi garb and external symbolic appearances among certain individuals in Ethiopia.

Finally, here is the concrete, unassailable evidence of actual Wahhabi/Saudi involvement in Ethiopia's religious affairs coming from the horse's mouth, so to speak, from personalities no less prominent than former senior officials of the National Ethiopian Majlis for Islamic Affairs (YeEthiopia YeIslimnna Gudayoch Teklalla Mikr Bet). According to a report that was recently published in The Reporter on Tahsas 19, 1996 E.C. (12/29/03), the two senior officials, namely, the former Secretary-General Ato (Mr.) Abdul Rezzaq and the former Chairman for Haj and Umra Services have revealed, in their open letter to the Ethiopian Prime Minister, H.E. Mr. Melles Zenawi himself, that Wahhabists were using 4 million Saudi Riyals obtained from Saudi Arabia in order to influence elections for membership of the Majlis with a view to ensuring that their fundamentalist followers would hold key positions in the council on all levels. This very interesting and extremely important article reveals further the highly corrupt methods including financial incentives used by the Wahhabists to influence not only elections but also the government bureaucracy.

The above disturbing and highly significant developments have further been corroborated by another news item that has just been published in The Monitor (Tahsas 30, 1996) (1/9/04) stating that members of the Ethiopian Majlis for Islamic Affairs have been dismissed for reasons of corruption. It is also interesting to note from the article that the loyalty of the Majlis' previous chairman, Haj Abdrahman Hussain is alleged to have been primarily for Saudi interests even at the expense of the interests of the Ethiopian Muslim society! . . . Christian Ethiopians have been facing religious persecution in Saudi Arabia. If evidence may be required regarding the harassment, imprisonment and maltreatment of Christians in Saudi Arabia (a presumably tolerant society?), one need go no further than check on numerous sources from various reliable publications and media reporting on the plight of desperate Christians who have been languishing in Saudi jails.

All Ethiopian workers, he added, suffer in Saudi Arabia:

If one still needs a further indication of the truth, one should view the Ethiopian movie entitled: "Hiywot Inde Waza" [loose translation: As If Life Were Mundane]; depicting the desperate plight of Ethiopian female workers in Saudi Arabia. Those who have worked in Saudi Arabia invariably confirm that the reality is worse than the horrors shown in the movie. The tragedy is that innocent Ethiopians have to suffer the indignity of Saudi society in order to overcome their economic difficulties. A Wahhabist society with a belief system that permits a husband to beat his wife for misbehaving would have no mercy on a female worker.

Calling all Ethiopians, whether Christians or Muslims, to resist Saudi-Wahhabi interference, he concludes as follows:

The responses to Alem Zelalem's article seem to miss the main point, namely, that there is a threat posed by Wahhabi fundamentalism in Ethiopia and that it should be resisted by all, whatever faith or religion they may be subscribing to. If there is any doubt about this, one should look at the case of Afghanistan which was taken by Wahhabists to a disastrous consequence from which that country is still struggling to survive. It is up to all Ethiopians to wake up in time and nip the Wahhabist mischief in the bud. The alternative of letting Wahhabist hegemony loose on the Ethiopian scene would have consequences that would be too dire to contemplate.

At this time, the confrontation between Wahhabism and Ethiopian-ness is far from over. It is integrally combined with other pressing regional issues, ethnic, political, strategic, cultural. The struggle between the Ethiopian interpretation of Islam and the *Wahhabiyya,* as shall be discussed in Chapter 8, has meanwhile acquired a global, intra-Islamic significance.

In both Ethiopia and Saudi Arabia, it is clear, religions will remain major shapers of identities and will continue to compete over the future of local societies. Beyond that assumption, it would be futile to guess in which direction these energies will flow.

## Notes

1. See Ahmed, "Islam and Islamic Discourse."
2. See also Ahmed, "Islamic Literature and Religious Revival"; Ahmed, "Islam and Islamic Discourse."
3. Sayyid Qutb's memories of the two years he spent in the United States (1949–1950), where he began to develop his radical anti-Western ideas, were published in 1985 in Saudi Arabia. See al-Khalidi, *Amrika min al-dahil bi-min-zar Sayyid Qutb*.
4. Ahmed, "Islam and Islamic Discourse."
5. Carmichael, "Contemporary Ethiopian Discourse on Islamic History."
6. Habib, *Eslamna enna yatalaqu nabiya yamuhammad tarik*, p. 56.
7. Ahmed, "Co-existence and/or Confrontation?"
8. See also Gori, "Una traduzione sulle origini dell'Islam in Etiopia."
9. Shaikh Al-'Amudi was often mentioned as involved in financing Osama bin Laden and other terrorist networks. Some of the rumors stemmed from confusing him (see, for example, *USA Today*, 29 October 1999) with 'Abd al-Rahman al-'Amudi, also of Ethiopian decent, and one of America's most prominent Muslim activists indicted in October 2003 for helping to finance Al-Qaida. (See *Washington Post*, 24 October 2003.) On 12 January 2000, the Eritrean embassy in Washington spread the news that Shaikh Al-'Amudi was connected to bin Laden and financed the Eritrean Islamic Jihad, all in the service of "the Ethiopian TPLF regime" (see www.AllAfrica.com).
10. Quoted from www.waltainfo.com/Conflict/BasicFacts/2003/August/State_05.htm.
11. The passage below is based also on Teitelbaum, *Holier Than Thou*, and Rabi, *Saudi Arabia: Islam, Oil, Politics*, chap. 7–9.
12. See, for example, a series of articles by leading Egyptian journalist Wa'il al-Ibrashi, in *Ruz al-Yusuf* (Cairo), 17, 24, 31 May 2003.
13. For the *fatwa*, see al-Shu'ayr, *Majmu' fatawa wa-maqalat mutanawi'a*, vol. 7, pp. 359–361. For an analysis, see al-'Atawna, "Shari'a and Politics in Saudi Arabia."
14. Al-Shaykh Darwish, "Ayam fi Makkale wa-mudun Tiqray," *Al-'Alam al-Islami* (Mecca), 21, 28 February, 14 March, 11 April, 25 April 1993.
15. *Al-'Alam al-Islami,* 28 February 1993.
16. Ahmed, "Islam and Islamic Discourse."
17. *Al-'Alam al-Islami* (Mecca), 11 October 1993, 11 July 1996.
18. See, for example, ibid., 20 July 1992, 10 June, 26 August 1996.
19. Ibid., 30 August 1993, 4 July, 5 December 1994, 10 June, 26 August 1996.
20. Ibid., 15 July 1996.
21. Ibid., 10 January 1994.

22. Ibid., 3 July, 7 September 1992, 11 March 1996.

23. Ibid., 5 August 1996, 14 July, 1 September 1997; *Al-Da'wa* (Riyadh), 22 August 1996.

24. See US Department of State, "International Religious Freedom Report 2004, Ethiopia," at www.state.gov/g/drl/ris/irf/2004.

25. See *Al-'Alam al-Islami* (Mecca), 30 December 1991, 19 September 1992, 5 April, 9 August 1993, 19 September 1994.

26. Ibid., 16 September 1991.

27. Ibid., 21 October 1991, 11 September 1995.

28. Ibid., 27 July 1998.

29. Oromos did not even come onto the Ethiopian historical stage until the sixteenth century when, in the wake of Gragn's depredations they moved from somewhere in the south into the heart of the country. The area of origin of the Oromos is still a subject of serious scholarly debate: was it northern Kenya, southern Ethiopia, south-central Somalia? What really was their "ethnogenesis"? There is substantial literature on this subject, but no widely accepted conclusion. Alleged connections between Oromifa and Arabic were never proven, and there has never been a significant body of Oromny writing in the Arabic script.

30. See Steven Stalinsky, "Preliminary Overview—Saudi Arabia's Education System: Curriculum, Spreading Saudi Education to the World and the Official Saudi Position on Education Policy," MEMRI Report no. 12, 20 December 2002, in http://memri.org/bin/articles.cgi?Page=archives&Area=sr&ID=SR01202. Quotations below are from this report. Also S. Stalinsky, "Inside Saudi Classroom," in www.nationalreview.com/comment/comment-stalinsky020703.asp; E. Doumato, "Manning the Barricades: Islam According to Saudi Arabia's School Texts," *Middle East Journal*, vol. 57, no. 2 (Spring 2003), pp. 230–247; D. Roy, "Saudi Arabian Education: Development Policy," *Middle Eastern Studies*, vol. 28, no. 3 (1992), pp. 477–508; Groiss, *The West, Christians and Jews in Saudi Arabian Schoolbooks*.

31. See Stalinsky, "Preliminary Overview."

32. Saudi Ministry of Education, *Ta'rikh sirat al-Rasul wal-da'wa al-islamiyya* [History of the Prophet's Biography and the Call for Islam], fourth year, elementary, 1999, pp. 35–36; *Al-Sira al-nabuwiyya wa-ta'rikh al-khulafa al-rashidin* [The Biography of the Prophet and History of the Righteous Caliphs], first year, intermediate, 2000, p. 27.

33. The 2001 edition of the above-mentioned *Ta'rikh sirat al-Rasul wal-da'wa al-islamiyya*, pp. 58–59.

34. Saudi Ministry of Education, *Al-Mutala'a al-'Arabiyya wa-qawa'id al-imla wal-khat*, 2001.

35. Saudi Ministry of Education, *Jazirat al-'Arab al-qadim wasirat al-nabyy*, 2001, pp. 25–27, 63–65.

36. Saudi Ministry of Education, *Al-Adab al-'arabi* [Arabic Literature], first year, secondary, 1999, pp. 65–66.

37. Saudi Ministry of Education, *Jughrafiyyat al-'alam al-islami* [Geography of the Islamic World], second year, intermediate, 1994, pp. 25–27.

38. Shaikh 'Abd al-Karim 'Abd al-Salam, "Limadha kanat al-hijra ila al-habasha?" *Majallat al-Jami`a al-Islamiyya bi-al-Madina,* Rajab 1403, pp. 215–223, in www.iu.edu.sa/Magazine/59/20.htm.

39. Bakr, *Ma'alim al-hijratayn ila ard al-Habasha.*

40. Al-Yusuf, *Ithyubya wa-al-'uruba wa-al-Islam 'ibra al-ta'rikh.*

41. These are Yusuf Ahmad, *Al-Islam fi al-Habasha,* Cairo, 1935 (see a discussion of this book in Erlich, *Ethiopia and the Middle East,* pp. 104–109, and in the 1960 underground book *The Wounded Islam in Ethiopia,* written by Abu Ahmad al-Ithyubi [a pseudonym] discussed in Chapter 4).

42. The Saudi claim that their involvement in Ethiopia is in the name of progress and democracy and that it is merely defensive is indeed hardly compatible with most of their activities. Nor are their basic concepts of Christianity, in Ethiopia and the world, compatible with their statements that their Islam is tolerant toward "the people of the book." Though Ethiopia is not allied with Israel as it was in the 1960s, the old Ethiopian Christian-Solomonian "Zionist" blend is occasionally mentioned in Saudi publications as proof of an assumed international anti-Islamic plot. In Addis Ababa's *mercato* Islamic bookstores, a Saudi book called *Zionism* is widely distributed. It makes no mention of Ethiopia but is apparently distributed to influence local youth (and, presumably, youth in other countries as well). Written in English, Dr. 'Abdallah al-Kahtany's *Zionism* has this to say on the Jews and their nature:

> The only evidence collected that Auschwitz was used as a death camp came from Rudolf Haus's [sic.] confessions that were extracted under severe torture and interrogation by British Intelligence. Such confessions can not be used as reliable evidence. Especially when having the fact that they contradict with professional opinions. The estimated number of Jews killed during the war was 300,000; much fewer than the number of Muslims killed in the Jewish Holocaust in Palestine. . . . [pp. 32–33] Genocide of Jews on the Hands of the World Zionist Movement . . . Monopolizing their strong grip on the media, the Zionists were able to make people (especially Americans and a large portion of Europeans), believe that the Nazis had eliminated six million Jews in a very short period of time. By doing so, they were able to derive sympathy from the majority of Americans towards the Jews, the Jewish cause, consequently winning them on their side. . . . [p. 34] There is very strong evidence that the Zionist leaders in charge of European Jewry were, one way or another, involved in escalating the death of Jews under German control during World War II. . . . [Their aim was] to push for the escalation of Jewish settlements in Palestine by bringing in young and skilled Jews from all over the world while eliminating the old and the disabled. . . . In the next chapter I will bring historical supporting evidence on some of the criminal practices perpetrated by prominent Zionist leaders against their own people during one of the supposedly decisive period in Jewish history. . . . [pp. 37–39] This being the mentality of the Zionist rescue officials, need-

less to say, the helpless children, old men and women were left to face
their doom in the Nazi concentration camps or in the ghettos under the
control of Zionist leaders. These leaders were in close contact with
World Zionist Organization and had close relations with high-ranking
Nazis. . . . Any action taken regarding the Jewish people in those days
was taken with the mutual consent of the Nazis and the Zionists. Both
of them considered the Jews as a commodity fit for bartering, to be
used as such to advance their heinous and ugly designs. [Chapter:
"Zionist Monopoly of Christian Sympathy," pp. 90–91]

43. See de Waal, *Islamism and Its Enemies in the Horn of Africa.* On
Sudan, see the following chapters, Alex de Waal and A. H. Abdel Salam,
"Islamism, State Power and Jihad in Sudan," pp. 71–113, and Alex de Waal,
"The Politics of Destabilization in the Horn," pp. 182–231. Also see Shay, *The
Red Sea Islamic Terror Triangle*.

44. See "Qisas ta'rikhiyya lil-matlubin" [Historical stories for those wanted, pursued by the authorities, "to raise the moral of Al-Qa'ida men through historical models"], at www.tawhed.ws.

45. See "Hawla tatbiq al-shari'a" at www.tawhed.ws.

46. See Alexander and Swetnan, *Usama bin Laden's al-Qaida,* Appendix
1, p. 1.

47. The following paragraphs on Al-Ittihad al-Islami, The Eritrean Islamic
Jihad, and the Islamic Oromo Liberation Front are based on Tadesse, *Al-Ittihad*;
Abraham Kinfe, *Somalia Calling*; Roland Marchal, "Islamic Political Dynamics
in the Somali Civil War"; Shay, *The Red Sea Islamic Terror Triangle*; Pirio,
"Radical Islam in the Greater Horn of Africa"; "The Horn of Africa: How Does
Somaliland Fit?" *The Somaliland Times,* 8 March 2003, at www.somaliland-
times.net; Ziv, "Al-Ittihad Al-Somali and Somalia"; Burr and Collins, *Alms for
Jihad*; Marquardt, "Al-Qaeda Threat to Ethiopia"; Shinn, "Terrorism in East
Africa and the Horn"; Shinn, "Promoting Stability in the Horn of Africa";
Shinn, "Ethiopia: Coping with Islamic Fundamentalism Before and After
September 11"; Gnamo, "Islam, the Orthodox Church and Oromo Nationalism
(Ethiopia)"; United States Institute of Peace, "Terrorism in the Horn of Africa";
"Counter-Terrorism in Somalia: Losing Hearts and Minds?" *Africa Report,* no.
95 (11 July 2005), at www.crisisgroup.org.

48. *Al-'Alam al-Islami,* 16 March 1992. For more on the IOLF, see *Al-
'Alam al-Islami,* 21 September 1992.

49. Paul Henze adds the following:

The destruction of Oromo traditional carved and painted tombstones
is, to the best of my knowledge, a very recent phenomenon which I
only became aware of during my little expedition in the fall of 2002. I
have been hunting out and photographing Oromo tombstones ever
since the early 1970s. I have observed them go through a fascinating
evolution during this time. In the early 1970s such tombstones in Bale
and southern Arussi usually featured only geometric symbols which

Oromo elders explained signified aspects of the deceased man's accomplishments in life (I have no recollection at this period of ever finding a female tomb). Earlier elaborately carved but unpainted tomb monuments are difficult to date but they may stem from the nineteenth century or even earlier but are no longer made. These never had Islamic symbolism, only animals and weapons, including firearms. Sometime after the mid-twentieth century Oromos began erecting square tombs with a high raised panel painted on both sides. Often all the sides of the square base were painted too or covered by colored designs. These tombs invariably had Amharic (only) inscriptions until the 1990s. There was a great efflorescence of such tomb-building during the Derg period all over the south and women began to be commemorated as well as men. These painted tombs were made both by Muslim and Christian Oromos. Neither had a great deal of religious symbolism, but almost all showed animals—bulls, horses, leopards, lions.

Oromos were very slow to use Latin Oromifa on tombs. Amharic was apparently regarded as a more formal, official language. It is only in recent years that we find Latin Oromifa inscriptions, but they do not yet predominate. In Arsi in 2002, I heard nothing of Islamic clergy advocating Arabic engraving. They were opposed to standing tombs in toto, and advocated flat burials with only a slab over the grave. The professional tomb painter we interviewed bemoaned the fact that demand for his services had recently declined sharply because of the activity of the "Wahhabis," as he referred to them. (Henze, personal commun.)

50. *The Indian Ocean Newsletter*, 6 September 1997.

51. German anthropologist Patrick Desplat studies the culture of contemporary politics of Islam in Harar. The information on the Oromos in this context is derived from his paper, "They Call Us Unbelievers, We Call Them Unbelievers," delivered at a Mainz University symposium, *Cultural and Linguistic Contacts*, 20–23 October 2004. I am grateful for additional information that he gave me on that occasion.

52. Galili, "The Religious Dimension and Separatism in the Contemporary Reshaping of Oromo Identity."

53. *The Indian Ocean Newsletter*, 31 July 1999.

54. Ibid., 7 October 2000.

55. See Alex de Waal, "Chasing Ghosts—The Rise and Fall of Militant Islam in the Horn of Africa."

56. See comprehensive analyses by Abbink, "An Historical-Anthropological Approach to Islam in Ethiopia"; Ahmed, "Co-existence and/or Confrontation?"

57. Kebede, "Religion, Civilization, and Human Rights."

58. See www.ethiomedia.com.

59. Ibid.

60. Ibid.

# 8

## Local Dilemmas,
## Global Perspectives

HUMAN BEINGS—INDIVIDUALS AND GROUPS—ARE AWARE OF THEIR own complexities. They consider themselves multidimensional beings who flexibly make conscious choices inspired by a reservoir of concepts. By the same token, they are also often inclined to ignore and even deny the versatile complexity of the "other." The historian, however, should know better. A serious observer of human affairs will usually find that history is the product of meetings among actors with multiple options. That the "other" is also complex and varied. That the "others" also act against a variety of conceptual backgrounds, expressing their own, often polarized, worlds. Historians are expected to understand this mutuality. Their interest is to comprehend multifaceted processes. Their importance lies in their effort to cope with the challenge of diversity. Their success is judged by their ability to tell history as produced by such dialectical dynamisms.

In this volume, I tried to follow the dialectics between politics and religiosity as a dimension in modern relations between an Islamic state and what used to be considered, until recently, a Christian one. I discussed the ever-changing interplay between three cultural systems: the Christian-Ethiopian, the Saudi-Wahhabi, and the Islamic-Ethiopian. None of these actors, we saw, was ever monolithic.

Ethiopian Orthodox Christianity underwent substantial changes during the seventy-five years we covered. Reaching its historical peak as a state religion under Haile Selassie, it was temporarily defeated in 1936–1941, then restored and reinvigorated, until finally, it lost its hegemony after the 1974 revolution. However, as a culture and as the identity of core Ethiopian societies and establishments, it is still very much there. For them, it is sure to remain a prime definition of the Ethiopian identity. The Christian-Ethiopian "self" was never one-dimensional. Existing in a state torn between a centralizing ethos and a decentralized environment, and a product of local cultures and imported dogmas, church and Christianity in Ethiopia often revolved around inner tensions. After 1941, but mainly under Mangistu and more so as of 1991, there emerged and developed a new dimension of Evangelical Christianity in Ethiopia, spearheaded by Pentecostalism, which stresses strict bible-centered life in a way quite different from mainstream, traditional Ethiopian culture. Relations between Ethiopian Orthodox Church members and Pentecostals have been marred by conflicts; many of the Orthodox view Pentecostalism as an alien religion.[1] The implications of this inner-Christian development on the general Christian-Islamic and on the Islamic-Islamic dynamism discussed above remained outside the scope of this study. In general, one may be impressed that the Pentecostals, driven by their more fundamental approach, are far less tolerant of the resurgence of Islam than the Orthodox, whose rather flexible set of beliefs had coexisted with local Islam for centuries. Ethiopian Pentecostals seem to perceive Islam as a foreign religion detrimental to Ethiopia's identity and national cause. Though they claim to view the Ethiopian Muslims with sympathy, they work to evangelize them, and many evangelical churches have intensified their efforts in Muslim-inhabited areas. Muslims, for their part, though they respect the stricter morals of the Pentecostals, are most suspicious of their intentions. Many Orthodox Christians say they view the Pentecostals as being more dangerous than Islam.

Islam in the Horn of Africa—at home in Ethiopia and in neighboring Middle Eastern countries—was perceived through a polarized set of Christian-Orthodox Ethiopian concepts. On one pole was the self-image of an isolated culture that strove for unity when facing the inherent enmity of a one-dimensional Islamic "other." This approach was called "the Ahmad Gragn syndrome," and we saw it manifested at major twentieth-century junctures. At the opposite pole was the self-image of a more pluralist Ethiopia with the urge to maintain contacts with the Middle East. This was labeled the "Egyptian Abuna" concept, signifying Christian-Ethiopia's opening to the neighborly lands of Islam, often combined with persistent, vivid elements of tolerance toward Ethiopia's Muslims. Indeed, all the aspects of interreligious relations discussed here reflect this dual Christian conceptualization, as it shaped, and was reshaped by, attitudes and politics.

At the beginning of the twenty-first century, it seems that most

Ethiopian Christians have emancipated themselves from the ancient siege consciousness and are ready to accept a pluralistically redefined, open Ethiopia. In spite of splits and tensions regarding the new federal system and its leadership, few voices call for the restoration of the Christian political hegemony. The overwhelming majority, it seems, favor interreligious affinity and the flourishing of religiosity outside of politics. From our perspective, however, we need to add that the "Gragn syndrome" has not entirely disappeared. Should interreligious relations be rendered political, the centuries-old Christian siege consciousness will most probably resurface. Nothing good can come of such an eventuality.

We followed Islam's diverse reservoir of attitudes toward Ethiopia. The initial polarized message of the formative Muhammad-*najashi* story, its ever-recurring debates and varied interpretations, helped in penetrating the nuanced conceptual world of Islam and discussing its dialectics with concrete political issues. The basic Saudi-Wahhabi concept of the Christian Ethiopian "other" clearly tends toward the negative option. From their early modern meeting in the 1930s, through the days of Mussolini, and on to the period of Mangistu Haile Mariam, Saudi policy and Wahhabi thinkers showed little consideration and even less grace when it came to Ethiopia as a Christian neighbor. Yet Saudi policy varied. It fluctuated among subversion, indifference, and expressions of friendliness. These attitudes were influenced by strategic considerations on one hand and by legacies of Wahhabism on the other. We have discussed the interplay between these religious and political concepts as well as the actual Wahhabi-Saudi influence on Ethiopian affairs. Here too, the picture was never monolithic. Saudi policymakers proved to be both ideological and pragmatic. In certain circumstances, Saudi Wahhabi scholars were ready to express moderation and accept Ethiopia. The radicalization of *Wahhabiyya* in the 1990s, or, rather, its new globalized militant wing, directly inspired the forces in Ethiopia and the Horn that worked toward Islam's political victory. Altogether, Saudi-Wahhabi concepts and policies wavered among three options: following diplomatic pragmatism and good neighborliness, systematically and patiently working to gradually Islamize Ethiopia, and enhancing subversion for the same purpose. After 11 September 2001, the Saudi state and the perpetrators of the third option overtly turned against one another. In our context, the government of Riyadh continued to develop constructive ties with Addis Ababa while Al-Qaida members continued to expand terrorist networks in the Horn. The MWL, led by the established Wahhabi scholars of the kingdom, began to raise voices of

Islamic moderation. In January 2005, the MWL held its Fifth Holy
Mecca Conference on "Intercultural Dialog: Aims and Areas." It ended
with a declaration that Islam, from its inception, stood for constructive
understandings with other cultures, and again the Prophet-*najashi* story
was central to the discussions. In sharp contrast to the 1983 "decision"
of the MWL's Islamic Jurisprudence Academy, which endorsed the concepts of *Islam al-najashi* and of total denial of non-Wahhabi scholarship, the 2005 declaration praised the model of Islamic-Christian coexistence in this formative episode. It made no mention of the contention
that Ethiopia's king had adopted Islam. Rather, it emphasized that his
Christian righteousness helped the true Muslims overcome the pagans of
Mecca.[2] The multidimensional Saudi involvement in Ethiopia persists,
and for all intents and purposes, the histories of both shores of the Red
Sea are today reintegrated. A most important aspect of the reemergence
of the Red Sea as a bridge between the Horn and Arabia is its impact on
Islam in Ethiopia.

Ethiopia's Islam, we have seen, also has many faces. Its current
resurgence, reorganization, partial Arabization, and reconnection to
global Islam further deepen its initial conceptual dilemmas. The old
issue of accepting or resisting the Christian hegemony has now changed
to participation in a multicultural Ethiopia or striving for victory there.
The new permissive system in Ethiopia and the newly imported Islamic
terminology are helping Ethiopia's Muslims to debate their options in
the classical Islamic-Ethiopian terms of the dual Prophet-*najashi* legacies. Most Ethiopian Muslims today interpret history in a way conducive to the rebuilding of a pluralist Ethiopian identity and state.
Others strive for Islamic victory, either peacefully or by force. The latter
are generally referred to as "Wahhabis," attesting to the accumulative
impact of Saudi involvement since 1991 (and indeed, as we saw, indirectly since the 1930s).

Having elaborated on the complexities of history as a game of endless variations, it is futile to risk a guess about the future. This book
deals with the politics of religion, in itself only part of the picture. The
Ethiopian perspective enabled us to examine Saudi history from a new
angle. We saw Ibn Sa'ud's formula at work in the 1930s, when the
state's concrete considerations were still only indirectly influenced by
religious circles. We saw Faysal's formula at work in the 1970s when
new, limitless resources enabled the seemingly convenient remobiliza-
tion of Wahhabism for both the internal power-game and the advance-
ment of foreign policy. We then followed developments since the 1980s
leading to the shattering of that balance. The Saudi removal from home

and "export" of its renewed, globalized, and radicalized Wahhabism—in the direction of Ethiopia, as well—has backfired, especially since 2001.[3] For Saudi Arabia to become stabilized, a new formula, balancing state and fundamental local Islam, has to be implemented. Until then, all options are open, with all the due implications on the regime's survival, and on Saudi influence in Ethiopia, in the region, and indeed, far beyond.

The politics of state and religion is central in today's Ethiopia, but it may become marginalized again and rendered secondary to other issues. Except for reemphasizing its importance, there is no way to say where the multidimensional interplay between Christians and Muslims is heading. Will its future be determined in Ethiopia's center or in the periphery? In Chapter 7, we cited some relevant voices from the center. We quoted writers and members of Ethiopia's intelligentsia who demonstrated both moderation and militancy on both sides. It is also premature for a historian to generalize about the comprehensive picture of Ethiopia's periphery today. Two anthropologists, Jon Abbink and Eloi Ficquet, have recently done work on Wallo, the region we referred to as a land of historical Christian-Islamic integration and tolerance. Both examined responses to the importation of Wahhabism from Arabia to Wallo, and both concluded that the local traditions of coexistence are, at present, resiliently resisting such fundamentalization.[4]

Harar, we have noted time and again, represented an Islam inspired by both Ethiopian and anti-Ethiopian historical legacies. In Mangistu's time, Harar became a demographic micro-cosmos reflecting the all-Ethiopian diversity, and due to the new political system introduced in 1991, its political interplay was energized. German anthropologist Patrick Desplat examined the inner Islamic tensions in Harar of the early 2000s. He found a community marked by heated debates and splits. On one hand, there was a small but active Wahhabi nucleus, combining local Oromos, Somalis, and Adaris, whose leaders had spent years in Saudi Arabia. On the other hand, there were the guardians of local Islam and local traditions, who apparently make up the majority. Both sides trade accusations about twisting Islam and serving foreign causes. "They call us infidels—and we call them infidels," Desplat quoted a leading shaikh who summarized the situation.[5] Behind such expressions of mutual stigmatization, and behind more subtle nuances manifesting antagonistic interpretations of Islam, a struggle is being conducted over the future of the town and of Ethiopia.

The internal Harari-Islamic story that we have followed throughout this book is relevant not only to our Ethiopian-Saudi story. It reflects today's global debate over the essence of Islam. In 1996, Shaikh 'Abdallah ibn Muhammad ibn Yusuf al-Harari, last mentioned at the end of Chapter 4, paid a visit to his native town of Harar. The aging scholar, sworn rival of Harar's first nucleus of Wahhabists during the 1940s, had gained international prominence during the forty-eight years since he left Ethiopia. After studying in various Middle Eastern capitals and earning scholarly prestige, in 1983 he established an Islamic association in Lebanon, popularly known as *Al-Ahbash* (the Ethiopians). Under his leadership, *Al-Ahbash* has become a leading factor in Lebanon's society and culture. Moreover, it became a transnational association with branches on five continents. Its global Islamic significance cannot be detailed here. (With my former student and colleague, Mustafa Kabha, I have analyzed it elsewhere).[6] *Al-Ahbash* has very few Ethiopian members; its nickname stems from their admiration for Shaikh 'Abdallah as a charismatic and reputed scholar. Behind this symbolic name, hundreds of thousands of "Ethiopians" the world over recycle and idealize the model of Islamic-Christian coexistence as transmitted from Ethiopia by the Harari shaikh. In over twenty books and in various *Al-Ahbash* publications, the key word is moderation, *i'tidal*. Shaikh 'Abdallah, in the eyes of his admirers, has become one of the Sunni world's leading scholars, but his initial, formative education is Ethiopian. From Harar, and by wandering around Ethiopia, he combined Sufi traditions with Sunni mainstream concepts and on this basis developed his ideas of a sober, moderate Islam capable of coexisting with Christians (and Jews). In Lebanon, also a land of Muslims and Christians, the shaikh succeeded in the 1980s to establish an Islamic community of local "Ethiopians." In the 1990s, as global Islam's dialogue with Western civilization became more sensitive, his ideas and *Al-Ahbash* branches were welcomed in Europe, the United States, and Australia. Moreover, an ideological war—in books, pamphlets, and mostly over the Internet—has developed between *Al-Ahbash* and the *Wahhabiyya*. It is arguably one of the more heated intra-Islamic debates on the essence of the religion conducted today.[7]

Shaikh 'Abdallah and his men accuse Ibn Taymiyya and his Wahhabi followers of being narrow-minded radicals who are ignorantly making a mockery of Islam and destroying its image. Wahhabis the world over respond harshly. They are trying to expose the "Ethiopians" as deviating from the true message of the Quran and the Sunna, as rigid Sufis verging on paganism, and as traitorous collaborators with infidels. *Wahhabiyya*, to reiterate, has in the 1990s become a term connoting various militants in the name of political Islam. The Wahhabi counterattack, begun in the 1980s by Saudi Arabian scholars, in the 1990s has become an all-Wahhabi transnational campaign. In the context of this stormy debate, Ethiopia is often mentioned. Some Wahhabi thinkers try, occasionally, to delegitimize Shaikh 'Abdallah as "a black foreigner" who comes from a land of underdeveloped Islam. The shaikh, for his part, describes Ethiopia as a model of Islam's supraracial purity and interreligious tolerance. Indeed, the Wahhabi-"Ethiopians" transnational clash continues to gain momentum.

When Shaikh 'Abdallah visited Harar in 1996, it was at the height of the conflict between the Ethiopian army and Al-Ittihad al-Islami together with the Islamic Oromo Liberation Front, forces that supported the Islamic militants in town. While the latter were being beaten in the field, the shaikh managed to reorganize the anti-Wahhabi majority in Harar. He inspired his followers to stigmatize the Wahhabis and left the local community with an Amharic translation of his main anti-Wahhabi book.[8] In 2003, the shaikh came from Beirut to Harar again to further promote his version of Islam in the town and in Ethiopia.

Shaikh 'Abdallah's lifetime nemesis, the aging Shaikh Yusuf 'Abd al-Rahman, is also still active and is also still connecting the local Harari story to international Islam. A resident of Medina since 1976, Shaikh Yusuf was much behind the Saudi Wahhabis' initial campaign in the 1980s against *Al-Ahbash*. Since 1991, Shaikh Yusuf has paid several visits to Harar, countering Shaikh 'Abdallah by preaching Wahhabi-style fundamentalism aimed to restore Harar's Islamic independence. However, as in the past—like in the days of *fitnat al-kulub* or the Ogaden War—Shaikh Yusuf continued to oppose the original Harari population's melting into an all-regional Islamic movement. Refusing to gamble on the jihadist movements of the Oromos or of the Somalis, he found himself confronting the militants. As in 1941, he now stands for advancing fundamental Islam in Harar through education, not through violence. In some ways, old Shaikh Yusuf's leadership in the early 2000s reflects the post–11 September moderation of the MWL, with which he was long associated.

The legacy of Ahmad Gragn and the call for Islam's victory over Ethiopia have not died in Harar. Though Al-Ittihad al-Islami, the IOLF, and the agents of Al-Qaida seem to have lost some ground in recent years, international Islamic terrorists still consider the Horn of Africa an operations base and a safe haven.[9] Their kind of Islam is still there, spreading in Harar as well and competing there against the "Ethiopian" messages of Shaikh 'Abdallah and the nonviolent fundamentalism of Shaikh Yusuf. Similarly and symbolically, the Islamic militants of Harar are also connected to the outside world. In 1991, young Hamdi Ishaq left the town to join his two brothers, Ramzi and Fathi, in Italy. In 1996, he moved to England, changed his name to Hussein 'Uthman, and, with false Somali documents, obtained British citizenship. On 21 July 2005, together with exiles from Somalia and Eritrea, he attempted to blow up a London Underground station in protest of Western aggression and in the service of Islam's global victory. Shortly before his arrest, his phone was used to call a number in Saudi Arabia.[10]

## Notes

1. See Eshete, "Growing Through the Storms."
2. See "Al-hiwar al-hadari wal-thaqafi: ahdafuhu wamajallatuhu," at www.themwl.org/Subjects.aspx?d=1&cidi=42&1=AR. See there also: 'Izz al-Din Ibrahim, "Ba'da arba'in sana min al-hiwar al-islami al-masihi."
3. See Teitelbaum, "Terrorist Challenge to Saudi Arabian Internal Security."
4. See Jon Abbink, "Transformations of Islam and Communal Relations in Wallo, Ethiopia"; Ficquet, "Interlaces of Mixity, Islam and Christianity in Wallo, Central Ethiopia." Another researcher, Terje Østebø, is currently working on a Ph.D. dissertation tentatively titled "Islam and Locality: The Study of Contemporary Islamic Discourse Among the Oromo People in Bale, Ethiopia," to be submitted to the Department of Religious Studies, Stockholm University. It is based on many years of field research and will focus on the contemporary religious discourse and the emergence of Wahhabi-Islam among the Oromo Muslims in Bale. His tentative findings are quite compatible with the more general story presented here. Initial introduction of Wahhabi concepts to Bale can be attributed to the work of Shaikh Muhammad Katiba, who studied in Harar—most probably with the local Wahhabi circles discussed in Chapter 4—and returned to Bale in 1945. The beginning of what can be defined as a Wahhabi movement among the Oromos of Bale, its conflict with local Sufism, and its efforts to influence the Oromos' nationalist movement—all referred to in Chapters 6 and 7—can be attributed to the work of Shaikh Abu Bakr Muhammad, who returned to Bale in 1969 from his studies in Saudi Arabia.

> Islam in Bale—he observed—has during the last part of the last century gone through radical changes. With its antecedents in the earlier decades of the same century, two stages of religious change can be identified, the first starting in the late 1960s, while the second has occurred in the post-Derg period (from 1991). The changes were in general caused by the emergence and growth of Wahhabi Islam, by which previous dominating religious perceptions and practices have been transformed. Refusing to label themselves as Wahhabis, the followers of *Wahhabiyya* prefered the term *tawhid;* interchangeably used as a term for the oneness of God and

as a term for the movement transforming Islam during the first stage of change. As for the second stage, the concept *ahl al-Sunna*—the community of the Sunna—is more frequently used by the followers of a more radical version of Wahhabism. . . .

The new political climate in the post-Derg period paved the way for increased religious activities among the Muslims in Bale. On one hand, this was a continuation of the changes introduced by the *tawhid*-movement, where returnees from Saudi Arabia played an important role. On the other hand, with the emergence of *ahl al-Sunna* also came a more radical version of Islam. This group gained support among the young generation of Muslims, and managed to challenge the mainstream leadership. In the first years after 1991, an ideology with political overtones appeared within this group. Although clearly visible, this was merely a fraction within the *ahl al-Sunna*, lacking resources and hardly connected to similar movements in the Islamic world. From the middle of the 1990s, the government, in coordination with the established religious leadership, managed to suppress this tendency. Key persons were either arrested or forced to leave Bale. Today the *ahl al-Sunna* is still a vibrant force within the Islamic community in Bale, although the political aspects are less visible. The movement seems to recruit most of its members from the rural schools and mosques. It targets the younger generation; advocating a religious piety in line with their *Wahhabiyya*-Salafiyyah ideology.

I am grateful to Terje Østebø for this information and his messages.

5. Desplat, "They Call Us Unbelievers, We Call Them Unbelievers."

6. See Kabha and Erlich, "*Al-Ahbash* and *Wahhabiyya*—Interpretations of Islam."

7. For a detailed analysis and for sources consulted, see ibid. The section below is based on this article.

8. See al-Harari, *Kamukhtasar Abdilah al-Harari mashaf ya'emnat kifl atchru tenatna.*

9. For a detailed update, see "Counter-Terrorism in Somalia: Losing Hearts and Minds?" *Africa Report*, no. 95 (11 July 2005), www.crisisgroup.org.

10. See Anna Pukas in Rome, and John Twomey in London, "Incredible Mobile Phone Trail to Bomber," *LexisNexis,* 2 August 2005.

# Bibliography

Abbink, Jon. "An Historical-Anthropological Approach to Islam in Ethiopia: Issues of Identity and Politics," *Journal of African Cultural Studies,* no. 2 (1998): 109–124.

———. "Transformations of Islam and Communal Relations in Wallo, Ethiopia," a paper presented at the conference *Islam, Disengagement of the State, and Globalization in Sub-Saharan Africa*, Paris, 12–14 May 2005.

'Abd al-Salam, 'Abd al-Karim. "Limadha kanat al-hijra ila al-habasha?" *Majallat al-Jami'a al-Islamiyya bi-al-Madina*, Rajab 1403 (April 1983): 215–223. Available at www.iu.edu.sa/Magazine/59/20.htm.

'Abd al-Wahhab, Muhammad. *Mukhtasar sirat al-rasul.* Cairo: 1956.

'Abd al-Wahhab, Sulayman bin 'Abdalla bin Muhammad. *Taysir al-'aziz al-hamid fi sharh kitab al-tawhid.* Riyadh: n.d.

'Abidin, 'Abd al-Majid. *Bayna al-Habasha wa-al-'arab.* Cairo: n.d.

Abir, Mordechai. *Ethiopia: The Era of the Princes.* London: Longmans, 1968.

Ahmed, Hussein. "Co-existence and/or Confrontation? Towards a Reappraisal of Christian–Muslim Encounter in Contemporary Ethiopia." Paper presented to the conference *Christian-Muslim Relations in Sub-Saharan Africa*, University of Birmingham, April 2004.

———. *Islam in Nineteenth-Century Wallo, Ethiopia: Revival, Reform, and Reaction.* Leiden: Brill, 2001.

———. "Islamic Literature and Religious Revival in Ethiopia (1991–1994)," *Islam et Societes au Sud du Sahara*, no. 12 (1998): 89–108.

———. "*Al-'Alam*: The History of an Ethiopian Arabic Weekly." In B. Zewde, R. Pankhurst, and T. Beyene, eds. *Proceedings of the 11th International Conference of Ethiopian Studies,* Addis Ababa, 1994, pp. 155–165.

———. "Islam and Islamic Discourse in Ethiopia (1973–1993)." In H. Marcus, ed., *New Trends in Ethiopian History, Papers of the 12th International Conference of Ethiopian Studies,* New Jersey, 1994, pp. 775–801.

———. "The Historiography of Islam in Ethiopia," *Journal of Islamic Studies,* vol. 3 (1992): 15–46.

————. "Traditional Muslim Education in Wallo." In *USSR Academy of Science, Proceedings of the Ninth International Congress of Ethiopian Studies,* Moscow, 1988, pp. 94–106.

Ahmed, Yusuf. *Al-Islam fi al-Habasha.* Cairo: 1935.

Al-'Atawna, Muhammad. "Shari'a and Politics in Saudi Arabia" (in Hebrew), *Jama'a,* vol. 8 (2001): 54–83.

Al-'Azm, Sadiq al-Mu'ayyid. *Rihlat al-Habasha.* Cairo: 1908.

Alexander, Yona, and Michael Swetnan. *Usama bin Laden's al-Qaida: A Profile of a Terrorist Network.* Ardsley, NY: 2001.

Al-Habashi, Sadiq. *Ithyubya fi 'asriha al-dhahabi, fi 'asr Hayla Silasi al-Awwal.* Cairo: 1954.

Al-Harari, 'Abdalla. *Kamukhtasar Abdilah al-Harari mashaf ya'emnat kifl atchru tenatna.* Harar: 2003. A summarized Amharic translation of his *Mukhtasar al-'aqida al-sunniya li-al-'Allama 'Abdalla al-Harari.* Malaysia: n.d.

Aliboni, Roberto. *The Red Sea Region: Local Actors and the Superpowers.* London and Sydney: 1985.

Al-Ithyubi, Abu Ahmad (pseudo.). *Al-Islam al-jarih fi al-Habasha.* Addis Ababa: 1960.

Al-Kahtany, 'Abdallah. *Zionism.* Riyadh: Al-Muntada al-Islami, 2000.

Al-Khalidi, Salah 'Abd al-Fattah, *Amrika min al-dahil bi-minzar Sayyid Qutb.* Jedda: 1985.

Al-Rumi, 'Abd al-'Aziz, Muhammad Baltaji, and Sayyid Hijab. *Mu'alafat al-Shaykh al-Imam Muhammad bin 'Abd al-Wahhab.* Riyadh: n.d.

Al-Salman, Muammad. *Rashid Rida wa-da'wat al-shaykh Muhammad bin 'Abd al-Wahhab.* Kuwait: 1988.

Al-Samara'i, 'Abd al-Jabar Mahmud. "Al-rasa'il allati ba'atha biha al-Nabi ila muluk al-duwwal al-mujawirah," *Al-Faysal,* no. 55 (November 1981): 71–81.

Al-Shu'ayr, Sa'd. *Majmu' fatawa wa-maqalat mutanawi'a.* Riyadh: n.d.

Al-Yusuf, Muhammad Al-Tayyib bin Yusuf. *Ithyubya wa-al-'uruba wa-al-Islam 'ibra al-ta'rikh.* Mecca: Meccan Publishing House, 1996.

Arslan, Shakib. *Al-Sayyid Rashid Rida, aw ikha arba'in sanah.* Beirut: 1937.

Aynor, Hanan S. "Crisis in Africa, Part II: Haile Selassie's Ethiopia." Unpublished manuscript.

Bakr, 'Ali al-Shaykh Ahmad. *Ma'alim al-hijratayn ila ard al-Habasha.* Riyadh: 1993.

Bergman, Ronen. "Israel and Africa: Military and Intelligence Liaisons." Doctoral thesis, Cambridge University, 2006.

Borruso, Paolo. "La crisi politica e religiosa dell'impero etiopico sotto l'occupazione fascista, 1936–1940," *Studi Piacentini,* no. 29 (2001): 57–111.

————. *L'Ultimo Impero Cristiano, politica e religione nell'Etiopia contemporanea (1916–1974).* Milano: 2002.

Buchan, James. "The Return of the Ikhwan." In David Holden and Richard Johns, eds., *The House of Saud,* 511–526. New York: 1981.

Buonasorte, Nicla. "La politica religiosa italiana in Africa Orientale dopo la conquista, 1936–1941," *Studi Piacentini,* no. 17 (1995): 53–114.

Burr, J. Millard, and Robert Collins, *Alms for Jihad: Charity and Terrorism in the Islamic World.* Cambridge: 2006.

Burton, Richard Francis. *First Footsteps in East Africa.* London: 1894.

Carmichael, Tim. "Approaching Ethiopian History: Addis Ababa and Local Governance in Harar, c. 1910 to 1950," Ph.D. diss., Michigan State University, 2001.

———. "Contemporary Ethiopian Discourse on Islamic History: The Politics of Historical Representation," *Islam et societes au sud du Sahara,* no. 10 (1996): 169–186.

Cerulli, Enrico. *L'Islam di Ieri e di Oggi.* Rome: 1971.

Cleveland, William. *Islam Against the West, Shakib Arslan and the Campaign for Islamic Nationalism.* Austin: University of Texas Press, 1985.

Coury, Ralph. *The Making of an Egyptian Arab Nationalist, The Early Years of Azzam Pasha, 1893–1936.* Reading, UK: 1998.

Crone, Patricia. "'Even an Ethiopian Slave': The Transformation of a Sunni Tradition," *Bulletin of the School of Oriental and African Studies (BSOAS),* 1994: 59–67.

Desplat, Patrick. "They Call Us Unbelievers, We Call Them Unbelievers . . . Understanding Religious Debate in Islam Through Cultural Contact." Paper presented at a Mainz University symposium, *Cultural and Linguistic Contacts,* 20–23 October 2004.

De Waal, Alex. "Chasing Ghosts—The Rise and Fall of Militant Islam in the Horn of Africa," *London Review of Books,* vol. 27, no. 16 (18 August 2005).

———, ed. *Islamism and Its Enemies in the Horn of Africa.* Addis Ababa: 2004.

Dimashqiyya, 'Abd al-Rahman, "Al-Ahbash du'at takfir," *Al-Muslimun* (Saudi Arabia), annexed to *Rasa'il* (11 December 1992): 140–141.

Dishon, Daniel, ed. *Middle East Record, 1960.* Tel Aviv: 1967.

Doumato, Eleanor A. "Manning the Barricades: Islam According to Saudi Arabia's School Texts," *Middle East Journal,* vol. 57, no. 2 (Spring 2003): 230–247.

Edris, Abdubasir. "Traditional Islamic Centers of Learning in Harar." B.A. diss., Department of History, Addis Ababa University, 1992. Available from the Institute of Ethiopian Studies.

Erlich, Haggai. "Islam and Ethiopia." In H. Erlich, ed., *Ethiopia: Christianity, Islam, Judaism,* 139–262 (in Hebrew). Tel Aviv: 2003.

———. *The Cross and the River: Ethiopia, Egypt, and the Nile.* Boulder: 2002.

———. "Periphery and Youth: Fascist Italy and the Middle East." In Stein Larsen, ed., *Fascism Outside Europe,* 393–423. Boulder: 2001.

———. "Identity and Church: Ethiopian-Egyptian Dialogue, 1924–1959," *International Journal of Middle East Studies,* vol. 32 (2000): 23–46.

———. "Ethiopia and Egypt, Ras Tafari in Cairo, 1924," *Aethiopica* (Hamburg), vol. 1 (1998): 64–84.

———. *Ethiopia and the Middle East.* Boulder: 1994.

———. "Mussolini in the 1920s, the Reluctant Imperialist." In Uriel Dann, ed., *The Great Powers in the Middle East, 1919–1939,* 213–222. New York: 1988.

————. *Ethiopia and the Challenge of Independence.* Boulder: 1986.

————. *The Struggle over Eritrea.* Stanford: 1983.

Eshete, Tibebe. "Growing Through the Storms: The History of the Evangelical Movement in Ethiopia, 1941–1991," Ph.D. thesis, Michigan State University, 2005.

Farias, Fernando de Moraes. "The Enslaved Barbarian." In John Ralph Willis, ed., *Slaves and Slavery in Muslim Africa,* vol. 2, 36–41. London: 1985.

Fernyhough, Timothy. "Slavery and the Slave Trade in Southern Ethiopia: A Historical Overview, ca. 1800–1935." In Harold G. Marcus, ed., *New Trends in Ethiopian Studies, Papers of the 12th International Conference of Ethiopian Studies,* Lawrenceville, 1994, pp. 680–708.

Ficquet, Eloi. "Interlaces of Mixity, Islam and Christianity in Wallo, Central Ethiopia," a paper presented at the symposium, *Cross and Crescent: Christian-Islamic Relations in Ethiopia,* Institute of Ethiopian Studies, Goethe Institute, Addis Ababa, 23–26 September 2002.

Foucher, Emile. "The Cult of Muslim Saints in Harar." In Bahru Zewde, R. Pankhurst, and Tedese Beyene, eds. *Proceedings of the 11th International Conference of Ethiopian Studies,* vol. 2, Addis Ababa, 1994, pp. 71–83.

Galili, Roi. "The Religious Dimension and Separatism in the Contemporary Reshaping of Oromo Identity" (in Hebrew). M.A. seminar paper, Tel Aviv University, 2004.

Gershoni, Israel. *Light in the Shade: Egypt and Fascism, 1922–1937* (in Hebrew). Tel Aviv: 1999.

Gershoni, Israel, and James Jankowski. *Redefining the Egyptian Nation, 1930–1945.* Cambridge: 1995.

Gnamo, Abbas. "Islam, the Orthodox Church, and Oromo Nationalism (Ethiopia)," *Cahier d'Etudes Africaines,* vol. 42 (2002): 109–114.

Goglia, Luigi. "Il Mufti e Mussolini: alcuni documenti italiani sui rapporti tra nazionalismo palestinese e fascismo negli anni trenta," *Storia Contemporanea,* vol. 17, no. 6 (December 1986).

Gori, Alessandro. "Arabic." In Siegbert Uhlig, ed., *Encylopaedia Aethiopica,* vol. 1, 301–304. Hamburg: 2003.

————. "Arabic Literature." In Siegbert Uhlig, ed., *Encyclopaedia Aethiopica,* vol. 1, 305–307. Hamburg: 2003.

————. "Una traduzione sulle origini dell'Islam in Etiopia," *Oriente Moderno* (2002): 431–440.

Gorman, Robert. *Political Conflict on the Horn of Africa.* Boulder: 1981.

Groiss, Amon. *The West, Christians, and Jews in Saudi Arabian Schoolbooks.* Report by the American Jewish Committee and the Center for Monitoring the Impact of Peace, New York, January 2003.

Habib, Hajji Muhammad Thani. *Eslamna enna yatalaqu nabiya yamuhammad tarik.* Addis Ababa: 1967, 1987, 1988.

Haile Selassie I. *My Life and Ethiopia's Progress 1892–1937.* Translated and annotated by Edward Ullendorff. Oxford: 1976.

Hamad, Muhammad Abu al-Qasim. *Al-Ab'ad al-dawliyya li-ma'arakat irtirya.* Beirut: 1974.

Hamza, Fuad. *Qalb jazirat al-'arab*. Riyadh: 1933 (new edition 1968).

Hassen, Mohammed. "Abba Gifaar II." In Siegbert Uhlig, ed., *Encylopaedia Aethiopica*, vol. 1, 15–16. Hamburg: 2003.

———. *The Oromo of Ethiopia: A History, 1570–1860*. Cambridge: 1990.

———. "The Relations Between Harar and the Surrounding Oromo, 1800–1887." B.A. thesis, Institute of Ethiopian Studies, 1973.

Hecht, Elisabeth Dorothea. "Cat in Harar." In Siegbert Uhlig, ed., *Encyclopaedia Aethiopica*, vol. 1, 698. Hamburg: 2003.

Henze, Paul. *Layers of Time: A History of Ethiopia*. London: 2000.

———. *The Horn of Africa from War to Peace*. New York: 1991.

Hill, George Birkbeck. *Colonel Gordon in Central Africa 1874–1879*. London: 1885.

Holtz, Avram, and Toby B. Holtz. "The Adventuresome Life of Mortiz Hall: A Biographical Study." In Piotr Scholtz, ed., *Orbis Aethiopicus, Studia in honorem Stanislaus Chojnacki*, 49–66. Albstadt: 1992.

Huntington, Samuel. *The Clash of Civilizations, and the Remaking of World Order*. New York: 1996.

Ibn Taymiyya, Taqi al-Din Ahmad. *Kutub warasa'il wafatawi* Ibn Taymiyya *fi al-fiqh*, Maktabat Ibn Taymiyya. Cairo: n.d.

———. *Sharh al-'umda fi al-fiqh*. Riyadh: 1992 (1413H).

'Inan, Muhammad 'Abdalla. *Mawaqif hasima fi ta'rikh al-islam*. Cairo: 1929 (fourth edition, 1962).

Jalata, Asafa. *Oromia & Ethiopia: State Formation and Ethnonational Conflict, 1868–1992*. Boulder: 1993.

Kabha, Mustafa, and Haggai Erlich. "*Al-Ahbash* and *Wahhabiyya*—Interpretations of Islam," *International Journal of Middle Eastern Studies* (2006): 519–538.

Kaplan, Steven. "Christianity—Imperial Religion Between Hegemony and Diversity." In Haggai Erlich, ed., *Ethiopia: Christianity, Islam, Judaism*, 17–138 (in Hebrew). Israel: The Open University, 2003.

Kebede, Solomon. "Religion, Civilization, and Human Rights: The Case of Islam." Privately distributed paper, Addis Ababa, 2001.

Khattab, Mahmud Shit. *Islam al-Najashi*, Mecca: Matba'at Rabitat al-'Alam al-Islami, 1982.

———. "Islam al-Najashi wal-i'timad 'ala al-masadir al-islamiyya fi al-dirasat al-lughaiyya wal-islamiyya," *Al-Faysal* (July 1982): 73–78.

Kinfe, Abraham. *Somalia Calling: The Crisis of Statehood and the Quest for Peace*. Addis Ababa: EIIPD, 2002.

Kostiner, Joseph, and Joshua Teitelbaum. "State Formation and the Saudi Monarchy." In Joseph Kostiner, ed., *Middle East Monarchies: The Challenge of Modernity*. Boulder: 2000.

Kramer, Martin. *Islam Assembled*. New York: 1986.

Lafin, John. *The Arabs as Master Slavers*. Englewood: 1982.

Legum, Colin, ed. *Africa Contemporary Record, Annual Survey, 1981–1982*. New York and London: 1982.

Levtzion, Nehemia. "Tnu'ot hitangdut vereforma baislam bame'a ha-18"

[Movements of Islamic reform and resistance in 18th century Islam], *Hamizrah Hehadash*, vol. 31 (1986): 48–70.

Lewis, Bernard. *Race and Slavery in the Middle East: A Historical Inquiry.* New York: 1990.

Lewis, Ioan M. *The Modern History of Somaliland, From Nation to State.* London: 1965.

Long, David E. "Saudi Arabia and the Horn of Africa." Unpublished paper, n.d.

Marchal, Roland. "Islamic Political Dynamics in the Somali Civil War." In Alex de Waal, *Islamism and Its Enemies in the Horn of Africa*, 114–146. Bloomington: Indiana University Press, 2004.

Marcus, Harold. *Haile Selassie I: The Formative Years, 1892–1936.* Berkeley: 1987.

Marquardt, Erich. "Al-Qaeda Threat to Ethiopia." Available at www.jamestown.org/authors.

Miers, Suzan. "Britain and the Suppression of Slavery in Ethiopia," *Slavery and Abolition*, no. 3 (1997): 257–288.

Miran, Jonathan. "A Historical Overview of Islam in Eritrea," *Die Welt des Islams*, no. 2 (2005): 177–215.

Moten, Rashid. "Islam in Ethiopia: An Analytical Survey." In Nura Alkali, ed., *Islam in Africa*, 221–231. Ibadan: 1993.

Muhammad, Akbar. "The Image of Africans in Arabic Literature: Some Unpublished Manuscripts." In John Ralph Willis, ed., *Slaves and Slavery in Muslim Africa*, vol. 1, 47–74. UK: Frank Cass, 1986.

Munro-Hay, Stuart. "Arabia: Relations in Ancient Times." In Siegbert Uhlig, ed., *Encylopaedia Aethiopica*, vol. 1, 294–300. Hamburg: 2003.

Nallino, Carlo A. *L'Arabia Saudiana.* Rome: 1939.

———. "Viaggio a Gedda, Relazione al Ministro degli Afari Esteri e appunti sul viaggio nell Arabia Saudiana (1938)." In *Istituto per l'Oriente*. Rome: Carte Private di C. A. Nallino, O/5.

O'Fahey, Sean. *Enigmatic Saint: Ahmad Ibn Idris and the Idrisi Tradition.* Evanston: 1990.

Pankhurst, Richard. *Economic History of Ethiopia.* Addis Ababa: 1968.

Perham, Margery. *The Government of Ethiopia.* Evanston: 1969.

Peters, Francis E. *The Hajj: The Muslim Pilgrimage to Mecca and the Holy Places.* Princeton: 1994.

Pirio, Gregory Alonso. "Radical Islam in the Greater Horn of Africa." Available at www.news.asmarino.com/Information/ 2005/2/xGregoryAlonsoPirio.

Pizzigallo, Matteo. *La Diplomazia dell'Amicizia, Italia e Arabia Saudita 1932–1942.* Naples: 2000.

Rabi, Uzi. *Saudi Arabia: Islam, Oil, Politics* (in Hebrew). Israel: The Open University, 2006.

Rahji Abdella. "The Kulub-Hannolato Movement by the Harari, 1946–1948." B.A. paper, Department of History, Addis Ababa University, November 1994. Available from the Institute of Ethiopian Studies.

Ricci, Lanfranco. "Cerulli, Enrico." In Siegbert Uhlig, ed., *Encylopaedia Aethiopica*, vol. 1, 708–709. Hamburg: 2003.

Roy, Delwin. "Saudi Arabian Education: Development Policy," *Middle Eastern Studies*, vol. 28, no. 3 (1992): 477–508.

Sabbe, Osman Saleh. *Ta'rikh irtirya*. Beirut: 1974.

Salis, Renzo Sertoli. *Italia, Europa, Arabia*. Milano: 1940.

Saminullah, Muhammad. "Forsaken Muslims of Ethiopia," *The Muslim World League Journal*, Rajab 1403 (April-May 1983): 41–45.

Saudi Arabia, Ministry of Education. *Jazirat al-Arab al-qadim wa-sirat al-Nabi*. 2001.

———. *Al-Sira al-nabuwiyya wa-ta'rikh al-khulafa al-rashidin*. First year, intermediate, 2000.

———. *Al-Adab al-'arabi*. First year, secondary, 1999.

———. *Ta'rikh sirat al-Rasul wa-al-da'wa al-islamiyya*. Fourth year, elementary, 1999.

———. *Jughrafiyyat al-'alam al-islami*, Second year, intermediate, 1994.

Sbacchi, Alberto. *Ethiopia Under Mussolini, Fascism and Colonial Experience*. London: 1985.

Segre, Claudio. "Liberal and Fascist Italy in the Middle East, 1919–1939." In Uriel Dann, ed., *The Great Powers in the Middle East, 1919–1939*, 199–212. New York: 1988.

Shaltut, Fahim Muhammad. "Fatra mushraqa lil-jihad al-islami fi al-Habasha." *Majallat al-Buhuth al-Islamiyya* (Riyadh) (June 1985): 249–268.

Shay, Shaul. *The Red Sea Islamic Terror Triangle: Sudan, Somalia, and Yemen* (in Hebrew). Herzliyya: 2004.

Shinn, David. "Promoting Stability in the Horn of Africa," *Economic Focus*, vol. 7 (January 2004): 1–8.

———. "Terrorism in East Africa and the Horn: An Overview," *The Journal of Conflict Studies*, vol. 23 (Fall 2003): 80–81.

———. "Ethiopia: Coping with Islamic Fundamentalism Before and After September 11," *CSIS Africa Notes*, no. 7 (February 2002).

Shumburo, Mahdi. "The Hannolato Movement and the Culub Insurrection (Recent Harari History, 1940–1960)," New York, 1992. Manuscript kept at the Institute of Ethiopian Studies.

Sivan, Emmanuel. *The Crash Within Islam* (in Hebrew). Tel Aviv: 2005.

———. "The Clash Within Islam," *Survival*, vol. 45 (Spring 2003).

———. *Radical Islam: Medieval Theology and Modern Politics*. New Haven and London: 1985.

Spencer, John. *Ethiopia at Bay, A Personal Account of the Haile Selassie Years*. Algonac, MI: 1984.

Stalinsky, Steven. "Inside Saudi Classroom." Available from www.nationalreview.com/comment/comment-stalinsky020703.asp.

———. "Preliminary Overview—Saudi Arabia's Education System: Curriculum, Spreading Saudi Education to the World and the Official Saudi Position on Education Policy." MEMRI report no. 12, 20 December 2002. Available from memri.org/bin/articles.cgi?Page=archives&Area=sr&ID=SR01202.

Stoffregen-Pedersen, Kirsten. "Bible Translation into Amharic." In Siegbert Uhlig, ed., *Encylopaedia Aethiopica*, vol. 1, 574–575. Hamburg: 2003.

Tadesse, Medhane. *Al-Ittihad, Political Islam and Black Economy in Somalia.* Addis Ababa: 2002.

Tafla, Bairu. "Abdullahi 'Ali Sadiq." In Siegbert Uhlig, ed., *Encyclopaedia Aethiopica*, vol. 1, 38. Hamburg: 2003.

Tawfiq, Muhammad 'Umar, *Min zikraiyat musafir.* Jedda: 1980.

Teitelbaum, Joshua. "Terrorist Challenge to Saudi Arabian Internal Security," *MERIA*, vol. 9, no. 3 (September 2005).

———. *Holier Than Thou: Saudi Arabia's Islamic Opposition.* Washington Institute for Near East Policy Paper No. 52, 2000.

———. "The Saudis and the Hajj, 1916–1933: A Religious Institution in Turbulent Times" (in English). M.A. thesis, School of History, Tel Aviv University, 1988.

Toledano, Ehud. *The Ottoman Slave Trade and Its Suppression.* Princeton: 1982.

Tuson, Penelope, and Burdett, Anita, eds. *PRO, Records of Saudi Arabia, Primary Documents 1902–1960.* London: 1992.

Ullendorf, Edward. *Ethiopia and the Bible.* London: 1968.

United States Institute of Peace. "Terrorism in the Horn of Africa." Special Report 113, Washington, D.C., January 2004.

Van Donzel, Emeri. "Correspondence Between Fasiladas and the Imam of Yemen." In Gideon Goldenberg, ed., *Proceedings of the Sixth International Conference of Ethiopian Studies*, Rotterdam, 1986, pp. 91–100.

———. *A Yemenite Embassy to Ethiopia, 1647–1649.* Stuttgart: 1986.

———. *Foreign Relations of Ethiopia, 1642–1700.* Leiden: 1979.

Voigt, Rainer. "Abyssinia." In Siegbert Uhlig, ed., *Encyclopaedia Aethiopica*, vol. 1, 59–65. Hamburg: 2003.

Wagner, Ewald. "Abadir 'Umar ar-Rida." In Siegbert Uhlig, ed., *Encylopaedia Aethiopica*, vol. 1, 4–5. Hamburg: 2003.

Warburg, Gabriel. *Islam, Sectarianism, and Politics in Sudan Since the Mahdiyya.* London: 2003.

Willis, John Ralph. *Slaves and Slavery in Muslim Africa*, vol. 1 and 2. London: 1985.

Yizraeli, Sara. *The Remaking of Saudi Arabia, The Struggle between King Sa'ud and Crown Prince Faysal, 1953–1962.* Dayan Center, Tel Aviv University, 1997.

Yusuf, 'Abd al-Rahman Isma'il. *Al-Rasa'il al-thalath* [The three messages]. Medina: 2002.

Yusuf, Muhammad Isma'il. *Qissat al-kulub* [The story of the club]. Cairo: 1997.

Zabiyan, Muhammad Tayasir. *Al-Habasha al-muslima—mushahadati fi diyar al-islam* [Bloodstained Palestine]. Damascus: 1937.

Zekaria, Ahmed. "Harar: The Land of Ziyara, Pilgrimage." In *First International Seminar of the Institute of Ethiopian Studies*, pp. 1–9.

Ziv, Shiri. "Al-Ittihad Al-Somali and Somalia" (in Hebrew). M.A. seminar paper, Tel Aviv University, 2005.

# Index

# About the Book

What is the significance of Islam's growing strength in Ethiopia? And what is the impetus for the Saudi financing of hundreds of new mosques and schools, welfare organizations, and the spread of the Arabic language in that country? Haggai Erlich explores the interplay of religion and international politics as it has shaped the development of modern Ethiopia and Saudi Arabia.

Tracing Saudi-Ethiopian relations from the 1930s to the present, Erlich highlights the nexus of concrete politics and the conceptual messages of religion. His fresh approach encompasses discussions of the options and dilemmas facing Ethiopians, both Christians and Muslims, across multiple decades; the Saudis' nuanced conceptualization of their Islamic "self" in contrast to Christian and Islamic "others"; and the present confrontation between Ethiopia's apolitical Islam and Wahhabi fundamentalism. It also provides new perspectives on the current dilemmas of the Wahhabi kingdom and the global implications of the evolving Saudi-Ethiopian relationship.

**Haggai Erlich** is professor emeritus of Middle East and African history at Tel Aviv University. Most recent of his numerous publications is *The Cross and the River: Ethiopia, Egypt, and the Nile.*